DELEUZE, BERGSON, MERLEAU-PONTY

DELEUZE, BERGSON, MERLEAU-PONTY

THE LOGIC AND PRAGMATICS OF CREATION, AFFECTIVE LIFE, AND PERCEPTION

———

DOROTHEA E. OLKOWSKI

INDIANA UNIVERSITY PRESS

This book is a publication of

Indiana University Press
Office of Scholarly Publishing
Herman B Wells Library 350
1320 East 10th Street
Bloomington, Indiana 47405 USA

iupress.org

Manufactured in the United States of America

Cataloging information is available from the Library of Congress.

ISBN 978-0-253-05468-5 (hardback)
ISBN 978-0-253-05469-2 (paperback)
ISBN 978-0-253-05470-8 (e-book)

1 2 3 4 5   26 25 24 23 22 21

CONTENTS

DELEUZE, BERGSON, MERLEAU-PONTY

Introduction

Deleuze, Bergson, Merleau-Ponty: A Three-Body Problem in Continental Philosophy

CAN ANYONE PREDICT HOW THREE entities will orbit one another in a repeating pattern? "Finding any solution is a daunting prospect. Three objects in space can be set off in infinite ways. Somehow, initial conditions—starting points, velocities, and so on—must be found that bring the objects back to those conditions so the whole dance can start over again."[1]

In some respects, solutions to the physical or astrophysical three-body problem are more easily obtained than solutions to the philosophical version of this problem. Of course, the ideas of Gilles Deleuze, Henri Bergson, and Maurice Merleau-Ponty—the three philosophers brought together in this book—do not literally orbit one another in physical space, yet, like the physical problem, our three-body problem appears to be a chaotic system where tiny perturbations may be amplified endlessly and precise predictions about final outcomes are likely impossible—not merely in the work of these three philosophers but also in the ideas of those who make use of these ideas in their own work. Even so, deliberating on and addressing the problems associated with the relationships between the ideas of these three philosophers is the principle problem this book works to resolve, exacerbated by the personae Deleuze-Guattari that must include Félix Guattari, whose engagement with Deleuze introduces another perturbation.

If the relationships existing between the three philosophers in the title is a true three-body problem, everything depends on a number of considerations, such as where our analysis starts, whether or not the three philosophers' ideas have the ideational equivalent of the same mass, and whether or not they are uniformly spaced in relation to one another. In other words, do we carry out a chronological analysis? Have each of the three philosophers' ideas had the same impact on other philosophies? And finally, to what extent do their ideas serve as chaotic attractors, not quite repeating one another but still resonating rhythmically?

It should be clear by now that a multitude of variables affect the trajectory of this book. Clearly, as well, choices had to be made about which ideas of each of these philosophers would be explored and given precedence. The most powerful body in this problem is Gilles Deleuze—not the person but the ideas as disturbed by those of Henri Bergson and Maurice Merleau-Ponty. Posing the problem in terms of chaotic attractors privileges the Deleuzean structure. Solving this problem has been only somewhat less difficult than solving the one facing celestial mechanics since Isaac Newton discovered it in the 1680s. For decades and even centuries, it went unresolved, but more recently (2017), more than six hundred new three-body periodic orbits were discovered by computer scientists in China.[2] We philosophers are limited in this regard. We may not be capable of six hundred or more different accounts of these ideas, but certainly there are many more than one.

I have pursued a particular set of ideas as central to our problem. I have examined the relationship between the creation of ideas and their actualization in relation to semiology, logic, and the cosmos in the philosophies of Deleuze, Bergson, and Merleau-Ponty. It is not a linear path. It is more a question of periodic orbits following strange and unrepeated trajectories that have been generally unpredictable. In other words, in spite of what I think I know or understand, I have, at every instance, sought to remain attentive to alternatives to my former views in order to consider ideas, concepts, orientations, problems, and solutions that could unexpectedly erupt and so alter the orientation of my own thinking within the context of the problem I have set out.

What, then, is the problem that implicates a three-body solution? To a certain extent, it is a problem raised by mathematicians, physicists, cognitive scientists, and philosophers of science whose ideas were taken up and utilized by the three philosophers addressed in this book. One aspect is the view that emerged, starting in approximately the sixteenth century, that science is autonomous, that it generates its own elements, that it stands outside time and outside the lived experience of a subject. This is how logic became the internal method directing the internal and indefinite progress of science and scientific discoveries. The limitation of this approach is that for science, external references would seem to be essential to complete the system. Concepts need to be tested and put into practice in the world.

Gottlob Frege carried the idea of autonomy from natural science into philosophy, claiming that if the truth value of a declarative sentence is its reference, then, on the one hand, all true sentences have the same reference, and, on the other hand, so do all false sentences. Deleuze's conclusion that "from this we see that in the reference of the sentence all that is specific is obliterated" may seem excessive to a logician but nevertheless points in the direction of the types of distinctions we are confronting.[3] Deleuze likewise acknowledges that it had become problematic for philosophy to place images or affects in consciousness and movements in space. Both Bergson and Merleau-Ponty address this in their work, especially in the form of mind-body dualism. Deleuze accepts their efforts, elaborates on them or rejects them, and radically reformulates the relevant concepts.

In chapter 1, we see how, in his work on cinema, Deleuze agrees that both Bergson and Merleau-Ponty questioned the juxtaposition of qualitative images and quantitative spaces, yet he seeks to resituate Bergson within the context of his own reflections on this matter. Deleuze recognizes the mathematical idea that space is homogeneous and infinitely divisible, but also the apparently contradictory Bergsonian position that movement must be indivisible and heterogeneous, and so introjects that each instant is mobile by means of the movement-image, a qualitative or affective change in the *Whole*. Phenomenology is far more difficult for Deleuze to reconcile with his own position, which is opposed to what he calls the natural perception of a perceiving subject in the world that is normative for phenomenology.

We should not expect these disagreements to be resolved in the sense of bringing the three philosophies into perfect alignment with one another. What we see is the manner in which Deleuze approaches their ideas, along with those of Charles Peirce, to conceptualize images in the form of affects and signs, which, in turn, become increasingly important in Deleuze's work. But first, the chapter situates these orientations within the philosophical tradition out of which such questions have arisen.

Chapter 2 takes this on directly. Kant's science of relations requires its axioms to have a possible object in outer intuition. Deleuze, along with modern mathematics, evades the three-dimensional limitations of the space of human experience. Deleuze and Guattari initially appear to follow in the footsteps of the formalist post-Euclidean mathematicians and logicians, yet in the end, they carry out a critique of formal logic. They focus, in particular, on Frege's extensional logic, which, they argue, lacks both endoconsistency and exoconsistency as well as self-reference and so loses all the characteristics of a philosophical concept and is able only to operate with trivial or insignificant propositions.

Deleuze and Guattari then turn to fuzzy logic: the logic of ambiguous or vague propositions, matters of opinion. Fuzzy sets are phenomenological in that they operate with aggregates of perceptions and affections immanent to a subject and to consciousness and differentiate by means of degrees. This implies that they are subjective judgments, or judgments of taste. Phenomenology, they argue, exceeds the limits of fuzzy logic in that it refers a transcendental subject—not merely an empirical subject—to its perceptive-affective variables and so produces concepts that are at least acts of transcendence—that is, *original opinions, Urdoxa*.

However, *Urdoxa* are not yet philosophical concepts, so Deleuze and Guattari next take up the intensional concept. We find it in the work of Rudolf Carnap and—originally and more to the point for Deleuze-Guattari—Charles Peirce. The intensional concept gives them a scientific or logical concept that allows for philosophical functions or significations that relate to the lived as virtual and not as empirically real. This discovery reveals the extent to which Peirce's logic has been at work in Deleuze and Deleuze-Guattari's philosophy from its earliest inception. Following Peirce, we can see Peircean concepts of Firstness, Secondness, and Thirdness taken up, transformed, and utilized across the works we are examining here.

Deleuze and Guattari examine the philosophy of Alain Badiou only briefly in this context, returning rapidly to a Peircean structure—that of the continuum, Deleuze's *ideal continuity*, the *mise-en-abyme* whose whole can be reflected in any of its parts. The continuum consists of virtual events, the *virtual chaos*, the potential through which states of affairs take effect as discontinuities, as signs, and as the actualization of qualities. We continue to use the Peircean affiliation to make sense of how Deleuze approaches both Bergson and Merleau-Ponty.

Chapter 3 begins with the analytic attack on Bergson's philosophy as dualist, implying that the identification of space with intellect reduces logic to a subset of geometry. Bertrand Russell developed and extended this attack to Bergson's concept of duration, arguing that we live in an unchanging mathematical temporality and that duration is merely a psychological illusion even as Bergson continued to deny Albert Einstein's claim that there is only one time, the time of physics. Russell accused Bergson of not understanding relativity, and Bergson was soon subject to scorn from many corners. Interestingly relevant to our discussion, Russell directed his harshest criticisms to Bergson's concept of continuity.

Merleau-Ponty stepped up to defend Bergson against his accusers by endorsing Bergson's conception of intuition against the charge of dualism. Intuition, Merleau-Ponty asserts, is a continuum between pure perception and pure memory; it is the double movement toward both matter and memory. He accuses Einstein of being stuck in the classical view of reality, which claims the world is governed by deterministic laws, and of being unable to face the prospect that the principles of quantum physics describe a world of probabilities. He further upholds Bergson's distinction between time perceived and time conceived—real time and measured time.

Following this, Deleuze takes up the cause of what he refers to as Bergsonism, making possible the revival of Bergson's philosophy within the context of his own. It appears that Deleuze's reading of Bergson's understanding of duration as heterogeneous accords with Peirce's conception of continuity. For Peirce, the continuum is synthetic, and as for Bergson, it cannot be reconstructed out of a sum of points. Additionally, we see that the three philosophers (Bergson, Peirce, and Deleuze) agree with respect to their understanding of discontinuity, yet Deleuze departs from his agreement with Bergson to assert a Husserlian-influenced concept. He posits that a Gestalt-like sensorial aggregate can produce a nonmathematical multiplicity superior in force to its elements. These suggestions are carried into the next chapter to articulate how they operate.

In chapter 4 we examine how Deleuze transforms Bergson's two senses of time (cinematographic time and duration) into his own concepts; namely, the movement-image and the time-image, which are what distinguishes movement from time. Any space in the movement-image is homogeneous with every other, and so seemingly measurable, but everything, including all bodies, is also an image. This dematerialization of bodies stems from the identity of matter and light, making matter into light existing in the form of blocks of space-time. In the same way, consciousness cannot be distinguished from images, meaning the light that constitutes it. Thus even the brain is one image among others; it is the interval between an action and a reaction, an effect of the images that pass through it.

This conception of the brain resembles Bergson's concept of an unconscious material point, which gathers and transmits all the affective influences from all points in the universe, but is it not something more? There must be some sort of organization to prevent the infinity of images reflecting one another on the plane of immanence from freezing into a single static image. Bergson relies on the concept of a zone of indetermination that arises after the reception of affective sensations that allows the organism to make a selection from the relevant images that constitute ontological memory.

For Deleuze it is images that associatively choose one another. He refers to this using the cinematic term *framing*. Framing is not, as in Bergson, the means whereby the body analyzes images for the sake of what actions it may carry out. Instead, Deleuze argues that images are received by other images and associated if relevant; otherwise, they pass unrecognized through the brain. Action is the process of associating images more closely or distancing them. Deleuze once again turns to Peirce and finds the conception of images as signs that relate cognitively to the three types of movement-image, and he creates several additional signs to serve his distinction between the movement-image and the time-image. The chapter concludes with an account of Merleau-Ponty's conception of cinema, which is taken up again in the following chapter.

Chapter 5 returns to Merleau-Ponty's philosophy to discover the extent to which it correlates with or differs from that of Bergson and Deleuze. We begin by asking what Merleau-Ponty's phrase "the primacy of perception" really means. He clarifies that both our ideas and our perceptions have a future and a past temporal horizon; both appear to themselves as temporal, and our temporality provides us with a route to follow; it gives us space. Thus, perception is not prior to temporality and is not a function of cognition.

Merleau-Ponty orients this on the concept of form or structure, which replaces a theory of physical forces and causes. He argues that forms or structures of physical matter, vital life, and mind will be invested with equal rights and that the physical world must in some way be the staging ground for behaviors. In physics, experiments verify a number of intersecting laws that operate within a cosmological structure posited as nature or natural laws, yet there must be structures or forms in natural laws and natural laws in structures, which are expressed as the limit toward which physical knowledge tends. Moreover, the physical form exists as an Idea—a signification—signifying an assemblage or ensemble of molecular facts, and it is also an object of perception.

Setting aside, although not renouncing, the precision of differential calculus and the ambiguity of lived experience, Merleau-Ponty proposes that the subject formulates an outline of multiplicity in place of the unity of an object in consciousness. This anonymous flux, the preobjective hold of our bodies on the world, is due to the temporal priority of the world—the so-called temporal wave—in relation to the perceiver. With this, Merleau-Ponty might be situating the perceiver in the position of the measuring apparatus of the two-slit experiment of quantum physics for which the wave collapses into a particle.

Merleau-Ponty goes on to link the physical world and the actions of a living being via his conception of freedom. Claiming that there is no freedom without a field (*champ*), Merleau-Ponty sets out three fields: matter, life, and signification, each of which interacts with the others. One is not free through causal physical forces or through psychological ones insofar as freedom requires a past and a future that belong to the temporal unity of one's current projects, which are always a molecular process and not molar mechanical causality. This is what sets us free from our first-person existence.

Although this language seems to reflect Deleuze's position, Deleuze is careful, in his analysis of the paintings of Francis Bacon and Paul Cézanne, to articulate the manner in which his own philosophy is not phenomenological. For Deleuze, sensations bypass the senses and directly attack the nervous system. This *vital power* is not the phenomenological Gestalt, which for Deleuze lacks the superior and powerful, direct and unmediated impact on the nervous system, and is unable to produce philosophical concepts. This leaves open the question of freedom. Does this imply that, for Deleuze, freedom is an impossibility precisely due to this vital power? This question takes us to the final chapter of the book.

In a previous book on Deleuze's philosophy (*The Universal [In the Realm of the Sensible]*), I argue that the philosophy set out by Deleuze leaves us at a sort of dead end—the limit point immanent to the classical dynamical system that governs Deleuze's conceptualization of nature, the socius, and living beings. I set out an alternative, post-Deleuzean, postclassical system governed by a unique model of temporalization as proposed by the physicists Fotini Markopolou and Lee Smolin. It was my position that this was necessary to evade the consequences of Deleuze's diagnosis of Western philosophy as articulated by Deleuze and Guattari in *Anti-Oedipus*. In chapter 6, I set out Deleuze and Guattari's own solution to the dilemma of *Anti-Oedipus*, which seems to me to predict the unending domination of capitalism and oedipalism. This solution lies in pragmatism and the Refrain.

The Refrain is part of the question of what a regime of signs can do. Art, science, and philosophy still have the ability to cut through the virtual chaos as forms of thought and creation in the struggle against opinion. In this, phenomenology cannot, for Deleuze, take us to concepts. Peirce's pragmatism does because for Peirce, thought must be aligned with its *conceivable* practical effects in the world and must be understood as a system of signs where each sign is determined through its effect on another sign or on other signs.

Deleuze and Guattari's development of these ideas points to their differences with Peirce and also implicates their view of the failure of formal logic. Embracing neither Peirce's skeletonized structure nor Frege's pure, syntactical ordering of units, they create a regime of signs that is an assemblage with two sides: semiotic systems and regimes of bodies. Freed from the domination of language and guided by the diagram and the Refrain, they venture into a new way of thinking—the creation of conceptual personae, machinic assemblages that are abstract machines of creation. Their goal is nothing less than to reach out into the Cosmos. The modern artist, poet, philosopher, or scientist discerns the immaterial, nonformal, and energetic forces of the Cosmos, which are material forces but molecularized, therefore now actually *immaterial*, non-visible to the artist and scientist and also not thinkable in themselves to the philosopher. With this, they recognize the necessity for Earth and its people to become cosmic, inhabitants not of Earth but of the Cosmos, a necessity to which, they argue, pragmatics can contribute in important ways.

A number of things have made this book possible, including the support and encouragement of generous friends such as Helen Fielding, whose intelligence and constant faith in my work have made her one of the brightest lights of my career and life; and also Noelle McAffee, a joyfully gifted and richly spirited friend and philosopher; Lyat Friedman, an energetic and creative thinker and friend; Joseph Kuzma, my brilliant colleague; Michael Eng, supportive and innovative in many arenas; Andrew Cutrofellow, whose canny insights and support for me and my work has meant so much; and the anonymous reviewer whose acuity and knowledge made this a far better book. I also thank the delightful Kyoo Lee, who invited me to the Symposium on Cosmic and Human Spacetime at KIAS, the Korean Institute for Advanced Studies, Seoul, South Korea, where the relevance of the anti-Bergsonian ideas of Russell came to prominence for me. I thank the University of Colorado at Colorado Springs for the 2018 sabbatical leave that allowed me to finish this book and for the Committee for Research and Creative Work's grant that allowed me to carry out research at the Merleau-Ponty archive in Paris. In addition, I have revisited a few key ideas I first set out in *Gilles Deleuze and the Ruin of Representation* (University of California Press, 1999) to differentiate the ideas that arose from Henri Bergson's creative mind from those of Deleuze's creative reading of Bergson. I have also made use of some previously published essays, namely, "Merleau-Ponty and the Temporality of Architecture," in *Merleau-Ponty: Space, Place, Architecture*, ed. Patricia M. Locke and Rachel McCann (Athens: Ohio University Press, 2016) and "Bergson and Film," in *Film, Theory, and Philosophy: The Key Thinkers*, ed. Felicity Colman (Durham, NC: Acumen Press, 2009). And always, as I put this work out into the world, I embrace Max and Emma, who are the present and the future, and who mean so much to me.

NOTES

1. Jon Cartwright, "Physicists Discover a Whopping 13 New Solutions to Three-Body Problem," *Science*, March 8, 2013, http://www.sciencemag.org /news/2013/03/physicists-discover-whopping-13-new-solutions-three-body problem. The thirteen new solutions discovered by physicists Milovan Šuvakov and Veljko Dmitrašinović at the Institute of Physics Belgrade can be viewed

at http://three-body.ipb.ac.rs. "Newton solved the two-body problem for the orbit of the Moon around the Earth and considered the effects of the Sun on this motion. This is perhaps the earliest appearance of the three-body problem. The first and simplest periodic exact solution to the three-body problem is the motion on collinear ellipses found by Euler (1767). Also Euler (1772) studied the motion of the Moon assuming that the Earth and the Sun orbited each other on circular orbits and that the Moon was massless. This approach is now known as the restricted three-body problem." From Juhan Frank, "PHYS 7221—The Three-Body Problem Special Lecture," Louisiana State University, October 11, 2006, http://www.phys.lsu.edu/faculty/gonzalez/Teaching/Phys7221 /ThreeBodyProblem.pdf.

2. XiaoMing Li and ShiJun Liao, "More Than Six Hundred New Families of Newtonian Periodic Planar Collisionless Three-Body Orbits," *Science China Physics, Mechanics & Astronomy* (2017), https://doi.org/10.1007 /s11433-017-9078-5.

3. Gottlob Frege, "On Sense and Reference," as reprinted in A. W. Moore, ed., *Meaning and Reference* (Oxford: Oxford University Press, 1993), 30.

ONE

Naturalism, Formalism, Phenomenology, and Semiology in Postmodern Philosophy

FOREIGN BODIES, FOREIGN MINDS

Embassytown, a novel by science fiction writer China Miéville, describes a species of nonhuman but intelligent beings who inhabit an alien planet, Arieka, at the farthest edge of the known universe.[1] The Ariekei are described as almost grotesquely alien, and their planet, invaded and inhabited by a contingent of human administrators and diplomats, presents an extreme version of the culture/nature distinction. Briefly stated, it is a story about fundamentalism in language brought about by an extreme commitment to reference and true propositions. On the human side, there is Embassytown, a small, enclosed, artificial environment where even the air has to be manufactured. Featuring brick and ivy, bureaucratic and planetary politics, it is a place where language does not refer to an outside because it is emblematic of a formal, syntactical expression of order, and so is not concerned with reference—that is, the truth or falsity of its statements.

But on the Ariekei side, it's all biological, consisting of polymers and "biorigged" flesh such that even their dwelling places and technology are purely biological. The Ariekei walk on four spiderlike legs ending in hooves; their bodies bear external spines, their heads, dark hair, and their faces, eye antlers. They have two mouths and two awkward coral-like wings, a giftwing for manipulation under the turn mouth and a fanwing, for hearing, behind the cut mouth. Wings and eye antlers all retract or furl and emerge like those of sea creatures or light-sensitive plants. The Ariekei are called "Hosts" by their human occupiers; mature Hosts are accompanied by battery creatures (Zelles), and the older ones grow edible sacs.

Communication between Ariekei and humans is difficult. The Ariekei consist of and are embedded in pure biology, pure nature. Ariekei language and thoughts are indistinguishable; they operate without the influence of artifice, including writing; thus their minds and language are profoundly naturalized. As a result, when a non-Ariekei speaks the Ariekei language, unless the speaker is somehow able to unite mind and language, Ariekei hear only noise. The meaning is not in the sound but only in the mind. Meaning is conveyed in thoughts so much so that words do not signify and are not symbolic—that is, words are their own referents.

The strange bodies of the Ariekei dictate that they speak simultaneously with their two harmonizing mouths, the "cut" above on the neck and the "turn" at the chest. Their language is the simultaneous enunciation of these sounds, which are representable as words written one over the other in the form of a fraction. Possibly because of their biological or material embeddedness and the indistinction between mind and word, the Ariekei language allows only affirmations, only true propositions. It gives them the capacity to speak of events that actually are taking place or have taken place in their biologically embedded world, and so the language allows them to tell no lies. Affirmation is the limiting limit of their semantics. This amounts to an extreme "naturalism" in language, whose philosophical formula stipulates that linguistic accounts must be built on empirical causal relations and natural law.[2] This is all the more the case for a species whose environment is "biorigged," its nest-like homes and towns consisting of apparently living plantlike materials bearing no resemblance to the cultivated geometries of the human parts of the city. Little surprise, then, that humans and Ariekei cannot even breathe the same air.

Lacking all cultural artifice, Ariekei have no signifiers that allow them to use a word to describe an action or object in a nonliteral, nonaffirmative manner. They cannot, for example, express disappointment by declaring "I felt crushed." Likewise, joy would not be articulated with phrases such as "I am flying high." For this species, such statements are lies.

At first this fidelity to truth in the form of affirmation is admirable, yet it is not absolute. Due to the extreme limitations of what can be expressed in this manner, the Ariekei eventually develop a mechanism to produce and use similes (saying that one thing is like another) for which the referent is a real and embodied event or action. The protagonist Avice is one of the similes. As a girl, she was given something unpleasant to eat; she ate it out of obedience, not choice, and suffered for this. Later, one of the Hosts said of her, "When we talk about talking . . . most of us are like the girl who ate what was given to her. But we might *choose* what we say with her."[3] Referring to Avice's act in this way, as a limitation, indicates that at least some Ariekei find even the similes too constraining, at best a kind of making do.[4]

The difficulty inherent in communicating with the Ariekei leads the human bureaucrats to breed a race of doubles, called Ambassadors, who can replicate the Ariekei process of speaking two words simultaneously. They originate as clones with massive amounts of empathy, approximating a unified mind, to produce "speech spoken by a thinker thinking thoughts."[5] Things go badly when some Ariekei begin to learn to turn the similes into contradictions at the same time that Bremen, the ruling planet, sends a special pair of Ambassadors whose "language" not only intoxicates the Ariekei but induces addiction to the sound of their voices, even as they say nothing more important than pleasantries and polite conversation. The addicted Ariekei begin to demand this "god-drug" and become incapable of taking care of themselves, their young, and their city.

Out of the chaos emerge two fundamentalist revolts, one against addiction and one against "lying." The revolts are led by other Ariekei along with certain humans who become leaders by advocating for the purity of truthful, affirmative propositions with evident external natural and empirical referents. The novel thus pits signifying against naturalistic affirmative truth telling and expression against the purity of reference in a political and religious context. For the addictive Ambassadors and the human bureaucrats who breed the double that administers the god-drug, language is pure artifice in the form of statements with signification but no empirically true affirmation or external reference. Their language, nothing more than a postmodern signifying chain pushed to its limits so as to mislead, is posited as a necessity in the political and cultural realm to the point of becoming addictive in its own context. Affirmative statements about events that have actually occurred remain largely outside the bureaucratic system of language. It becomes the task of nonbureaucratic humans to teach the Ariekei to signify using metaphors in order to release them from their addiction but also to make good on some conception of reference within Embassytown to keep it from being overrun by the powerful forces of Bremen.

SIGNIFYING AND SIGNS

The case for chains of signifiers and the overdetermination of meaning is often thought to be one of the chief accomplishments of postmodern philosophy. British literary scholar Alan Kirby claims that a defining trait of postmodern philosophy is its concern with the elusiveness of meaning and knowledge.[6] Postmodernism, he writes, treated contemporary culture as a spectacle before which individuals were powerless to act but nevertheless were able to problematize questions about the real. These observations align with those of the French postmodern theorist Jean-Francois Lyotard, who famously describes the postmodern condition as the debunking of grand philosophical, scientific, political, religious, and historical narratives. Nevertheless, while there are still university courses that teach the literature of this debunking—for example, "Postmodern Fictions"—they are rare.

Kirby comments that outside of academia, postmodernism is dead, dead and buried. He claims that celebrated authors like Nabokov, Gibson, and B. S. Johnson, along with philosophers such as Derrida, Foucault, and Baudrillard, are no longer relevant to a generation accustomed to interacting, inventing, or directing their texts and drinking in the illusion that they are somehow controlling or at least managing their place in quick bites of online and reality TV worlds, the more banal the better. Such so-called pseudomodernism is said to have reactivated the individual along with the once-abandoned grand narratives and have taken the place of postmodernism. Pseudomodernism, he argues, is greatly inferior, and instead of calling reality into question, it takes itself for the real even while engendering nothing but the desire to return to the infantile state of being consumed by one's activities. This territorialization is problematic.

Perhaps the technological and social revolutions of the last ten or more years leave little doubt about the veracity of this claim, but if we have definitively left something called postmodernism behind, it seems we still do not know what it is and to what extent it may or may not have contributed to the current state of affairs. This is the complaint made as long ago as June 2011 by British ethologist and evolutionary biologist Richard Dawkins on his Richard Dawkins Foundation for Reason and Science website. Dawkins and others, like physicist Alan Sokal, are making claims about postmodernism strikingly similar to Kirby's criticism of pseudomodernism. When Dawkins puts a question on his website asking what "critical theory" might be, the clearest answer he gets from any commenter is that critical theory includes structuralism, poststructuralism, and postmodernism and that it is the provenance of "a few scruffy radicals."[7]

The problem is that this is not a definition, much less an explanation. Dawkins is left like the poor Duck in *Alice in Wonderland*, who just wants to know what *it* means when the Mouse, who is telling a dry tale, says, "Stigand, the patriotic archbishop of Canterbury, found it advisable."[8] For the Duck, *it* refers to something specific, like a frog or a worm. Like the Duck, Dawkins offers up crisp definitions of the biological concepts *Lamarckian* and *mutationism*—definitions that are clear and concise, as well as informative and, as far as possible, truth telling. Like the Ariekei language, these terms are supposed to refer to nature, to the world outside of language that is empirically verifiable in all its aspects. Given the impossibility of such clear and concise naturalistic definitions for postmodernism, Dawkins asks if it is possible that words like *postmodern* mean nothing at all.

Even Kirby, who defends postmodernism as ironic, knowing, and playful—part of a world where a multiplicity of ideologies, worldviews, and voices can be heard—provides more of a description than a definition or explanation. Nevertheless, this failure to fill the gap does not mean Dawkins is right. It may simply mean that when and where postmodernism and associated concepts have been defined, its defenders have not been able to understand it well enough to translate its canonical terms into informative definitions. Still, whether or not one is an advocate of postmodernism, it is philosophically, historically, and culturally important to have a clear definition and/or explanation. Of course, there is always the risk that the Dawkins of the world won't find even the most accurate explanations reasonable or sensible, but certainly it is worth the effort of reaching across the wider and wider abyss to try.

Coming on the tail of the infamous Sokal hoax, where the physicist submitted a postmodern parody of science to a cultural studies journal that published it as authentic, criticisms like Dawkins's, as well as the responses to them, convinced many readers that postmodernism is a nebulous mishmash of free associations from scruffy intellectuals, a swirl of metaphors verging on lies. However, the truly astounding fact about postmodernism is that, whatever it became in the hands of enthusiasts, it originated as more or less what many of its recent practitioners and critics say it is not—that is, it began as a formal system or series of formal systems.[9] Formal systems are often not well known or understood outside mathematics and computer and natural science, but they are pervasive across social sciences and humanities and in cultures that, unlike the Ariekei, are not grounded in a pure naturalism. However, it is quite possible that the postmodern call for the undoing of master narratives may not have recognized the formal basis of its own call for the radicalization of theory. Let us then begin by clarifying the formal structures that give way to contemporary demands for nonnaturalistic and nonrepresentational modes of thought.

SCIENCE IS INDEPENDENT OF BOTH THE HUMAN MIND AND BEING

In *Postmodern Philosophy and the Scientific Turn*, I use the phrase "the scientific turn" to characterize a philosophical paradigm widely utilized in twentieth- and twenty-first-century Continental philosophy but that, I argue, originated primarily in Analytic philosophy as a turn toward the language of logic and toward discrete and formal computation in the philosophy of language and philosophy of mind. I made the claim that a number of significant postmodern philosophers and theorists embraced this turn but referred to it as "the linguistic turn," and I argued that the linguistic turn, like its correlate in Analytic philosophy, finds its theoretical roots in a methodology broadly construed as mathematical or logical formalism.

The modern move toward formalist thinking began in the sixteenth century with the work of Francis Vieta (1540–1603), who introduced abstraction in the form of letters into algebra.[10] It was embraced by Bernhard Bolzano (1741–1848), who argued that science is a demonstrative system—a demonstrated theory that dispenses with verification. In the twentieth century, the French philosopher of science Jean Cavaillès (1903–1944) argued similarly that science is independent of both the human mind and being-in-itself and becomes an "object *sui generis.*"[11] This is not trivial, for it indicates that science is not one object among others in a cultural milieu but that it is autonomous, capable of generating its own intelligible elements, and that different sciences are unified by their common inclusion in this one system, "a self-enclosed dynamism" without beginning or end; science is also outside of time, especially outside the "lived experience of a consciousness."[12] Science is understood to be an unending and unstoppable conceptual becoming, independent of what the scientist herself understands. As Cavaillès states, for all the natural sciences, including the biological sciences, "growth occurs without external borrowing. . . . [thus] there is a break between *sensation or right opinion* and science."[13] This is why the structure of science is and only can be demonstration defined as logic, "the internal rule which directs it posits each of its steps," as well as its essential traits: unity, necessary indefinite progression, and closure upon itself.[14]

However, unlike the logical positivists, Cavaillès does not accept the idea that the theory of science is logic alone, for that position ends up abandoning even truth as correspondence and is left with coherence theory, which stipulates that so-called atomic statements or judgments of perception—the reported sensations of a particular observer at a specific moment in time, formerly said to be irrefutable and therefore foundational—are really only the result of syntactical commitments—that is, the arrangement of signs.[15] As noted previously, this is how the corrupt human politicians on Ariekei speak to one another; they speak by arranging signs in relation to one another and evade even the slightest reference to the naturalistic external state of affairs. The general weakness with this approach is that syntactical formalization cannot complete itself by itself; it cannot help but refer to objects, so the system is not, in fact, self-enclosed.[16]

For philosophers like Cavaillès, the logic of a formal system requires an ontology to complete it; in addition to the formal system, it requires reference to an exteriority, to objects, and not just to other signs in the system.[17] But for hardened formalists, "all external questions are 'metaphysical' and therefore nonsensical," so the term *external* refers only to systems of signs or, at most, to marks on paper, foregoing the necessity that signs are not objects that imply a reference to an external actuality.[18]

Although Cavaillès stood in opposition to logical positivism, he is thought to have been influenced by mathematician David Hilbert's formalism.[19] Both argue that the truth of mathematics is in the demonstration, in the method of mathematics, so that science cannot be the product of the intentions of scientists. It is, instead, science itself that demonstrates what is true or not, so "the credit should and does go to science itself."[20] Thus, mathematical objects—such as "the square root of −1"—are merely the product of the mathematical system that produces them, and outside this formal-linguistic context, they are meaningless. The conclusion here is that until and unless such formulations become objects of study, they represent no idea.[21]

If mathematical language extends itself, introducing its own formal idealizations, then the universe of mathematical objects is always in the process of formation, a conceptual becoming that cannot be stopped and will always be beyond the reach of individuals.[22] As the mathematician Vladimir Tasić points out, the same thing can be said about "truth," especially the claim that "all truth changes all the time," a statement that cannot itself be proven to be true since no formal language can formulate its own theory of truth, and even higher concepts of truth are needed to do this.[23] The implication is that if mathematics is always and endlessly formulating its own object, mathematical truth cannot possibly be formulated by finite human understanding. Gödel's incompleteness theorem expresses this by claiming that higher concepts will have to be continued into the transfinite as part of a conceptual continuum that never ends.[24] And yet, even Gödel notes that such concepts are put to the test, judged in human practice, in the lifeworld—in the cultural, social, and intellectual milieu.

Cavaillès's chosen task seems to have been to reconcile formal logic with worldly applications—in a sense, to bring the Ariekei together with the human politicians: "Through the detour of abstract axiomatics, the formalist elevates himself to the general theory of formal systems and succeeds in constituting systems in which the structure has completely eliminated the content."[25]

For this reason Cavaillès rejected at least some aspects of Edmund Husserl's account of the relation between mathematics and the physical world, which, for Cavaillès, remained too much embedded in such a logical empiricism. He states that, essentially, if it is the case that "physical theory is simply an empty mathematical form applied to the invariant intuitive contents of the lifeworld," mathematics does not truly augment our knowledge of the lifeworld but merely idealizes our power to predict.[26] In other words, this is the old problem of the Kantian schematism, which is supposed to bring together an empirical intuition and a radically heterogeneous concept.

After Cavaillès's death at the hands of the Nazis, Georges Canguilhem wrote a book on the work and life of Cavaillès, and in 1948, Canguilhem became the director of the Institut d'histoire des sciences at the Sorbonne. Canguilhem also served from 1964 to 1968 as the president of the Jury d'Agrégation in philosophy, which provided him with institutional influence over the teaching of philosophy and helped consolidate the future influence of students.[27] Among these students were Gilles Deleuze, Michel Foucault, Louis Althusser, and Jacques Derrida. With this in mind, in subsequent chapters we will look more closely at ideas Cavaillès grappled with that seem to have made their way into the philosophy of Gilles Deleuze.

POSTMODERN PHILOSOPHY, DELEUZE, BERGSON, AND MERLEAU-PONTY

As stated previously, for philosophers like Cavaillès, the logic of a formal system requires an ontology to complete it. This means there must be reference to exteriority—to objects and not only to other signs in the system. Although Gottlob Frege may have judged this as missing the point of a purely logical language, the task has been taken up by competing factions of philosophers, at one point characterized by Gilles Deleuze as either materialists or idealists. Materialism, often referred to as physicalism, is the doctrine that everything that exists is physical. Idealism clearly assumes the contrary position: that all that is real is either the content of one's mind or at least its effect. Currently, throughout philosophy, it appears the materialists are in ascendance over the idealists.

In *Cinema 1: The Movement-Image*, Deleuze addresses the materialist and idealist positions by citing what he calls a "crisis of psychology," which arose at a point in time when he believes it became impossible for philosophers to continue to place "images in consciousness and movements in space."[28] Deleuze notes that this juxtaposition of qualitative images and quantitative spaces was brought into question by both Henri Bergson and Maurice Merleau-Ponty. For Bergson, the matter was couched in the language of temporal duration and extensive spatiality. For Merleau-Ponty, what was at stake was a matter of the split between empiricism and what he refers to as intellectualism. It has been pointed out that this choice of terms is unfortunate as it does not accurately reflect the operative language of contemporary discussions, which tend to refer to either empiricist sense-data theories or neurophysiological physicalism.[29]

Lawrence Hass argues convincingly that "intellectualists (such as Kant) and empiricists alike have held essentially the same theory, that is, Descartes' theory."[30] This is the theory that material objects cause sensations in the mind or brain, which then represents these sensations as objects. Hass adds that in contemporary philosophy, this view is present wherever a philosopher provides a list of sensory *qualities* such as "cold, hot, white, sour, hard, bitter, red."[31] He contrasts this with what he argues is Merleau-Ponty's view, which is that any so-called sensible is a matter of perceptual complexity in a larger field.[32] Nevertheless, Deleuze utilizes the Bergsonian and Merleau-Pontyean language of materialism versus idealism or intellectualism to refer to the idea of a consciousness constituted out of pure material movements as opposed to a universe constituted from pure images in consciousness.[33]

In this context, Deleuze refers first to Bergson and Husserl, as each sought to overcome this opposition rooted in mind-body dualism. Deleuze's own overcoming of the opposition of materialism and intellectualism led him to a concept he attributes to cinema: the *movement-image*. Deleuze recognizes Bergson's objection to cinema as an "ambiguous ally" in overcoming dualism. However, utilizing the concept of the movement-image, Deleuze offers a reading of Bergson that resituates Bergson's philosophy in proximity to his own on this matter. He then turns abruptly from Husserl to Merleau-Ponty, who, he states, attempts "only incidentally a confrontation between cinema and phenomenology."[34] Although framed in the context of Deleuze's account of cinema's movement-image, these comments are important with respect to the question of Deleuze's relationship to both Bergson and Merleau-Ponty.

Undoubtedly each of the three is engaged in the undoing of dualism— understood as the relation between thought and movement—by slightly different means but each in accordance with the problematics set out at the beginning of this chapter, that is, providing an explanation of the relation between empiricist and formalist approaches to reality. If the structures of logic—its true assertions and formalist propositions—define or determine the real, does such a reconciliation arise only in relation to a theory of empiricist sense-data? Moreover, can either of these approaches be reconciled with movement and change? Or, like the Ariekei, will we have to recognize as lies any statement or construct that arises on the basis of movement and change and so allows for statements that may not be able to be expressed as true assertions?

For Bergson, this understanding does not start from logical constructs but from the image of one's own body, which arises as one image among many in the material world. An image is neither representation nor thing—perhaps we may refer to it as an affect or a sensibility, not yet a perception. An image arises in relation to the afferent nerves transmitting disturbances to nerve centers and efferent nerves transmitting from the nerve centers to the body's periphery and setting it in motion, thereby changing surrounding images.[35] The body is able to be distinguished from all the other images insofar as it is the center of action in relation to all the other images. Additionally, it is distinguishable as a zone of affective life that does not automatically or mechanically respond to the material forces of the universe that affect it.[36] Thus, for Bergson, the body image is a center of action or nonaction, an open zone of indetermination from which there is the option of acting back into the world or not acting at all. As such, it is not a mathematical point.[37] Deleuze's take on Bergson's situating of the body as the central image is that "you may say that my body is matter or that it is an image."[38] This is to say, as well, that the body or matter and what he will refer to as the movement-image are identical. This is an approach that will take us from here all the way to the final chapter of this book.

Deleuze recognizes that what he calls Bergson's first thesis on movement is the idea that space (as conceived by mathematics) is infinitely divisible and therefore homogeneous but movement is indivisible and heterogeneous and so cannot be reconstituted out of either positions in space or instants in time.[39] From this it follows, for Bergson, that because cinema is constituted of immobile sections (shots called any-instant-whatevers) to which movement is added, it does not meet his understanding of movement. Deleuze objects that each section is in fact mobile so that movement is not added to immobile sections because, even though every shot is fixed, spatial, and immobile, the means by which the shot becomes cinema, namely the projector, constitutes a movement-image.[40]

He correlates this with what he calls Bergson's third thesis regarding duration: "Not only is the instant an immobile section of movement, but movement is a mobile section of duration, that is, of the Whole."[41] Movement is therefore a change in quality. Deleuze does not name the qualities—hot, cold, red, white—but, like sense-data theorists, he refers to changes of quality. Additionally, he says that movement—such as pouring sugar into a glass—expresses a change in the *whole*, a qualitative transition. For his part, Bergson did not affirm that an instant of time is an immobile section of movement and that movement is a mobile section of duration, for this would imply that an instant, an immobile section, is part of duration or is duration.

Bergson is clear that duration cannot be reconstituted out of a series of immobile sections. The universe endures, it elaborates the absolutely new, but it is not the whole. What endures is the world, and the world, according to Bergson, is Open; it is not the given or givable, and so it is not the whole. The duration of sugar dissolving in a glass of water coincides with the duration of the one who watches and waits for it to dissolve; thus, duration is immanent to the open universe, which includes the observer.[42] Deleuze wrangles with Bergson's concepts in a manner that must be addressed, and later chapters of this book will take up the distinctions set out here in order to clarify the reasons for Deleuze's reading of Bergson and to distinguish it from Bergson's own conceptualizations.

With respect to Merleau-Ponty, Deleuze argues that phenomenology establishes "'natural perception' and its conditions" as its norm.[43] He states that "hence movement, perceived or made, must be understood not of course in the sense of an intelligible form (Idea) which would be *actualized* in a content, but as a sensible form (Gestalt), which organizes the perceptive field as a function of a situated intentional consciousness."[44] First, we might want to pay attention to the distinction—if there is one—between actualizing an Idea and the formalist process of projecting or applying a formal structure onto an empirical world. Second, this raises the question of what is meant by natural perception. Merleau-Ponty calls it the undoing of classical psychology and physiology, which is to say the overthrow of sense-data theory, the idea of perception as a "mosaic of sensations" apprehended, as Descartes argued, by an inspection of the mind or held together by judgment that keeps all the separate data together.[45]

Thus, natural perception, according to Merleau-Ponty, is perception of a *whole*—"the interrelationships and structure of a whole"—which is a "spontaneous" way of seeing as opposed to an "analytical structure"—that is, the perception of isolated elements.[46] This is the case for sound as much as for sight since a melody is not a sum of sounds but a perceived whole that can survive even being transposed from one key to another. Often sound or even touch melds with vision so we may perceive a "wooly blue" rug or, as the artist Paul Cézanne claimed, find color in shapes.[47] In each case, it is the whole that creates a certain amount of constancy even amid changes in lighting that alter the color of objects, motion (such as when sitting on an unmoving train next to one that starts to move so it is unclear which is moving and which is still), or the shifting figure-ground of an optical illusion. Merleau-Ponty's point is that we anchor ourselves in objects in the world even if they are unstable and not the other way around because our perceptions are not fragmented sense-data that the mind orders.[48]

This is not exactly what Deleuze seems to say when he insists that for phenomenology, anchoring in the world is not the effect of *objects* asserting themselves but of a perceiving subject that is strictly a consciousness of the world and so organizes that world as the function of its situated intentional consciousness. Deleuze's own view emerges here when his criticism extends to the idea that for phenomenology, the sensible form, the Gestalt, organizes the perceptual field for the situated intentional consciousness. This is apparently in place of his own preference, which is that of an intelligible form (Idea) "*actualized in a content.*"[49] What is key here is the concept of actualization. This is not the usual formalist account of the relation between concepts and the world but can be seen as a reformulation of formalism in Deleuzian terms, namely the *actualization* of an Idea in a content rather than the projection of a formal equation onto a material or empirical reality. Content may or may not be material or empirical but may be any type of sign, a broad concept whose implications we will examine in later chapters. For Merleau-Ponty, "objects and lighting form a system which tends toward a certain constancy and a certain level of stability," but this does not occur through "the operation of the intelligence but through the very configuration of the field."[50]

It is for the same reasons, Merleau-Ponty continues, that the self-evidence of introspection has been thrown into doubt. Introspection—the interior examination of our own emotions in order to understand those of others—gives us almost nothing because anger, shame, love, and hate are not inner realities or hidden psychic facts. They are types of behavior and styles of conduct visible and felt from the *outside*, just as emotions are *disorganizing* reactions, variations on our relations with others.[51]

When Merleau-Ponty applies these phenomenological concepts to film, he addresses it as a perceptual object that is, as Deleuze concurs, a temporal Gestalt, a whole.[52] He argues that the viewer's understanding of any single scene depends on what precedes it so that the same image can be read in a variety of ways. This "rhythm" exists as much for the sound in film as for the visuals as both require an internal organization invented by the film's "creator," especially as sound, including music, transforms the whole.[53]

It appears that Merleau-Ponty's and Deleuze's ideas may resonate with one another, so why does Deleuze object so strenuously to Merleau-Ponty's phenomenology? One area in which Merleau-Ponty and Deleuze evidently differ is with respect to the question of meaning. Merleau-Ponty asks what a film signifies, what it means, and Deleuze, as will be evident in chapter 5, most point-edly does not. Nevertheless, when Merleau-Ponty notes that films have stories and ideas, he cautions that the joy of art does not lie in representing because "the film does not mean anything but itself."[54] There is no external referent for the film. Its meaning appears to be immanent to the film itself. With respect to our perception of films, Merleau-Ponty states that we see film images from the outside as behaviors, not as thoughts.

Clearly, for Deleuze, film images should not be translated into behaviors. They are images and signs. Films consist of movement-images, time-images, affection-images, and a range of different signs—opsigns, sonsigns, chrono-signs, lectosigns, and noosigns, all of which make possible a semiology of the cinema.[55] Of course, we must also ask what Merleau-Ponty means by behavior (*comportment*) since, for him, it is clear that symbolic and mental activities count as "forms of behavior" in which signs are related to other signs and not merely to objects.[56]

These differences appear to be amplified by Merleau-Ponty's claim that art and philosophy differ because "art is not meant to be a showcase for ideas and . . . contemporary philosophy consists not in stringing concepts together but in describing the mingling of consciousness with the world, its involvement with a body, and its coexistence with others."[57] This statement gives us the opportunity to ask to what extent Deleuze is really at odds with the idea that consciousness is "thrown into the world, subject to the gaze of others."[58] It is possible that Deleuze might agree with Merleau-Ponty's claim that philoso-phers and filmmakers share the view of the world that the inside is also outside, but the manner in which this outside and inside are identified may be a crucial point of distinction between these two philosophers.[59] We will take these ques-tions up in the chapters that follow; these questions will repeatedly return us to the matter of the relation between thought and world, matter and mind or memory, and what is at stake in this for Deleuze, Bergson, and Merleau-Ponty.

NOTES

1. China Miéville, *Embassytown* (London: Del Rey, 2012).

2. Joseph Rouse, "Naturalism and Scientific Practices: A Concluding Scientific Postscript," in *Naturalized Epistemology and Philosophy of Science*, ed. Chienkuo Michael Mi and Ruey-lin Chen (Amsterdam: Rodopi, 2007), 61–86, 64.

3. Miéville, *Embassytown*, 211.

4. Miéville, *Embassytown*, 211.

5. Miéville, *Embassytown*, 107.

6. Alan Kirby, "The Death of Postmodernism and Beyond," *Philosophy Now*, no. 58 (November/December 2006), https://philosophynow.org/issues/58.

7. See "The Richard Dawkins Foundation," https://www.richarddawkins .net.

8. Lewis Carroll, *The Philosopher's Alice in Wonderland and Through the Looking-Glass*, introduction and notes by Peter Heath (New York: St. Martin's Press, 1974), 30.

9. See Dorothea Olkowski, *Postmodern Philosophy and the Scientific Turn* (Bloomington: Indiana University Press, 2011), chap. 1, for an analysis of the Sokal hoax.

10. Florian Cajori, "A History of the Arithmetical Methods of Approximation to the Roots of Numerical Equations of One Unknown Quantity," in Colorado College Publication, General Series no. 51, Science Series vol. 12 (November 1910): 182.

11. Jean Cavaillès, *On Logic and the Theory of Science*, 2nd ed. (Paris: Presses Universitaires de France, 1960), in *Phenomenology and the Natural Sciences: Essays and Translations*, ed. Theodore J. Kisiel and Joseph J. Kockelmans (Evanston, IL: Northwestern University Press, 1970), 370, 371.

12. Cavaillès, *On Logic*, 371–372; Joseph Rouse, "Naturalism and Scientific Practices: A Concluding Scientific Postscript," Division I Faculty Publications, Paper 20 (2007), 60–86, 64, accessed January 2018, http://wesscholar.wesleyan .edu/div1facpubs/20.

13. Cavaillès, *On Logic*, 372. Emphasis added.

14. Cavaillès, *On Logic*, 373.

15. Cavaillès, *On Logic*, 350. This type of sentence is called a protocol sentence.

> If we want to know whether a given sentence is meaningful or not, we must decide whether or not we associate with it a method of verification, for the meaning of a sentence lies in the method that we would employ to verify or falsify it. This means that we must specify the conditions under which it would be possible to verify the sentence. In stating what those conditions are, of course, we must use sentences. Unless we want to be involved in an infinite regress (or a circle), there must be some sentences that we can verify directly, which will then form the foundation for verifying other sentences. Those sentences are the protocol sentences. Protocol sentences were taken (initially at least) to express conditions whose obtaining or not is directly verifiable.

K. Ludwig, "Carnap, Neurath, and Schlick on Protocol Sentences," *Noûs* 21, no. 4 (1987): 457–470, http://www.jstor.org/stable/2215667.

16. Cavaillès, *On Logic*, 350.

17. Cavaillès, *On Logic*, 350.

18. Cavaillès, *On Logic*, 350.

19. Vladimir Tasić, *Mathematics and the Roots of Postmodern Thought* (Oxford: Oxford University Press, 2001), 85.

20. Tasić, *Mathematics and the Roots*, 87, 88. Emphasis added.

21. Tasić, *Mathematics and the Roots*, 86, 87.

22. Tasić, *Mathematics and the Roots*, 88, 89.

23. Tasić, *Mathematics and the Roots*, 88.

24. Tasić, *Mathematics and the Roots*, 88.

25. Jean Ladrière, "Mathematics in a Philosophy of the Sciences," trans. Theodore J. Kisiel, in *Phenomenology and the Natural Sciences: Essays and Translations*, ed. Theodore J. Kisiel and Joseph J. Kockelmans (Evanston, IL: Northwestern University Press, 1970), 472.

26. Cavaillès, *On Logic*, 351.

27. Peter Halliward, *Concept and Form: The "Cahiers pour l'Analyse" and Contemporary French Thought*, accessed January 2018, http://cahiers.kingston .ac.uk/names/canguilhem.html.

28. Gilles Deleuze, *Cinema 1: The Movement-Image*, trans. Hugh Tomlinson and Barbara Habberjam (Minneapolis: University of Minnesota Press, 1986), 56. Originally published in French as *Cinéma 1: L'Image-Movement* (Paris: Les Éditions de Minuit, 1983).

29. See Lawrence Hass, *Merleau-Ponty's Philosophy* (Bloomington: Indiana University Press, 2008), 27.

30. Hass, *Merleau-Ponty's Philosophy*, 28.

31. Hass, *Merleau-Ponty's Philosophy*, 29.

32. Hass, *Merleau-Ponty's Philosophy*, 31.

33. Deleuze, *Cinema 1*, 56.

34. Deleuze, *Cinema 1*, 57.

35. For my account of Bergson's concept of the image, see Dorothea Olkowski, *Gilles Deleuze and the Ruin of Representation* (Berkeley: University of California Press, 1999), 95–97.

36. Henri Bergson, *Matter and Memory*, trans. N. M. Paul and W. S. Palmer (New York: Zone Books, 1988), 168–169; Henri Bergson, *Oeuvres* (Paris: Presses Universitaires de France, 1963), 48–49, 53.

37. "The body image is exposed to the action of external causes that may threaten to disintegrate it. Some of these causes are reflected, producing perception, the measure of our possible action on things and their action on us. As such, perception expresses *virtual action*, for there is always a distance between one body and another. When that distance decreases to zero, the body absorbs the action of external causes. This is affection, for it is then our own body that is sensed and the action upon ourselves is real action. The totality

of perceived images subsists even if our own body is no longer present but to annihilate the body is to destroy sensation which is simply a modification of the image called body." See Dorothea Olkowski, "Bergson and Film," in *Film, Theory, and Philosophy: The Key Thinkers*, ed. Felicity Colman (Durham, NC: Acumen Press, 2009).

38. Deleuze, *Cinema 1*, 59.

39. Deleuze, *Cinema 1*, 1.

40. Deleuze, *Cinema 1*, 2–3.

41. Deleuze, *Cinema 1*, 8.

42. Henri Bergson, *Creative Evolution*, trans. Arthur Mitchell (Lanham, MD: University Press of America, 1983), 10–11. Published in French in Bergson, *Oeuvres*.

43. Deleuze, *Cinema 1*, 57.

44. Deleuze, *Cinema 1*, 57. Emphasis added.

45. Maurice Merleau-Ponty, *Sense and Non-Sense*, trans. Patricia Allen Dreyfus (Evanston, IL: Northwestern University Press, 1992), 50.

46. Merleau-Ponty, *Sense and Non-Sense*, 49.

47. Merleau-Ponty, *Sense and Non-Sense*, 51.

48. Merleau-Ponty, *Sense and Non-Sense*, 52.

49. Deleuze, *Cinema 1*, 57.

50. Merleau-Ponty, *Sense and Non-Sense*, 51.

51. Merleau-Ponty, *Sense and Non-Sense*, 52–53.

52. Merleau-Ponty, *Sense and Non-Sense*, 54.

53. Merleau-Ponty, *Sense and Non-Sense*, 55, 56.

54. Merleau-Ponty, *Sense and Non-Sense*, 57.

55. Gilles Deleuze, *Cinema 2: The Time-Image*, trans. Hugh Tomlinson and Barbara Habberjam (Minneapolis: University of Minnesota Press, 1989), 25. Originally published in French as *Cinéma II: l'Image-temps* (Paris: Les Éditions de Minuit, 1985).

56. Maurice Merleau-Ponty, *The Structure of Behavior*, trans. Alden L. Fisher (Boston: Beacon Press, 1963), 121. Deleuze takes his assessment of phenomenology and film not from Merleau-Ponty but from Albert Lattay's *Logique du cinema*, which, he states, is "phenomenologically inspired." See Deleuze, *Cinema 1*, 226n3.

57. Merleau-Ponty, *Sense and Non-Sense*, 59.

58. Merleau-Ponty, *Sense and Non-Sense*, 59.

59. Merleau-Ponty, *Sense and Non-Sense*, 59.

TWO

Deleuze and Guattari's Critique of Logic

LOGICAL FUNCTIONS OR CONCEPTS?

The point was made in the first chapter that the mixing of formalist symbolic systems with ontology and empirical verification violates the principles of formalist systems according to which "all external questions are 'metaphysical' and therefore nonsensical."[1] Given this, the term *external* comes to refer only to systems of signs or, at most, marks on paper. From an alternative perspective, it also violates the sensible foundations of lived experience, where systems arise in relation to the intentional structures of a consciousness or a lived body. The two systems are incompatible and incommensurate, but it was also noted that it has been the goal of numerous contemporary and postmodern philosophers, beginning with Cavaillès, to bring these systems together. Perhaps this is our illusion. If so, it is the specific genius of Gilles Deleuze to have recognized this.

As I have argued previously, Deleuze is explicit about this in his criticism of Kant's account of the axioms of intuition. The axioms of intuition are extensive magnitudes, thus they are geometric; they are a priori synthetic propositions, spontaneous and active judgments, thus, axiomatic. In other words, they are postulates of thought, essential intuitions of the nature of space given a priori that must be confirmed by outer intuition.

However, for Deleuze, that the axioms of intuition must be confirmed by outer intuition represents a limitation that he, along with modern mathematics, does away with. For Deleuze, the idea that Kant's science of relations requires its axioms to have a possible object in outer intuition is problematic because it is limiting. Out of all logically possible geometric relations, only those that may actually be constructed can be such an object. This requirement limits

Kant to Euclidean geometry, the one space of human experience.[2] Our human intuition of spatial relations reveals the finitude of human understanding when it is limited by sensibility, as only spatial axioms tied to sensibility would obtain objective validity. This limitation was overcome by mathematicians who proved that there are geometries beyond those of the physical space of our experience.[3]

This leads to the development of a Riemannian geometry, applicable to the surface of a sphere where the straight line of its axioms refers to the endless (because circular) but finite (because circular) circles on the circumference of that sphere.[4] Most importantly, for our purposes, "the creation of non-Euclidean geometry brought into clear light a distinction that had always been implicit but never recognized—the distinction between a mathematical space and physical space."[5] Mathematical space is the space of scientific theory different in kind from the physical space, whose axioms are supported by sensation, as the latter are (as Kant's antinomies imply) purely subjective constructions as opposed to the objective constructions of mathematical space.

In essence, to bring these two together in a manner that privileges the naturalistic and empirical world is, for Deleuze, a grave error he believes even Husserl fell prone to, making it exceedingly difficult for his followers as well as his critics to recover from that slippage. Deleuze follows the lead of the post-Euclidean mathematicians, whose objective constructions of mathematical space provide an abstract and mathematical understanding of any question that is interesting, remarkable, or unusual. Nevertheless, in *What Is Philosophy?*, Deleuze and Guattari take a stand against formalist mathematics' counterpart, formal logic, as set out by Frege and Russell. The direction of their critique is implicit throughout their work, and although it is seldom explicitly addressed, we may find it in specific types of formulations.

In *What Is Philosophy?*, Frege is recognized for extending logic by drawing on the mathematical notion of a function and thereby removing logic from its familiar framework as a set of relations between subjects and their predications. Deleuze and Guattari's account of Frege does not cite secondary sources, and some of their comments on Frege may appear excessive or inflammatory to a realist, analytically inclined logician.[6] Nevertheless, I would argue that, in general, their position on Frege is relevant for their definition of a concept. One of Frege's "innovations" is "dispensing with differing acts of judgment (affirming, denying), in favor of one kind of judgment (affirmation) and differing kinds of propositions," thereby formalizing only the logically essential features of ordinary language, taking the logic of propositions as basic, rejecting the subject-predicate distinction, and formulating and introducing an adequate conception of quantification.[7]

Specifically, Frege replaces the subject term and the predicate term of a proposition with the notions of concept and object respectively.[8] "In place of the subject-predicate distinction Frege introduces that of function and argument. . . . The traditional account understands every sentence as ascribing something [property or meaning] to a subject."[9] Frege uses the terms *function* and *argument* to refer to certain kinds of expression—they are parts of sentences and not conceptual content—but sometimes he also uses function to refer to numbers or quantities: "If in an expression . . . a simple or complex sign occurs in one or more places, and we consider it replaceable in one or more of these places by something, but everywhere by the same thing, then we call the part of the expression which hereby appears as unchangeable the function and the replaceable part its argument."[10] General statements are then statements about functions and not about objects as in ordinary language. The distinction between function and argument is the difference between the fixed and the variable parts of an expression. It is purely syntactical in simple expressions that are determinate in a particular sentence. The statement "All men are mortal" is a statement about this particular function: "If *a* is a man, then *a* is mortal," and the statement "Some men are Greeks" is a statement about the function "*A* is a man and *a* is Greek," which indicates that "not all sentences resulting from substitutions for the letter *a* are false."[11]

A second crucial aspect of Frege's logic is his treatment of concepts. For Aristotle, the formation of concepts is the disjunction or conjunction of pre-existing concepts, and the validity of an argument depends on relationships between concepts—that is, the form of the propositions in which they are placed.[12] Immanuel Kant's analytic-synthetic distinction defines analyticity as "the *unity* of the act of bringing various representations under one representation," for "in every judgment there is a concept which holds of many representations.[13] For Kant, "concepts, as predicates of possible judgments, relate to some representation of a *not yet determined* object. The concept body . . . is therefore the predicate of a possible judgment, for instance, 'every metal is a body.'"[14] For Kant, the Table of Judgments is the key to what he calls the "function of thought."[15] The four types of judgments conform to "the technical distinctions ordinarily recognized by logicians," and they form a part of "the clue to the discovery of all pure concepts of the understanding."[16] Synthesis, as pure and a priori, gives us pure concepts of the understanding, and the act of putting different representations together and grasping them in one act is attributed to the power of imagination. Nevertheless, although the Table of Judgments does not provide any content for concepts, it is only by means of analysis (judgments) that different representations may be brought together under a concept.[17] Concepts require judgments, and the unity of judgments is independent of the content of concepts. Nevertheless, concepts and judgments alone do not give us knowledge. Knowledge requires sensible intuitions without which concepts are empty and blind.

Frege saw Immanuel Kant's analytic-synthetic distinction as an advance on Aristotle with respect to the truths of Euclidean geometry, which are both synthetic and a priori and whose axioms are self-evident and govern anything that is spatially intuitable, whether perceived or imagined.[18] And while such axioms are broadly applicable, the laws of logic, such as the law that every object is identical to itself, are said to hold in the domain of everything that is thinkable, not only in the realm of numbers.[19] Such logical truths are, for Frege, a priori but not synthetic; they are analytic but *not* in the Kantian sense. Moreover, as for the concepts of Deleuze and Guattari, such truths call for neither intuitions nor sensible experience as their source.[20] Frege seems to make the point that it is the argument form and not any particular concept-expression that serves logical truths, although it seems to be unclear what makes a truth analytic other than it is derivable from only definitions and logic.[21] Possibly to address this, Frege asserts that just as a specific property can hold for a sequence of natural numbers (1, 2, 3, etc.), it can also hold for *any* sequence where, if the initial premise is true, every member of the sequence must also be true. This can be verified sensibly but only to establish the truth of the premises.[22]

It has also been argued that Frege's logic is designed to express conceptual content only and nothing else.[23] Does this imply that what Frege means by concept is different from or similar to what Deleuze and Guattari mean by concept? In later work Frege states that the meaning of a word requires a context, prioritizing the sentence meaning over that of a word. So the following seems to hold for Frege: "In the sentence 'Bismark is dead,' the expression 'is dead,' occurring as part, designates a concept. If a sentence contains two proper names or more, the part of the sentence lying outside any two of the names designates a relation. The expression 'is north of,' for example, occurring in 'Canada is north of Mexico,' designates a relation."[24]

Frege came to the position that numbers and names are objects because they have identity; they are the same no matter how they are specified, and he distinguishes logical objects from concepts, which must be objective and nonpsychological and require a logical regimentation so they are able to function regardless of the situation.[25] This turns out to be more difficult than it might appear: "The identification of a science, on his view, requires all concepts of the science to be defined from primitive terms and all arguments to be replaced by gapless proofs from primitive terms. . . . Frege means not only to introduce a new general requirement—that each science must, ultimately, be systematized—he also means to introduce the first systematic science, a systematic science of logic."[26] The existing system, as Frege finds it, appears to be still presystematic insofar as the concept of number is not yet fixed and the use of numerals does not yet pick out particular objects. Nevertheless, the truth values of the elements of arithmetic, for example, have to be assumed in order to proceed at all.[27] Moreover, up to a point, it appears to be difficult to distinguish what Frege means by *concept* as opposed to *function* or even if it is the case that every concept is also a function.[28] Frege eventually seems to have addressed these problems so that it is possible to give a clearer picture of what he means by the word *concept* or at least to distinguish it from Deleuze and Guattari's use of the term.

Deleuze and Guattari maintain, specifically, that Frege wishes to make the concept into a logical function that has the truth value of either true or false and that he replaced the notions of the subject and predicate position of a proposition with the notions of argument and function.[29] Functions are said to be incomplete, like a frame waiting to be filled with a picture. Originally, Frege writes, "a function of x was taken to be a mathematical expression containing x, a formula containing the letter x."[30] However, it became clear that 2 x 1 is the same function as 3 x 1 even though the numbers vary and that both are different functions than 2 − 1.

Moreover, concepts as functions are extensional (referred to as having value-range), and logic is concerned only with truth—that is, affirmation. The concept "being human" is now understood as a function that has the "true" as value for any argument that is human. For example, "'Socrates is a man,' instead of being treated as a relation between terms (SaM), is treated as the *application of the concept* 'is a man' (Mx) to the *object* Socrates (s), yielding a value (a truth value) denoted by the sentence 'Ms'."[31] "Is a man" could be replaced by any other proposition. It defines a value for the variable x. Relations are treated in an analogous manner. The relation "is less than" ($L\,x, y$) utilizes pairs of objects and always has one of two truth values, True ($L\,3, 5$ = True) and False ($L\,5, 3$ = False).[32] Concepts, in this structure, are always incomplete; they can be completed by an object, marked by the placeholding free variable x, but objects are complete self-subsistent entities.[33]

The set of a function's truth values, what is true or false when something is plugged into x (the argument), constitute the concept's extension—the members of the set, which Deleuze and Guattari refer to as the exoreference, the proper names that allow for attribution. Conditions of reference are the concept's intension—logical descriptions or states of affairs, such as "morning star" and "evening star" for the planet Venus.[34]

Deleuze and Guattari argue that Frege's logic is extensional, meaning he treats concepts as *identical* when they have the same extension. Moreover, "every concept is defined over the whole universe of objects," and any concept (Fx) can be True only if the negation ($\neg Fx$) of it is False. Only one can be true; the Law of Excluded Middle holds, and it is this that provides self-consistency.[35] Moreover, the extension of the concept "$\neg Fx$" (*not-Fx*) is relative to the whole universe of possible objects of the concept "Fx," In other words, the true concept "Fx" carries with it the identity and individuation of all its members—its full extension—but its negation would consist of quite heterogeneous classes or sets and so cannot support identity.

For each concept, there is an object in the universe that is its full extension, and this concept is also an object over and above its members, and, as an object, it too must have a concept. Thus, Frege's universe contains classes, classes of classes, classes of classes of classes, indefinitely, a strongly hierarchical and highly complex picture. As well, the universe is the universe of all possible objects, which are, however, conceived of as actual, leading to the problem—the contradiction, actually—of the universe as a completed totality with deterministic membership *and* the universe as an object that would have to belong to itself (a logical contradiction).[36]

Frege argued that arithmetical objects, meaning numbers, are logical objects so that all true statements about these objects can be resolved by appeal to definitions derived from logical laws.[37] He accepted that the concept of number should be elucidated by reference to sets, but he hoped to reduce the mathematical concept of sets to that of classes, which are logical objects in a pure logical theory. The classes and classes of classes are planned for calculating, for determining the truth value of each universal statement of identity as well as the consistency of the entire system.

However, given the nested nature of classes, the system cannot proceed to infinity without canceling the truth value of every class along the way, as no ultimate class ever appears, throwing them all into question. As Deleuze and Guattari express this, "Proof of the consistency of arithmetic cannot be represented within the system ... [and] the system comes up against true statements that are nevertheless not demonstrable, are undecidable."[38] In other words, the system lacks both endoconsistency and exoconsistency.

It can be seen, as well, that "sentences have no self-reference, as the paradox 'I lie' shows."[39] The "liar paradox" is an example of a statement that refers to itself; it is its own referent. Additionally, anything is self-referential if it contains itself or, rather, a copy of itself. Continental philosophers refer to this as *mise-en-abyme*, often characterized as two mirrors facing one another and producing infinite reflections in each. The succinct expression of this paradox is as follows: "Let R be the set of all sets which are not members of themselves. Then R is neither a member of itself nor not a member of itself."[40]

The conclusion Deleuze and Guattari reach is that "*in becoming propositional, the concept loses all the characteristics it possessed as philosophical concept.*"[41] These include self-reference, endoconsistency, and exoconsistency. When the concept is turned into a function that is defined mathematically or propositionally, something new has been invented. For any sentence "*x* is human," being human transitions into a value for the variable *x*. What is at stake is the function's truth value, its true affirmative propositions, which are its extension (membership). The philosophical concept disappears into a function for a set of objects that make up its extension: "The reduction of the concept to the function inevitably deprives it of all its specific characteristics that refer back to another dimension."[42]

Thought refers by constituting or modifying states of affairs or bodies by means of performatives such as "I promise *x*." Living beings refer phenomenologically through modifications of perception, sensation, and action. By contrast, formal logic produces only the "empty reference" of truth value—the true or the false—which is then applied to already constituted states of affairs, trivial factual propositions such as "Napoleon was defeated at Waterloo."[43] Its propositions are what Deleuze and Guattari refer to as *prospects*—that is, informative propositions that are nothing more than "an ordered, oblique deformation of reference."[44] In other words, logical propositions operate with insignificant cases such as "Socrates is a man" or "Napoleon was the emperor of France," which require detachment from all psychological and sociological considerations in order to recognize truth and only truth in a proposition. Logic's preoccupation with strings of linked propositions prevents it from creating and solving real philosophical problems because problems are not propositional.[45] Philosophical problems, they concede, must be related to a reference. The question that remains is how to do this without falling into the very methods of which Deleuze and Guattari are so critical.

FROM FUZZY LOGIC TO PHENOMENOLOGY

Deleuze and Guattari are quick to note that after killing off the philosophical concepts, logic sometimes allows them to reemerge, but not as scientific functions, logical propositions, or elements of discursive systems and not as having a reference. To understand this claim, it is necessary to distinguish a number of what they consider to be failed attempts to reestablish concepts following their reduction by formal logic.

Leaving aside the well-defined sets of "physico-mathematical states of affairs," logic admits to what are called fuzzy sets, or subsets, "a rapprochement between the precision of classical mathematics and the pervasive imprecision of the real world."[46] Classical logic, addressed previously, replaces natural languages, which are ambiguous and vague, with crisp and unambiguous formal terms, but fuzzy logic was developed precisely to deal with ambiguous and vague propositions. For logicians, fuzzy sets are thus defined by contrast with classical logic: "For a mathematician, what does the word *fuzzy* signify (or synonymous words)? This will mean that an element is a member of a subset only in an uncertain fashion. . . . An element may then belong more or less to a subset. The theory of fuzzy subsets at least allows the structuring of all that which is separated by frontiers only a little precise, as thought, language, perception among men."[47]

In Deleuze and Guattari's terms, fuzzy sets are aggregates of perceptions and affections immanent to a subject and to consciousness, and they are characterized as qualitative or intensive multiplicities—"intensity explicated in extensity."[48] Redness or baldness, for example, are matters of degree; at stake here are "How red?" or "How bald?"

Such questions, for Deleuze and Guattari, are purely a matter of *opinion*, meaning subjective evaluations, judgments of taste, or empirical judgments. Far from producing relief, opinions are highly suspect as they arise out of the union of formal and empirical properties Deleuze and Guattari have warned against for philosophical concepts. Given that fuzzy sets are subsets of crisp, classical sets, one option is to make an about-face and return to the classical world with its paradoxes and exclusions. Alternatively, one can begin to delineate the basic features of a philosophical concept, such as the requirement that a concept belongs to a subject and not to a set or that it will be a function of the lived and so does not reference states of affairs in the manner of scientific-logical functions.

This approach leads us directly to the so-called transcendental phenomenology of Edmund Husserl, who discovered the subject's acts of transcendence that are *"capable of constituting new functions of variables or conceptual references."*[49] Husserl sought to purify consciousness of empirical and naturalistic assumptions by means of a transcendental-phenomenological reduction.[50] He begins with the psychological reduction, which focuses on consciousness and its experiences by suspending the natural attitude and so excluding the world beyond.[51] The second, or transcendental reduction rigorously eliminates empirical and naturalistic assumptions from consciousness by bracketing one's own ego and its intentions, thereby making way for the third, or eidetic reduction.[52]

Eidetic reduction seeks general types or essences by means of imaginatively varying individuals in the search for what is essential for physical things as well as social phenomena.[53]

Husserl's transcendental phenomenology, as Deleuze and Guattari state, made possible concepts such as Heidegger's "being-in-the-world" and Merleau-Ponty's "flesh." These concepts are not merely reflective of lived experience but refer the *transcendental subject* to lived experience; in other words, they are major functions that find in "perceptive-affective variables" their respective trajectories of truth. Thus, they are not just fuzzy sets, which are merely empirical judgments and opinions that serve as a bridge between classical logical concepts and phenomenological concepts that are "'significations' of the potential totality of the lived."[54] Phenomenological concepts are not simply *doxa*; they are *Urdoxa*, "original opinions as propositions," acts of transcendence.[55]

Nevertheless, this still does not capture what Deleuze and Guattari mean by *concept* in the philosophical sense. They argue that the phenomenological concept achieves universal and necessary features by "denaturing immanence"; in other words, it is immanent to a subject whose acts—that is, whose functions—are concepts relative to its *lived* plane of immanence.[56] What is missing, for Deleuze and Guattari, is something like immanence to *nature*.

They point to the Analytic-Continental divide between the scientific-logical concept and the phenomenological-philosophical concept represented in North American philosophy programs, admitting that the latter is left with little room to operate by the "logical horse," the Analytic rhinoceros at war with the Continental bird.[57] Yet Deleuze and Guattari will have neither; that is, they reject features of both—specifically scientific functions and logical propositions, as well as discursive or signifying concepts—in favor of what they refer to as an *intensional* concept.[58] Deleuze and Guattari do not refer to Rudolf Carnap in their account of intensional concepts, yet Carnap introduced a formal account of the intensional concept in the analytic tradition. A brief account of it is enlightening; however, as we will see shortly, Carnap's was not the original version of intensional concepts.

INTENSIONAL CONCEPTS

Frege's distinction between sense (intension) and reference (extension) eventually gave rise to the development of intensional identity rather than truth, as expressed in the work of Rudolph Carnap. The statement "*x* is blue" has the property of being blue, its intension, and the class of blue things as its extension, its membership in the class. The statement "Lake Michigan is blue" has the predicate "is blue" as its intension but the truth value "is true" as its extension.[59] Carnap utilized this distinction to solve "antinomies of identity" such as are found in the well-known expressions "morning star" and "evening star," both of which refer to the planet Venus and so have the same extension but different intensions.[60] He proposed that analyticity could be found in intensional identity rather than in truth.

Carnap expresses this in his own terms and distinguishes intension from noncognitive meaning components that are related to psychological effects such as emphasis, emotion, and motivation: "The technical term 'intension,' which I use here instead of the ambiguous word 'meaning,' is meant to apply only to the cognitive or designative meaning component.... [The] determination of truth presupposes knowledge of meaning (in addition to knowledge of facts); now, cognitive meaning may be roughly characterized as that meaning component which is relevant for the determination of truth."[61] Another crucial component of Carnap's definition of intension is that even when there is complete agreement among linguists as to the extension—the membership of a specific predicate in a region or even in the whole world—it remains the case that the linguists may "ascribe to the predicate different intensions."[62]

Carnap then distinguishes between his own "*intensionalist thesis in pragmatics*," which claims that the intension is an empirical hypothesis testable by observations of language behavior, and the "*extensionalist thesis*" (attributed to W. V. O. Quine) that the assignment of intensions is not a question of fact but a matter of choice, with no question of "right or wrong."[63] The distinction between these two theses is nontrivial. For the extensionalist thesis, for example, the German word *Pferd*, based on the study of an individual's speaking behavior, could be translated indifferently as *horse* or *unicorn*. Since the extension is the same (*Pferd*) for the two meanings (intensions), there is no way to empirically decide between the two. Moreover, classes with empty extensions, such as *unicorn* or *goblin*, would not be able to be tested at all.

The intensionalist, by contrast, would not simply investigate a specific individual example but would examine *all logically possible cases*, including cases that causally are impossible, meaning excluded by the known laws of nature of the universe.[64] Again, the implications of this are nontrivial, especially for Deleuze and Guattari. For example, if the laws of nature require "if P then Q," one would be asked to consider that things may be P but not Q. For Carnap, the intension of any predicate is determined by its "range," those possible kinds of objects for which it holds. This means that the intensionalist has to test responses to descriptions of strange sorts of animals, such as "man and lion, man and hawk, etc.," where the ignorance of such species is not relevant.

Even though intensional vagueness as to whether or not they can be "human" is unresolved, "tests concerning intension are independent of questions of existence."[65] The implication is that what is at stake is the creation of alternative plans of action, various reports of the same events, dreams, legends, and fairy tales—that is, creations of all kinds in any possible world.

INTENSIONAL CONCEPTS AND THE EVENT:
CHARLES PEIRCE

What seems to be essential for Deleuze and Guattari's construction of the intensional concept is what may be taken for the rule of immanence. As Carnap articulates it, "That X is able to use a language L means that X has a certain system of *interconnected dispositions* for certain linguistic responses."[66] Vagueness in the system puts in doubt decisions as to whether or not any particular intensions are able to be affirmed or denied. Perhaps we may say that, in such a case, *differentiation* is at work.

The intensional approach is characterized by Carnap with two different possible methods or dispositions in the use of concepts. The first is behavioristic, meaning it is empirically tested—for example, driving a car in order to observe its performance. But the second, *the method of structure analysis,* calls for investigating a situation, an event, in enough detail (including any relevant general laws of physics or physiology) to derive its characteristic responses. In other words, study the internal structure of the car, especially its motor, and, using physical laws, calculate its response under certain conditions.[67] The former method is, on Deleuze and Guattari's account, distinctly phenomenological; the latter, it appears, corresponds to their notion of the philosophical concept as intensional concept.

Deleuze and Guattari indicate their hesitation to depend on either the generosity or regrets of logicians, yet they call for a "precarious balance" between "scientifico-logical concepts [Frege, maybe Quine] and phenomenological-philosophical concepts [Husserl, probably Merleau-Ponty]."[68] They go on to promote the idea of a scientific or logical concept that allows for philosophical functions, meaning significations that relate to the lived, but only as *virtual,* not as empirically real. Lacking reference but organized, it seems, by the method of structure analysis, a concept arises in relation to the consistency of its internal components, condensing but also accumulating its components.[69]

The intensional concept is described as the "event as pure sense."[70] Its meaning is given formally without denoting lived experience or scientific states of affairs, thus it lacks conditions of reference in general. It consists of multiple variations, but its consistency is defined by *internal components* to the sign event in which it appears. This situates the intensive concept outside the mundane propositions in which it might have been enshrined as well as outside the propositional function, variables, and truth value of prospects.[71]

An earlier and likely more relevant source than Carnap for the development of the intensional concept is Charles Peirce. Peirce quickly points out that intension is likely to be confused with intensity, and so he prefers to use the term *comprehension*. Others, he notes, have referred to the intensional concept as internal quantity, force (creating lively representations in the mind), connotation (only when used in reference to essential characters implied by a definition), forms, attributes, depth, matter, and content.[72] Peirce chooses from among these options to refer to intension as depth and correlatively to refer to extension as breadth: "By the informed breadth of a term, I shall mean all the real things of which it is predicable, with logical truth on the whole in a supposed state of information. By the phrase 'on the whole' I mean to indicate that all the information at hand must be taken into account, and that those things only of which there is on the whole reason to believe that a term is truly predicable are to be reckoned as part of its breadth."[73]

Extension, or informed breadth, lies between the one extreme of knowing no facts but knowing only the meaning of terms and the other extreme, an absolute intuition of qualities—that is, knowledge of forms themselves. The former situation, essential depth, is defined as really conceivable qualities predicated of a term in its definition.[74] The latter, substantial depth, is defined as the real concrete form belonging to everything of which a term is predicable with absolute truth.[75]

Earlier in his work, Deleuze overtly connects his concept of intension to Peirce's by means of the concept of *generality*. Generality belongs to the order of *laws* that determines *resemblances* among subjects and equivalences to terms it designates. It is defined by the exchange or substitution of particulars.[76] Generality of the particular "stands opposed to repetition as universality of the singular" and carries the first time, the singular, to the nth power.[77] Nevertheless, the two, generality and repetition, are intimately connected. Generality is of the order of laws, which determine resemblances and equivalents, but every constant of one law is a variable of an even more general law and thus experiences its own powerlessness, its "utmost transitoriness"—uniting, for example, "the change of the water and the permanence of the river," which itself is nevertheless a variable in relation to other more general laws.[78]

Repetition—it is important to note—is possible only in relation to law, affirming itself only against law. It does not exist on its own without generality.

It is the "singularity opposed to the general, a universality opposed to the particular, a distinctive opposed to the ordinary, an instantaneity opposed to variation, and an eternity opposed to permanence."[79] Scientific experiments set up specific similar conditions that seek to establish only resemblances and equalities termed natural law. Moral law is no different except that it operates as the basis of "good" habits.[80] Repetition overturns the law either through mock submission (irony, masochism), by revealing its ultimate consequences, or suspending it by finding exceptions (humor).[81] In the realm of concepts, Deleuze's argument derives directly from Peirce. Generality produces representation, but the intensional concept is the effect of repetition.

For Peirce, law—say, a physical law as a possibility, as the unrealized idea of a quality that acts as a sign (qualisign)—is what he designates *Firstness*. *Secondness* is applied in specific cases—a reality that is a brute action without law, an existent acting as a sign (sinsign). The desire to connect the first with the second is *Thirdness*, a law acting as a sign (legisign). As Thirdness, law is a matter of thought and meaning or interpretation; it is a mental operation such as the laws of dynamics, which predict how bodies will move after forces have been defined.[82]

For Peirce, this makes thought an active factor in the real world that may modify laws. Regarding various natural laws—gravitation, elasticity, electricity, chemistry—Peirce asks the following: "Now who will deliberately say that our knowledge of these laws is sufficient to make us reasonably confident that they are absolutely eternal and immutable, and that they escape the great law of evolution? Each hereditary character is a law, but it is subject to development and to decay."[83] Moreover, every "sign [including Thirdness], or *representamen*, is something which stands to somebody for something in some respect or capacity. It addresses somebody, that is, creates in the mind of that person an equivalent sign, or perhaps a more developed sign. That sign which it creates I call the *interpretant* of the first sign."[84] In the case of Thirdness, the sign refers to an object that is an idea, somewhat like a Platonic idea insofar as it is the same idea even at different times. Furthermore, "The interpretant, the 'third' element of semiosis, in turn acts as a sign/representamen (a first), to determine another interpretant (another third), through the *Same* object (a second)—and so on . . ." unless an end is reached.[85]

As such, Thirdness has the character of *generality*, which Deleuze refers to as "the exchange or substitution of particulars . . . each of which can be replaced by any other particular idea which *resembles* it in relation to a given word."[86] Deleuze does not use the term *Thirdness* in *Difference and Repetition* but instead uses the term *repetition* in active and passive syntheses, yet it is as an open version of Thirdness—an unending evolution—that repetition forms a rich domain of signs and those signs give rise to Ideas, which in turn are subject to an infinite regress.[87] As Deleuze states, "Each passive synthesis constitutes a sign which is interpreted or deployed in active syntheses."[88]

This operates in nature as well as thought, for organic syntheses of elements contract, and every organism is the sum of such contractions, which constitute its primary sensibility. Along with perceptual syntheses, organic syntheses are redeployed in active psycho-organic syntheses of memory and intelligence. Each passive synthesis, each contraction, constitutes a sign that is interpreted and deployed in active syntheses. The formation of a "self" arises as a contemplation as "we learn, form behavior, and form ourselves . . . through contemplation."[89]

This is Deleuze's version of Thirdness. Contraction is our habit of living manifesting the primary habits that we are, the sensory-motor habits of our psyche, but it is through contemplation that we contract as imaginations, generalities, affirmations, and self-satisfactions.[90] Through and through, we are Thirdness: "Underneath the self which acts are little selves which contemplate and which render possible both the action and the active subject. We speak of our 'self' only in virtue of these thousands of little witnesses which contemplate within us; it is always *a third party* who says 'me.'"[91]

Generalization is usually defined in logic as an increase of extension (breadth) and a decrease of intension (depth) without a change of information, as opposed to abstraction, which decreases depth without affecting breadth.[92] However, for Peirce, when generalization is understood strictly, it increases depth because it is the reflection upon a number of cases yielding a description applicable to them all. It is an increase of definiteness of conceptions applied to known things.[93] For example: "Science ought to try the simplest hypothesis first, with little regard to its probability or improbability, although regard ought to be paid to its consonance with other hypotheses, already accepted. This, like all the logical propositions I shall enunciate, is not a mere private impression of mine: it is a mathematically necessary deduction from unimpeachable generalizations of universally admitted facts of observation."[94] Thus, to protest against generalization is to protest against thought itself—it is to protest against the *intensional concept*—as it is the one and primary fundamental law of mental action.[95] This implies that facts are in themselves disconnected and that it is the mind that unites them.[96] "Hence, to say that of *the real*, objective facts some *general* character can be predicated, is to assert the reality of a general," a "virtual prediction" that is, in the end, verified.[97]

Nevertheless, Peirce's conception of generalization differs from Deleuze's in certain important respects. For Peirce, generalization (Thirdness) assumes that the future is continuous with the present and that it compels assent among thinking subjects. In other words, "the future is a general form, a formal possibility that, though it may 'little resemble even the perceptual facts,' and whose coincidence with the 'matter' of future cases remains to be tested, *does* resemble conceived facts."[98] This will not be the case for Deleuze, who, with Guattari, rejects any resemblance between conceptualizations in favor of difference among ideas and disjunction in the realm of the sensible.

This is why Deleuze's use of these concepts insists upon the disjunction or discordant harmony of the faculties. Concepts, he argues, only ever designate possibilities, but his reasons for this differ from those of Peirce. Concepts designate possibilities because thought begins as *mis-sophia*, the original violence forced on thought out of absolute necessity through trespass, violence, and the enemy.[99] In the creation of concepts, the enemy is a rival invoking competitive distrust and *agon*, the Greek concept of struggle, contest, and conflict.[100] It is a necessity that destroys any thought that presupposes itself by situating thought within thinking; thus, it destroys the cogito. However, the necessity that forces thought is the object of an encounter that is not directly sensed but is a sign: a sign of wonder, love, hatred, or suffering; a sign of Socrates, a temple, or his demon, when the latter are understood as signs, as the "being of" some sensible.[101]

The *being of* the sensible cannot be grasped by the senses or by any faculty as it is *imperceptible*, not because it is too small or too far for the senses but because eventually it can be grasped as thought and only as thought—the being of the intelligible—and never as an object of empirical sensibility.[102] Sensibility is raised to the level of a transcendental exercise that is imperceptible to the senses and cannot be apprehended and so recognized as an object by the faculties.[103]

For Peirce, this immediate but vague encounter—unrecognizable as an object for Deleuze—precedes integration and differentiation and cannot yet be articulately thought. Thus, it is a quality (Firstness). But it is (as was noted previously) a quality that acts as a sign (qualisign)—that by which the given is given—and so is commensurate with how Peirce understands it. As indeterminate, sensibility, like Firstness, is freed of any particular quality and remains therefore a sphere of potentiality.[104] For Peirce, the immediate encounter of Firstness is that of possibilities or potentialities for signs, and so, due to its vagueness, the sign entails a "failure of the principle of contradiction."[105] Peirce specifies, "The whole of consciousness is made up of qualities of feeling," pure Firstness, of which we can have no "idea" insofar as feeling is instantaneous.[106]

Yet brute actuality appears. What is real insists upon forcing its way into recognition as something *other* than the mind's creation—as brute fact, a unique event, whether in the form of experience or information.[107] For Peirce this actuality, or Secondness, may be internal or degenerate—one idea connected by the mind to another—or not, in which case it consists of external facts, the action of one thing upon another.[108] The real is either a modification of things (action) or a consciousness of the overwhelming effect of things on us (perception).[109] But let us not forget that Secondness arises from the feeling (Firstness) of resistance and so from an awareness of what is not-self and from the feeling of struggle. This is the manner in which the real forces its way into our recognition.[110]

For Peirce, consciousness of feeling allows for judgment but not for assertion of truth or falsity. Take the statement "this appears red": "It takes some time to write this sentence, to utter it, or even to think it. It must refer to the state of the percept at the time that it, the judgment, began to be made. But the judgment does not exist until it is completely made. It thus only refers to a memory of the past; and all memory is possibly fallible and subject to criticism and control."[111] Nevertheless, Peirce asserts that "in the flow of time in the mind, the past appears to act directly on the future, its effect being called memory."[112] So we see that his interest lies in making assertions (not merely judgments) that can be regarded as law because they are binding for the future.

By contrast, Deleuze accepts the struggle arising from sensibility without engaging Secondness. He argues that Immanuel Kant's error came when he declared that concepts without intuitions are blind. Deleuze remains within the conflicts of sensibility insofar as they are precisely what give rise to the mind's creations. For Deleuze, struggle and conflict are the feeling of what happens when the sensible cannot be grasped, when it cannot be referred to an object of experience able to be recalled, imagined, or perceived by the faculties. It perplexes the soul and poses a problem for memory. Mere empirical memory only grasps what must have been seen, heard, imagined, or thought. But what Deleuze calls "transcendental memory" grasps the being of the past—that which can only be recalled, the forgotten thing that appears to memory, which apprehends it.[113]

And so, in the conflict between one's own perceptual sensibilities, what is left is no longer a *cogito*, a thinking self. No distinction can be made between self and not-self. What is left is a *fractured I* that is forced to pose a problem. In its trauma, the fractured I does not qualify its sensations by placing them in relation to anything that can be recalled, seen, heard, imagined, or thought. It seeks, instead, to think and recall that which has never been empirical, that which is transcendental with respect to both sensibility and memory.[114]

In this way, with Deleuze, we reach the third characteristic of *mis-sophia*. Transcendental memory forces thought to grasp that which can *only* be thought: "the Essence," the *being of* the intelligible that is both the final power of thought and the unthinkable.[115]

For Peirce, this third stage is Thirdness; it is also what he refers to as *consistency*, "a rule to which future events have a tendency to conform."[116] Thirdness consists of ideas such as generality, infinity, continuity, diffusion, growth, and intelligence.[117] It is the recognition of thought as an active force in the world without which no argument would have any power.[118] Thirdness is part of a triadic process, "a process of experimentally attaining truths grounded in the recognition of what is already known to us driven by the establishment, through laws, of generals or universals, and oriented toward communication within a community of like-minded thinkers."[119]

However, although grounded in fact and oriented toward a definitive end, this process is evolutionary. Peirce articulates this in terms of his desire for continuity, but even for Peirce, continuity can be problematic.

> Can we, then, ever be sure that anything in the real world is continuous? Of course, I am not asking for an absolute certainty; but can we ever say that it is so with any ordinary degree of security? This is a vitally important question. I think that we have one positive direct evidence of continuity and on the first line but one. It is this. We are immediately aware only of our present feelings—not of the future, nor of the past. The past is known to us by present memory, the future by present suggestion. But before we can interpret the memory or the suggestion, they are past; before we can interpret the present feeling which means memory, or the present feeling that means suggestion, since that interpretation takes time, that feeling has ceased to be present and is now past. So we can reach no conclusion from the present but only from the past.[120]

For Deleuze such uncertainty is manifest in the doctrine of the faculties. Each faculty is forced to the extreme point of its dissolution, grasping what is empirically ungraspable. It is the discordance that Kant characterizes as the sublime wherein something is communicated *continuously* but from one disjointed faculty to the next.[121]

THE LIMITS OF LOGIC AND PHENOMENOLOGY

Deleuze and Guattari permit the scientific-logical concept to retain its own independent sphere, but the phenomenological concept is more or less driven to irrelevance if not extinction. How so? As noted previously, logical concepts—prospects—designate the elements of the proposition, including function, variables, and truth value. By analogy, the phenomenological concept has been confused with the prospect because its concepts refer the transcendental subject to lived experience; in other words, they refer to major functions that find their respective trajectories of truth in *perceptive-affective variables*. "What *opinion* [*doxa*] produces is a particular relationship between an external perception as the state of a subject and an internal affection as the passage from one state to another (exo- and endoreference)."[122]

When phenomenology chooses a quality common to several perceived objects and aligns it with an affection common to some experiencing subjects who grasp the quality, the result of this correspondence is *opinion not concept*. It is a function or proposition whose arguments are perceptions and affections, a function of lived experience. Deleuze and Guattari ridicule this as aligned with the Western democratic popular conception of philosophy where rival opinions are offered over trivial matters such as preferring cats or dogs or the particular quality of cheese or wine at dinner—specifically dinner at Mr. Rorty's house, since it is Richard Rorty, above all, whose bourgeois liberal point of view takes such discussions to be philosophy. Each of these contestations requires a perceptive-affective lived situation from which an abstract perceptual quality is chosen and its effect on the generic subject debated. Opinions may then be grounded in recognizing a perceptual quality, an affection, and rival views of the appropriate quality are posited. That we call these elements contemplation, reflection, and communication means, for Deleuze and Guattari, nothing more than that "truth" is the opinion of one's own group, especially if it is in the majority.[123] Thus *doxa* is always *orthodoxa*.

Given this situation, what options do we have? The ancient Greek philosophers are chastised for confronting one another to compete merely in the realm of opinion and for objecting to the Sophists only because they could not find the true in an opinion. Plato's search for true opinion by means of the beautiful in nature and the good in minds ends with the acceptance of transcendent knowledge and so fails the test of immanence of the philosophical concepts.[124] Phenomenology also seeks the good and the beautiful but in art and culture, where they are the expression of transcendence within the lived subject. But the expression of transcendence is said to be merely the communication that "Europeanizes" the rest of the world. In a manner similar to Carnap's critique of empirical verification, Deleuze and Guattari's somewhat harsh conclusion is that in invoking the lived, by making immanence the immanence to a subject, phenomenology produces a subject that extracts clichés from perceptions and affections and does not then overturn opinion to replace it with the concept.[125]

On the other side of this philosophical divide, Deleuze and Guattari situate the theory of Alain Badiou, which they note is complex and confess that "we may have oversimplified it."[126] Essentially, for Deleuze and Guattari, the relationship between Badiou's formal, mathematical structures and philosophical concepts is first that the latter float in an empty transcendence and second that there must be at least two types of multiplicities—functions and concepts or states of affairs and virtual events—whereas Badiou claims the set is "any multiplicity whatever."[127] These criticisms are echoed in greater detail by philosophers and mathematicians who express concern regarding three aspects of Badiou's theory: one, that Badiou's set-theoretical models for ontology are a priori commitments, not necessary truths of the set theory; two, that with respect to his philosophical and political claims, Badiou confuses contingent attributes of informal models with necessary consequences of the axioms; and three, that the axioms of set theory themselves dictate strict limitations on the kinds of objects they can and cannot be applied to, especially with respect to anything meaningful for humans.[128]

This critique is addressed to the claim coming from Badiou that one and only one particular axiomatization of set theory provides "'the legislative Ideas of the multiple,' 'the first principles of being,' and 'the law of Ideas.'"[129] In short, "Badiou's heaven of ideas contains only the ZFC axioms [Zermelo-Fraenkel axioms, including the axiom of choice] plus all objects that can be logically derived from them."[130] Additionally, Badiou postulates the existence of empty sets and stipulates that the empty set is axiomatic, by which he means that the cosmos is created (not deduced) out of nothing. "But if we are logical readers rather than dogmatic ones, we will pause to note that there is nothing necessary about such an origin ex nihilo"; it is a choice with no mathematical or logical necessity.[131]

In the end, it appears to be the case as well that there is no justification within set theory for the alignment of the power set (the set of all subsets of a set) with the politics of the state, of Zermelo's axiom of choice with freedom, and of the equation of historical events (the French Revolution) with the "infinite multiples" characterizing the "event."[132] Characterization of the event as a set that contains itself is particularly problematic as this *mise-en-abyme* requires that one already has the set in order to define it, a profoundly nonmathematical procedure giving pause to the claim that Badiou's ontology *is* mathematics.[133] The practice of basing philosophical claims on contingent aspects of mathematical models goes back to the Pythagoreans, who have been widely accused of making an unsubstantiated leap from mathematics to cosmology, ontology, and theology.[134] Apparently, George Cantor, who discovered transfinite numbers, was no less fascinated by the jump to theological ideas.

A major restriction on these directions is that "ZF set theory admits objects and sets of a very restricted sort: numbers, structures, and in general those objects that are, or are taken to be, always the same and not affected by any conceivable event. It does not so much matter here whether we assume such objects and sets as given and independent of our minds."[135] These objects—like Leibniz's monads—are inert or unaffected. This aspect of mathematical objects is illuminated by one of the ZF axioms, the axiom of union, which states that the elements of x and the elements of y must not interact when they are brought together, otherwise they will lose their identity. As has been argued, this operates unproblematically for mathematics but not for mixing bottles of certain chemicals or for the duality of waves and particles in the two-slit experiment of quantum physics. Similarly, two ideas brought together seldom remain uncontaminated and generally produce more thought than even those two.[136]

As Deleuze and Guattari express this, "A state of affairs cannot be separated from the potential through which it takes effect and without which it would have no activity or development."[137] Although there are well-informed philosophers who are philosophically *friends* of Badiou and fully endorse the contingent or metaphorical treatment of natural numbers as "normal," as well as "the political register of the 'state' metaphor," it is clear that Deleuze and Guattari are not among their number.[138]

Badiou borrows key concepts (especially inconsistent multiplicity and the generic) from George Cantor's and Paul Cohen's set theory.[139] Against this, Deleuze is credited with taking his cues from Salomon Maimon, Hoëné Wronski, and Jean Bordas-Demoulin, each of whom utilize the differential relation (dy/dx), as well as Albert Lautman, who suggests the "calculus of problems."[140] Differential calculus has been used to find solutions to problems that are biological, physical, psychical, or sociological. And for Deleuze, "Solutions are like the *discontinuities* compatible with differential equations, engendered on the basis of an *ideal continuity* in accordance with the conditions of the problem."[141]

Using differential calculus, Deleuze favors the structure offered by dynamical systems, which account for the evolution of something over time and are therefore genetic. Every point in the genesis is a specific state, and the set of all the points is a state space. But mathematical state space, although infinitely dimensional, is not actually continuous. Even if its states are infinitely small, they are still discrete. Nevertheless, in *Difference and Repetition*, Deleuze argues that the Idea is "an n-dimensional, continuous, defined multiplicity," where dimensions refer to variables upon which a phenomenon depends and continuity is "a set of relations between changes in these variables."[142]

CONTINUITY AND DIALECTIC

This last is a curious statement, and, once again, although Charles Peirce is not specifically cited in this particular context, the statement resonates deeply with Peirce's conception of the continuum. According to Peirce, continuity is generality, "the possible is general, and continuity and generality are two names for the same absence of distinction of individuals."[143] In fact, for Peirce, continuity is generality that is understood as conformity to one Idea—that is, the continuum is "all that is possible" in a field so crowded that units lose identity and so become continuous.[144] As a result, the continuum is *supermultitudinous*, a collection so great that its constituents have no hypothetical existence except in their relations to one another, which are expressive of the continuum and not distinct.[145] This seems to be what Deleuze is aiming at by using the term *ideal continuity* cited previously, especially because the continuum is reflexive and so cannot be composed of points; it is *mise-en-abyme*—that is, the whole can be reflected in any of its parts.[146] This implies that the continuum is synthetic, unable to be analytically reconstructed, and also inextensible, unable to be divided, thus unable to be composed of points.[147] As Peirce states, "A continuum, where it *is* continuous and unbroken, contains no definite parts; . . . its parts are created in the act of defining them and the precise definition of them breaks the continuity."[148] In other words, given that the continuum consists of real and general possibilities that far exceed anything that exists, "existence is a rupture," a discontinuity.[149] Peirce's account thus fills in the structure of Deleuze's claim that solutions are like discontinuities, as a discontinuity implies an existence that is the fulfillment of a possibility.

Like Peirce, Deleuze insists that the continuum—the multiplicity that consists of virtual events or, as he calls it, "virtual chaos"—is the "potential" through which states of affairs take effect.[150] For Peirce, the richness and possibilities of the continuum far exceed the realm of existents.[151] Moreover, the continuum has multiple dimensions and a plasticity that never ruptures.[152] Points of time or space are "ideal limit[s]," the mathematical notion of limit being something approached infinitely closely without ever actually reaching it in dividing time or space.[153] Or, as Deleuze and Guattari understand it, "states of affairs leave the virtual chaos on conditions constituted by the limit (reference): they are actualities, even though they may not yet be bodies or even things, units, or sets."[154]

In the broader context, Deleuze has argued that "ideal connections constitutive of the problematic (dialectical) Idea are *incarnated in real relations* which are constituted by mathematical theories and carried over into problems in the form of solutions," where the solutions are like *discontinuities*.[155] In his early work, Deleuze locates the concept of the problematic in relation to differential calculus, stating that "solutions are like the discontinuities compatible with differential equations, engendered on the basis of an ideal continuity," where the latter is situated as the trajectory that traces the calculated speed and direction of an entity.[156]

But even there, he notes that differential calculus is a mathematical instrument, making it difficult to see in it the "Platonic evidence of a dialectic superior to mathematics."[157] That is, is there not a problematic Idea superior to mathematical formulations? This question gives rise to an alternative reading of Plato's Ideas as Thirdness, their manifestations as Secondness, and their qualities-signs as Firstness. As Deleuze states, "We must therefore distinguish between Justice, which is the ground [Thirdness]; the quality of justice [Firstness], which is the object of the claim possessed by that which grounds; and the just, who are the claimants [Secondness] who participate unequally in the object."[158]

This is the dialectic. This is also the structure that allows something to be grasped as a sign and the structure of the Idea that differentiates; it is the generality that actualizes quality. So when Deleuze argues that problems are always dialectical, this appears to be what he means. By contrast, solutions are mathematical, physical, biological, or sociological. Nevertheless, it is maintained that mathematics "finds its sense in the revelation of a dialectic which points beyond mathematics," even though "we cannot even suppose that . . . differential calculus is the only mathematical expression of problems as such."[159] Still, continuity in the development of mathematics has made "differences in kind between differential calculus and other instruments merely secondary."[160] This is because, as Deleuze argues, the dialectical Idea, the problematic, is a system of differential relations, and dialectical Ideas are the differentials of thought [Thirdness] engendered or incarnated in various domains [Secondness], each of which is characterized by its own differential calculus as determined by the problematic Idea.

One way of understanding this preference for differentials is to recognize that, for Deleuze, there are "different orders of Ideas *presupposed* by one another . . . (Ideas of Ideas, etc.)," and "mathematics appears with the fields of solutions in which dialectical Ideas of the *last order* are incarnated" ("last order" referring to the highest order), but other Ideas are incarnated in modes of expression corresponding to different sciences.[161]

Additionally, it is the case that the continuity of the trajectories of differential calculus correlates with Peirce's conception of Firstness—that is, Peirce's global continuum (which correlates with mathematical phase space) and the general continuum (the trajectories in phase space), which is the realm of potentiality (the last order Idea and lower order Ideas for Deleuze)—Secondness (the incarnations of Ideas through differentiation, probably quantitability for Deleuze); and Thirdness (the qualities of Ideas, qualitability for Deleuze).[162] Citing Peirce: "Continuity is thus a special kind of generality, or conformity to one Idea. More specifically, it is a homogeneity, or generality among all of a certain kind of parts of one whole. Still more specifically, the characters which are the same in all the parts are a certain kind of relationship of each part to all the coordinate parts; that is, it is a regularity."[163]

MULTIPLICITIES

These formulations lead to the claim that Ideas are multiplicities, an organization of the many without unity that bypasses both contradiction and contraries. Here we see the crucial role of the differential insofar as *multiplicity is difference and differentiation*. It is the differential relation, its *n*-dimensions consisting of the variables or coordinates of various phenomena, elements reciprocally determined along trajectories established by means of differential calculus.[164] It was noted previously that when sensibility is referred to the being of the sensible, the latter is imperceptible to the senses and cannot be recognized by any faculties; this perplexes the soul and poses a problem.[165] Deleuze calls this a "sign," and it correlates with Peirce's Firstness, the unrealized idea of a quality we are immediately aware of, which as chance and possibility does not conform to common sense and good sense.

Peirce defines Firstness as present, immediate, vivid, and prior to differentiation.[166] Secondness indicates facts, existence, actuality, action, and reaction. Thirdness, the "perfect third," is plastic, relative, and continuous, and "every kind of sign, representative, or deputy, everything which for any purpose stands instead of something else, whatever is helpful, or mediates between a man and his wish, is a Third."[167] Thirdness can therefore be understood to involve "mediation, order, law, continuity, knowledge, ternary relation, triad, generality, necessity."[168]

Like Peirce, Deleuze insists that "we can only know through signs, and, . . . we can only know those signs through diverse correlations of . . . conceivable effects in interpretation contexts."[169] Not surprisingly, then, there are three conditions that allow an Idea to emerge: first, potentiality or virtuality; second, reciprocal determination or juxtaposition, thus internal multiplicity without external reference; and third, an ideal connection, a differential relation actualized in spatiotemporal relations as its elements are incarnated in terms and forms.[170]

In short, Ideas arise in a structure that moves from the virtual to its actualization, from conditions of a problem to cases of its solution, and their genesis is a static genesis, the correlate of passive synthesis.[171] Examples of the emergence of the Idea include the emergence of atoms—objective elements of thought— as a physical Idea; the emergence of the concept of an organism—the relations between anatomical and atomic elements considered abstractly and thus independently of their forms and functions—as a biological Idea; and the social Idea—such as abstract labor, the expression of relations of productivity and property—as a Marxist Idea.[172]

In *What Is Philosophy?* actual states of affairs and virtual events are said to be two types of multiplicities (an organization of the many without unity). States of affairs are characterized as actualizations of virtual chaos (Peirce's continuum). Although they are mixtures, states of affairs are not yet bodies, things, units, or sets but merely masses of independent variables, particles (the elements of molecules) and their trajectories, or signs-speeds. In part, Deleuze and Guattari rely on the Stoic account of bodies with physical qualities, actions and passions, and *corresponding* states of affairs, which are determined by bodies but exist independently of the act that forms them.[173]

Deleuze and Guattari's account reflects their opposition to Aristotle's logic, which relies on hierarchical essences and classes, and instead embraces the Stoic approach to reality as consisting of events that are causally linked.[174] Nevertheless, Deleuze also seems intent on breaking apart even causal relations in order to overcome the Platonic difficulty surrounding the causal relationship between Ideas and material things. When bodies mix and penetrate one another—like a drop of wine in the ocean—they determine quantitative and qualitative states of affairs, such as "the red of iron, the green of a tree."[175] But states of affairs that are determined by mixtures in the depth of bodies are not merely distinguished from so-called incorporeal events. Any indication of a causal relation between states of affairs and these so-called surface effects of bodily mixtures is denied. Incorporeal events are expressed linguistically and conceptually as "to become red" or "to become green."[176]

This matters to Deleuze because it separates cause from effect, the causal relationship assumed to exist between bodies and Ideas. Bodies or states of affairs mix with one another and causally affect *one another*. Incorporeal events, however, follow laws; they are ideational and incorporeal; they are Ideas.[177] Incorporeal events are thus expressible in propositions and are connected to other events as relations between propositions. Such "dialectics" may look like dualism but more accurately can be called a duality, the boundary between things and propositions, the surface between bodily depths and incorporeal events.[178]

ARCHITECTONICS

We can now see that the problem raised at the beginning of this chapter has once again come fully into view. The problem is how to characterize the relationship between things and thought without resorting to dualism or certain versions of idealism. As stated previously, the continuum is a multiplicity that consists of virtual events, Deleuze's "virtual chaos," defined as the "potential" through which states of affairs take effect.[179] Furthermore, as Peirce defines it, the richness and possibilities of the continuum far exceed the realm of existents.[180] The continuum cannot be constructed starting from existents or particulars, and neither can the virtual chaos. But the state of affairs is inseparable from the potential through which it takes effect and that sustains its activity and development. The continuum, the virtual chaos, continues to act as a catalyst in the face of new or unanticipated problems.[181]

Living things, claim Deleuze and Guattari, pass from a state of affairs with potential to bodies that condition sensibility actualized in living beings—bodies whose perceptions are bodily states induced by other bodies, whose affections are the passing from state to state, and whose increase or decrease of potential arrives through the action of other bodies.[182] By relating this back to Peirce's semiotics, the meaning of Deleuze and Deleuze-Guattari's structure can be made more clear.

The issue this brings to light is how this affiliation with Peirce's pragmatics and the theory of signs is synchronized with Deleuze's reading of Bergson and Merleau-Ponty. Seemingly at odds with Peirce's semiology, what does Deleuze do with Bergson to align the two? In addition, both chapter 1 and this chapter note the extent to which Deleuze objects to phenomenology—especially what he takes to be the phenomenology of Merleau-Ponty. With our readings of Deleuze and logic along with Deleuze and Bergson, we will revisit this critique of phenomenology to determine the extent to which (if at all) Deleuze and phenomenology are commensurate with one another. So let us begin with Deleuze and Bergson—where we will also find Merleau-Pontean interventions—and move from there to Deleuze and Merleau-Ponty.

NOTES

1. Jean Cavaillès, *On Logic and the Theory of Science,* 2nd ed. (Paris: Presses Universitaires de France, 1960), in *Phenomenology and the Natural Sciences: Essays and Translations,* ed. Theodore J. Kisiel and Joseph J. Kockelmans (Evanston, IL: Northwestern University Press, 1970), 350.

2. Keith Devlin, *Mathematics: The Science of Patterns: The Search for Order in Life, Mind, and the Universe* (New York: Scientific American Library, 1994), 93.

3. Morris Klein, *Mathematics in Western Culture* (New York: Galaxy, 1964), 417.

4. Klein, *Mathematics*, 425, 426.

5. Klein, *Mathematics*, 428.

6. There is an active debate between the historical approach of Hans Sluga and the analytical approach of Michael Dummett. See Michael Resnick, review of *Gottlob Frege*, by Hans Sluga (London: Routledge Press, 1980), *The Philosophical Review* 92, no. 1 (1983): 122. Resnick argues that "Sluga can argue convincingly that Frege's philosophy evolved not in response to transcendental or objective idealism but rather against naturalism and an attendant subjective idealism," 122. In a separate review, Linda Wetzel adds that "Michael Resnik argues convincingly that Sluga's conception of Frege as an objective idealist is true of the Frege of the *Grundlagen*, but Dummett's realist conception is a more appropriate one for the later Frege." See "Reviewed Work(s): Frege and the Philosophy of Mathematics by Michael D. Resnik," review by Linda Wetzel, *The Philosophical Review* 92, no. 1 (1983): 114–116.

7. Resnick, *The Philosophical Review*, 123.

8. Mary Tiles, *Mathematics and the Image of Reason* (London: Routledge Press, 1991), 140.

9. Hans Sluga, *Gottlob Frege*, The Arguments of the Philosophers Series (London: Routledge & Kegan Paul, 1980), 84–85. See also, William Marshall, "Frege's Theory of Functions and Objects," *The Philosophical Review* 62, no. 3 (1953): 375.

10. Gottlob Frege, *Begrijffsscrift*, ed. I. Angelelli (Hildesheim, Germany: Halle a. S.: Louis Nebert, 1964), 15. Cited in Sluga, *Frege*, 86. Sluga notes that Frege later changed this terminology.

11. Sluga, *Frege*, 87, 88.

12. Joan Weiner, *Frege Explained: From Arithmetic to Analytic Philosophy* (Chicago: Open Court Press, 2004), 18, and Sluga, *Frege*, 89.

13. Immanuel Kant, *Critique of Pure Reason*, trans. Norman Kemp Smith (New York: St. Martin's Press, 1965), A68. Emphasis added.

14. Kant, *Critique*, A69. Cited in Sluga, *Frege*, 91. Emphasis added.

15. Kant, *Critique*, A70.

16. Kant, *Critique*, A70, A76.

17. Kant, *Critique*, A77–A78.

18. Weiner, *Frege Explained*, 11–12, 14.

19. Weiner, *Frege Explained*, 15.

20. Weiner, *Frege Explained*, 21.

21. Weiner, *Frege Explained*, 17, 19.

22. Weiner, *Frege Explained*, 22–23.

23. Weiner, *Frege Explained*, 30.

24. Marshall, *Frege's Theory*, 375. Weiner, *Frege Explained*, 51.

25. Weiner, *Frege Explained*, 56, 57.

26. Weiner, *Frege Explained*, 68.

27. Weiner, *Frege Explained*, 67–68.

28. See Weiner, *Frege Explained*, 71–73, for a clear and beautiful articulation of this problem.

29. Weiner points out that Frege's goal is to establish a logically perfect language, which is not possible in natural language. Weiner, *Frege Explained*, 79, 102.

30. Gottlob Frege, "Function and Concept," trans. Peter Geach, accessed November 2017, http://fitelson.org/proseminar/frege_fac.pdf.

31. Mary Tiles, *The Philosophy of Set Theory: An Introduction to Cantor's Paradise* (London: Blackwell, 1989), 140. Emphasis added.

32. Tiles, *The Philosophy of Set Theory*, 140.

33. Tiles, *The Philosophy of Set Theory*, 140.

34. Gilles Deleuze and Félix Guattari, *What Is Philosophy?*, trans. Hugh Tomlinson and Graham Burchell (New York: Columbia University Press, 1994), 136, 137. Originally published in French as *Qu'est-ce que la philosophie?* (Paris: Les Editions de Minuit, 1991).

35. Deleuze and Guattari, *What Is Philosophy?*, 137.

36. Tiles, *The Philosophy of Set Theory*, 152–154.

37. Tiles, *The Philosophy of Set Theory*, 138.

38. Deleuze and Guattari, *What Is Philosophy?*, 137.

39. Deleuze and Guattari, *What Is Philosophy?*, 137.

40. Eric W. Weisstein, "Russell's Antinomy," *MathWorld*—A Wolfram Web Resource, accessed January 2018, http://mathworld.wolfram.com/RussellsAntinomy.html. Symbolically, this is expressed as: let $R = \{x : x \notin x\}$. Then $R \in R$ if and only if $R \notin R$.

41. Deleuze and Guattari, *What Is Philosophy?*, 137–138.

42. Deleuze and Guattari, *What Is Philosophy?*, 138.

43. Deleuze and Guattari, *What Is Philosophy?*, 138.

44. Deleuze and Guattari, *What Is Philosophy?*, 139.

45. Deleuze and Guattari, *What Is Philosophy?*, 139.

46. L. A. Zadeh, forward to *An Introduction to the Theory of Fuzzy Subsets*, by A. Kaufmann, vol. 1, trans. D. L. Swanson (New York: Academic Press, 1975), ix.

47. A. Kaufmann, *An Introduction to the Theory of Fuzzy Subsets*, vol. 1, trans. D. L. Swanson (New York: Academic Press, 1975), xii.

48. Gilles Deleuze, *Difference and Repetition*, trans. Paul Patton (New York: Columbia University Press, 1994), 230. Originally published in French as *Différence et Répétition* (Paris: Presses Universitaires de France, 1968).

49. Deleuze and Guattari, *What Is Philosophy?*, 142.

50. David Woodruff Smith and Ronald McIntyre, *Husserl and Intentionality: A Study of Mind, Meaning, and Language* (Dordrecht, Netherlands: D. Reidel Publishing, 1982), 94.

51. Smith and McIntyre, *Husserl and Intentionality*, 96. Edmund Husserl, *Ideas Pertaining to a Pure Phenomenology and to a Phenomenological Philosophy*, trans. Frederick Kersten (Dordrecht, Netherlands: Kluwer, 1982), 31–32.

52. Smith and McIntyre, *Husserl and Intentionality*, 97. Husserl, *Ideas*, 33, 51, 54, 57.

53. Smith and McIntyre, *Husserl and Intentionality*, 101. Husserl, *Ideas*, 2–26, 69–70.

54. Deleuze and Guattari, *What Is Philosophy?*, 142.

55. Deleuze and Guattari, *What Is Philosophy?*, 142; Edmund Husserl, *Cartesian Meditations*, trans. Dorian Cairns (The Hague, Netherlands: Marinus Nijhoff, 1960), 55–56; Edmund Husserl, *Ideas: General Introduction to Pure Phenomenology*, trans. W. R. Boyce Gibson (New York: Humanities Press), 103–104.

56. Deleuze and Guattari, *What Is Philosophy?*, 143.

57. Deleuze and Guattari, *What Is Philosophy?*, 143.

58. Deleuze and Guattari, *What Is Philosophy?*, 143.

59. Steve Awody, "Carnap's Quest for Analyticity," in *Cambridge Companion to Carnap*, ed. Richard Creath and Michael Friedman (Cambridge: Cambridge University Press, 2007), 240.

60. Awody, "Carnap's Quest," 241.

61. Rudolf Carnap, *Meaning and Necessity: A Study in the Semantics of Modal Logic*, 2nd ed. (Chicago: University of Chicago Press, 1956), 236–237.

62. Carnap, *Meaning and Necessity*, 237.

63. Carnap, *Meaning and Necessity*, 237.

64. Carnap, *Meaning and Necessity*, 237. "Pairs of expressions that always have the same semantic value [in all 'possible worlds'] are intensionally equivalent." Awody, "Carnap's Quest," 241.

65. Carnap, *Meaning and Necessity*, 240.

66. Carnap, *Meaning and Necessity*, 242.

67. Carnap, *Meaning and Necessity*, 243.

68. Deleuze and Guattari, *What Is Philosophy?*, 143.

69. Deleuze and Guattari, *What Is Philosophy?*, 144.

70. Deleuze and Guattari, *What Is Philosophy?*, 144.

71. Deleuze and Guattari, *What Is Philosophy?*, 144.

72. Charles Sanders Peirce, *The Collected Papers of Charles Sanders Peirce*, ed. Charles Hartshorne, Paul Weiss, and Arthur Burks (Cambridge, MA: Harvard University Press, 1931–1935, 1958), 2.393–2.394.

73. Peirce, *The Collected Papers*, 2.407.

74. Peirce, *The Collected Papers*, 2.410.

75. Peirce, *The Collected Papers*, 2.414.

76. Deleuze, *Difference and Repetition*, 2.

77. Deleuze, *Difference and Repetition*, 2.

78. Deleuze, *Difference and Repetition*, 2.

79. Deleuze, *Difference and Repetition*, 2–3.

80. Deleuze, *Difference and Repetition*, 4.

81. Deleuze, *Difference and Repetition*, 5.

82. Peirce, *The Collected Papers*, 1.342, 1.346.

83. Peirce, *The Collected Papers*, 1.348.

84. Peirce, *The Collected Papers*, 2.228.

85. Kamini Vellodi, "Diagrammatic Thought: Two Forms of Contructivism in C. S. Peirce and Gilles Deleuze," *Parrhesia*, no. 19 (2014): 79–95, 10. Vellodi is clear that, for Peirce, an end will be reached, but I prefer to leave the system open, even at the risk of attributing to Peirce a belief he does not hold.

86. Deleuze, *Difference and Repetition*, 1.

87. Peirce, *The Collected Papers*, 1.339.

88. Deleuze and Guattari, *What Is Philosophy?*, 73.

89. Deleuze, *Difference and Repetition*, 73.

90. Deleuze and Guattari, *What Is Philosophy?*, 74.

91. Deleuze and Guattari, *What Is Philosophy?*, 75. Emphasis added.

92. Peirce, *The Collected Papers*, 2.422.

93. Peirce, *The Collected Papers*, 2.426.

94. Peirce, *The Collected Papers*, 4.1.

95. Peirce, *The Collected Papers*, 2.263, 6.21.

96. Peirce, *The Collected Papers*, 6.99.

97. Peirce, *The Collected Papers*, 6.100, 8.155.

98. Vellodi, "Diagrammatic Thought," 79–95.

99. Deleuze, *Difference and Repetition*, 139.

100. Deleuze and Guattari, *What Is Philosophy?*, 4.5.

101. Deleuze, *Difference and Repetition*, R 139.

102. Deleuze, *Difference and Repetition*, 140–141. Later chapters explain why Deleuze refers to this as the "Essence."

103. Deleuze, *Difference and Repetition*, 140.

104. Peirce, *The Collected Papers*, 6.196.

105. Peirce, *The Collected Papers*, 5.505. Cited in Fernando Zalamea, *Peirce's Continuum: A Methodological and Mathematical Approach* (Boston: Docent, 2012), http://acervopeirceano.org/wp-content/uploads/2011/09/Zalamea -Peirces-Continuum.pdf, 27.

106. Peirce, *The Collected Papers*, 1.327, 1.309.

107. Peirce, *The Collected Papers*, 1.325, 1.537.

108. Peirce, *The Collected Papers*, 1.365.

109. Peirce, *The Collected Papers*, 1.324.

110. Peirce, *The Collected Papers*, 1.322, 1.325.

111. Peirce, *The Collected Papers*, 5.544.

112. Peirce, *The Collected Papers*, 1.325.

113. Deleuze, *Difference and Repetition*, 140.

114. Deleuze, *Difference and Repetition*, 140.

115. Deleuze, *Difference and Repetition*, 141.

116. Peirce, *The Collected Papers*, 1.26.

117. Peirce, *The Collected Papers*, 1.340.

118. Peirce, *The Collected Papers*, 1.348–1.349.

119. Vellodi, "Diagrammatic Thought," 6.

120. Peirce, *The Collected Papers*, 1.167.

121. Deleuze, *Difference and Repetition*, 143, 146.

122. Deleuze and Guattari, *What Is Philosophy?*, 144.

123. Deleuze and Guattari, *What Is Philosophy?*, 145–146.

124. Deleuze and Guattari, *What Is Philosophy?*, 147, 148.

125. Deleuze and Guattari, *What Is Philosophy?*, 150.

126. Deleuze and Guattari, *What Is Philosophy?*, 228–229n11.

127. Deleuze and Guattari, *What Is Philosophy?*, 152.

128. Ricardo L. Nirenberg and David Nirenberg, "Badiou's Number: A Critique of Mathematics as Ontology," *Critical Inquiry* 37 (Summer 2011): 585–586.

129. Nirenberg and Nirenberg, "Badiou's Number," 588. Alain Badiou, *Being and Event*, trans. Oliver Feltham (London: Bloomsbury Academic, 2013), 59, 60, 66.

130. Nirenberg and Nirenberg, "Badiou's Number," 590.

131. Nirenberg and Nirenberg, "Badiou's Number," 590.

132. Nirenberg and Nirenberg, "Badiou's Number," 596, 598. Badiou, *Being and Event*, 95, 98, 178, 180.

133. Nirenberg and Nirenberg, "Badiou's Number," 598–599.

134. Nirenberg and Nirenberg, "Badiou's Number," 603.

135. Nirenberg and Nirenberg, "Badiou's Number, 606.

136. Nirenberg and Nirenberg, "Badiou's Number, 608, 609.

137. Deleuze and Guattari, *What Is Philosophy?*, 153.

138. See Paul Livingston, *The Politics of Logic: Badiou, Wittgenstein, and the Consequences of Formalism* (New York: Routledge Press, 2011), 46. Livingston's argument, that formal reasoning—including the formal and mathematical approaches of symbolic logic, mathematical set theory, category theory, and computational theory—has important political consequences, is important but notably difficult to prove.

139. Nirenberg and Nirenberg, "Badiou's Number," 583.

140. Simon B. Duffy, *Deleuze and the History of Mathematics: In Defense of the New* (London: Bloomsbury, 2014), 76, 131.

141. Deleuze, *Difference and Repetition*, 179. Emphasis added.

142. Deleuze, *Difference and Repetition*, 182.

143. Zalamea, *Peirce's Continuum*, 10; Peirce, *The Collected Papers*, 4.172.

144. Zalamea, *Peirce's Continuum*, 15; Peirce, *The Collected Papers*, 7.535n6; Charles Peirce, *Reasoning and the Logic of Things* (Cambridge, MA: Harvard University Press, 1989), 160; Charles Peirce, *New Elements of Mathematics* (The Hague, Netherlands: Mouton, 1976), 3.388.

145. Zalamea, *Peirce's Continuum*, 12; Peirce, *New Elements*, 3.86–3.87, 3.95.

146. Zalamea, *Peirce's Continuum*, 13; Charles Peirce, *Writings*, ed. Nathan Houser (Bloomington: Indiana University Press, 1982–2000), 3.103. Deleuze, *Difference and Repetition*, 179. Emphasis added.

147. Zalamea, *Peirce's Continuum*, 14.

148. Zalamea, *Peirce's Continuum*, 15; Peirce, *The Collected Papers*, 6.168.

149. Zalamea, *Peirce's Continuum*, 15.

150. Deleuze and Guattari, *What Is Philosophy?*, 153.

151. Zalamea, *Peirce's Continuum*, 15.

152. Peirce, *The Collected Papers*, 38. Deleuze does not appear to follow Peirce into the "logic of vagueness," bypassing excluding the law of the excluded middle in favor of the concept of virtuality (Peirce, *The Collected Papers*, 52).

153. Peirce, *The Collected Papers*, 59.

154. Deleuze and Guattari, *What Is Philosophy?*, 153.

155. Deleuze, *Difference and Repetition*, 179.

156. Deleuze, *Difference and Repetition*, 179.

157. Deleuze, *Difference and Repetition*, 179.

158. Deleuze, *Difference and Repetition*, 62. Thus, Deleuze notes the neo-Platonists designate the Imparticipable, the Participated, and the Participants.

159. Deleuze, *Difference and Repetition*, 179.

160. Deleuze, *Difference and Repetition*, 181.

161. Deleuze, *Difference and Repetition*, 181. Emphases added.

162. These correlates have been teased out of Deleuze, *Difference and Repetition*, 181, and Zalamea, *Peirce's Continuum*, 16.

163. Peirce, *The Collected Papers* 7.535n6. Cited in Zalamea, *Peirce's Continuum*, 17.

164. Deleuze, *Difference and Repetition*, 182–183.

165. Deleuze, *Difference and Repetition*, 140.

166. Peirce, *The Collected Papers*, 1.357. Cited in Zalamea, *Peirce's Continuum*, 49.

167. Peirce, *The Collected Papers*, 1.322; Charles Sanders Pierce, *Writings*, vol. 5 of 7, ed. Nathan Houser (Bloomington: Indiana University Press, 1982–2000), 300–301. Cited in Zalamea, *Peirce's Continuum*, 50.

168. Zalamea, *Peirce's Continuum*, 50.

169. Zalamea, *Peirce's Continuum*, 47.

170. Deleuze, *Difference and Repetition*, 183.

171. Deleuze, *Difference and Repetition*, 183.

172. Deleuze, *Difference and Repetition*, 185–186.

173. Gilles Deleuze, *The Logic of Sense*, trans. Mark Lester with Charles Stivale and Constantin V. Boundas, ed. Constantin Boundas (New York: Columbia University Press, 1990), 4. The conception of logic based on *Sachverhalt* (states of affairs) arose within the circle of philosophers influenced by Brentano and Husserl. "Bolzano, Frege and Husserl, by banishing thoughts from the mind, created the preconditions for the development of logic in the modern sense. By defending a view of thoughts or propositions as ideal or abstract entities, they made possible a conception of propositions as entities capable of being manipulated in different ways in formal theories." Barry Smith, "Logic and the *Sachverhalt*," *The Monist* 72, no. 1 (January 1989), 52–69, http://ontology.buffalo.edu/smith/articles/logsvh.html.

174. Jeffrey Barnouw, *Propositional Perception: Phantasia, Predication and Sign in Plato, Aristotle and the Stoics* (Lanham, MD: University Press of America, 2002), 154.

175. Deleuze, *The Logic of Sense*, 6.

176. Deleuze, *The Logic of Sense*, 6.

177. Deleuze, *The Logic of Sense*, 7.

178. Deleuze, *The Logic of Sense*, 8.

179. Deleuze and Guattari, *What Is Philosophy?*, 153.

180. Zalamea, *Peirce's Continuum*, 15.

181. Deleuze and Guattari, *What Is Philosophy?*, 153.

182. Deleuze and Guattari, *What Is Philosophy?*, 154.

THREE

Bergson and Bergsonism

BERGSON AND RUSSELL

For many years Continental philosophers stepped lightly around the philosophy of Henri Bergson. To some extent, this occurred in relation to the rise of Martin Heidegger's philosophy, which, in turn, gave way to existentialism.[1] But just as powerfully, and also somewhat ironically, some of the Continental rejection of Bergson may have been fostered by the criticisms levied against him by Bertrand Russell, who strongly opposed Bergson's prioritization of geometry over logic.[2] Russell's criticisms of Bergson began to appear after Bergson's lectures of 1911 at University College London, during which time Bergson was also presented with an honorary doctorate at Oxford University.[3] Russell characterized Bergson's philosophy as a dualist opposition between life and matter derived from the distinction Bergson drew between the tendencies of instinct or intuition and intellect.[4] Since, for Bergson, time as duration arises with instinct or intuition, and does not separate the world into distinct entities, while space as intellect does precisely this, Russell argued—in the manner of Einstein—that this is an error insofar as time is purely mathematical, a "homogeneous aggregate of the outer one joined to other moments," and so the concept of duration makes no sense.[5]

Following this, Russell questions Bergson's account of space as extension, the idea that every plurality of separate units involves space. For Russell, if the view that all separateness implies space were to be accepted, it could be used deductively to prove that space is involved wherever there is obvious separateness, no matter how little other reason for suspecting such a thing. Even worse, from Russell's point of view, is that if it is also the case that all abstract ideas involve space, then logic, which uses abstract ideas, would be reduced to an offshoot of geometry.[6]

Resonant with Gilles Deleuze's later interpretation of Bergson is Russell's objection to Bergson's criticism of the cinematographic representation of the world because, as Russell insists, the mathematics of differential calculus and dynamical systems does, in fact, conceive of change as a series of otherwise static states. Against this, it may be maintained that, for Bergson, cinematographic motion will never express continuity if by continuity we mean the heterogeneous interpenetration of past and present in duration.[7] In part, Russell attributes Bergson's objection to cinematographic representation to his failure to understand Zeno's paradoxes of motion. Russell endorses the hypothesis that we live in an unchanging mathematical world for which apparently different times actually coexist as atomic and externally connected units, even though he comes to realize that this idea cannot be verified.[8] By contrast, Bergson's view is that "the paradoxes appear from the erroneous presupposition that movement and time are infinitely divisible, that is, that their indivisible parts are geometrical points and non-durational instances."[9]

Bergson's philosophical importance has also been obscured by the disagreement with physicist Albert Einstein, regarding Bergson's challenge to relativity theory concerning the roles of philosophy and physics with respect to the nature of time. Bergson's stubborn persistence in voicing his objections to Einstein's claim that there is only one time—the time of the physicists and mathematicians—and Einstein's conclusion that the philosopher's time does not exist produced a mountain of accusations against Bergson that he did not understand relativity and did not understand the true nature of reality.[10]

The so-called twins argument was originally put forth by the French scientist Paul Langevin on behalf of Einstein. He described not twins but only a "voyager" taking off from Earth in an imaginary rocket. However, the version of this argument that became popular is often stated in well-known terms: "According to the theory of relativity, two twins (one which traveled in outer space at speeds close to the speed of light, and another one who remained on Earth) come back to Earth to find that time slowed down for the twin who had traveled. The twin who stayed would have aged more rapidly; the traveling twin would be younger. Their clocks and calendars would show different dates and times."[11] This formulation raises the question of whether the delay in time is only measured by the clock—that is, the traveling clock that slows—or if it is experienced biologically as well as psychologically by the traveler who, in the special theory, does not return to Earth, as this involves processes not accounted for by the special theory. Langevin persisted in making an equivalence between the physical process and the biological and psychological ones but met with resistance from other theorists.[12]

Einstein's theories of relativity have been called theories of timelessness.[13] Einstein's initial approach to relativity utilized operationalism—that is, not asking about what is real or not real but asking how an observer or different observers would measure what they observe.[14] Einstein initially made no special claim for this interpretation of his conception of the time of relativity as entailing biological as well as psychological time dilation. Yet he eventually argued that any conception of time other than that of relativity does not exist because time is and must be an objective event independent of individuals.[15] What Einstein discovered has been called the *relativity of simultaneity*; it is the question of whether two events distant from one another can be said to take place at the same time. He concluded that two observers moving with respect to one another will not agree about whether two distant events are simultaneous.[16] "But two events can be so far apart in space and take place so close in time that no signal can reach from one to the other. . . . Einstein showed that in these cases you can't state whether they're simultaneous or one happened before or after the other. Both answers are possible depending on the motion of the observers carrying the clocks by which time is measured."[17] In special relativity two observers do not agree; moreover, there is no way to tell which observer is in motion and which is not, resulting in the complete undoing of the idea that there is a real "now," thus refuting time as real.[18] However, the one thing that can be verified is the causal structure of events such that "what is physically real in the universe is its causal structure" and only its causal structure; the physical phenomenon is real.[19]

This leads inevitably to the conclusion that there can be no reference to any experience of future, past, or present. In this timeless block universe, what is real is the whole causal history of the universe, and any temporal event is merely a geometric point in spacetime.[20] General relativity seems only to have reinforced the view of time as an illusion since "given the initial conditions, Einstein's equations determine the whole future geometry of a particular spacetime and everything it contains."[21] Moreover, even though matter influences geometry and, in turn, geometry influences matter, they are hypothesized to remain in equilibrium, a rejection of the idea of absolute space and time but an embrace of a timeless, deterministic universe.[22] How is it, then, that the universe is full of moving stars, black holes, and gravitational waves, none of which contribute to a static and stable universe but, quite the opposite, all of which point to the universe as temporal, as having a history? Privileging evolution and change over determinism and the block universe would affirm that time is fundamental, which is Bergson's position.[23]

Russell's unrestrained criticism of Bergson's philosophy as antiscientific metaphysics was taken up by many philosophers and physicists of the time who sought to defeat Bergson's conception of time and intuition with what they perceived to be a rational, scientific worldview.[24] This occurred in spite of Bergson's ongoing insistence that he had no objections to the theory of relativity and did not actually reject Einstein's formulation of the simultaneity of time—the claim that there is only one real and universal time, which is actually timelessness, and can be interpreted to allow for the claim that two events that seemed to occur simultaneously according to one observer were not necessarily simultaneous for the other due to time dilation at high velocities.[25]

Much of the criticism of Bergson seems to have come from what was widely perceived to be a glaring error in his understanding of relativity theory. Some of his statements appear to be incorrect, and later attempts to ameliorate them failed. Because Bergson was interested in the relationship of clocks to the concrete quality of duration as an experienced now, it is clear that he rejected the Newtonian idea of an absolute space and time that need to be filled with some content.[26] He maintained that there is no distinction between duration and its content, and this is the meaning of his use of the term *image*, a concept that expresses duration as intuition. Some of Bergson's colleagues recognized this and affirmed the validity of his interest in "the questions of *how, why, and under what circumstances* should the clock delays described by relativity theory be unambiguously considered as real temporal changes."[27]

Bergson's target was always determinism. His version of novelty requires heterogeneity, or "multiplicity without divisibility and succession without separation," which is qualitative multiplicity, but the causal order of classical science is timeless.[28] Bergson agreed with the theory that acceleration produced the difference in the two observers' times but concluded that this is not *"real time"* since one twin had been propelled into space while the other remained at home, differences that cannot be ignored and, in fact, matter a great deal.[29] No doubt this is connected to his view that "time is at first identical with the continuity of our inner life ... memory, but not personal memory. . . . It is a memory within change itself, a memory that prolongs the before into the after."[30]

Unfortunately, Bergson also stated of Langevin's example that only one observer's clock could be real and the other is merely its mirror image.[31] He reasoned correctly that each observer perceives her local time with no dilation but incorrectly that she cannot perceive time dilation outside her own system.[32] Further, he confused the reciprocity of appearances due to velocity—that there is no privileged frame of reference—in special relativity with the parameters of general theory, which takes into account the effects of differing gravitational fields—that is, the different measuring of time in the two systems.³³ This led to the perception that Bergson was reasserting Newtonian time because he confused duration and the unity of a cosmic duration with metrical, measured unity, thereby contradicting his own position on the nature of time.³⁴

In the second edition of *Duration and Simultaneity*, Bergson referred to "Time" with a capital *T* as the time of philosophy in order to distinguish it from small *t* "time," the time of physics. When he wrote, in *Duration and Simultaneity*, that for Time there is no difference between a system in motion and one that is stationary, this was again taken by many as evidence for his lack of understanding of the physics of relativity.³⁵ This claim appears to be "completely at odds with the concept of time dilation in the theory of relativity and so a great deal depends on whether one accepts or not that Bergson truly did not understand the relevance of this statement."³⁶ In many ways, Bergson never really recovered from the judgments against him. Critics included physicists and philosophers such as Hans Richenbach, Paul Langevin, Ernst Cassirer, Roman Ingarden, Max Horkeimer, Rudolf Carnap, Jean Becquerel, Émile Meyerson, and, of course, Bertrand Russell.³⁷

On March 11, 1913, the philosopher Bertrand Russell addressed a group called The Heretics at Trinity College on "The Philosophy of Bergson." The address was then published in the journal *The Monist* in July of that year. Invited to reply, Bergson ceded that invitation to his advocate, Wildon Carr, whose response was published alongside Russell's text. Russell's comments are more than observation; they are a full-out attack on what was called "*le Bergsonism.*"³⁸ Russell was not the first to participate in the anti-Bergson manifestation but made up for it with the strength of his objections, accusing Bergson of anti-intellectualism, antirationalism, irrationality, antiscientism, and even collaboration with the Vichy government in France, in spite of the fact that Bergson was Jewish and had advocated for the United States to enter the war against Germany.³⁹

Russell's harsh criticisms appear to have set off an intense and partisan debate that fed the flames of the newly ignited and now ongoing Analytic-Continental divide.⁴⁰ It is clear that, "in Russell's work one finds the prototype of an attempted application of the new logico-philosophical methods of analysis to doing philosophy, and in particular to a certain 'traditional' way of philosophizing."⁴¹ Moreover, Russell's accusation, that Bergson represents "old" philosophy, has recently been heard coming from the lips of a contemporary philosopherwhohastakenupRussell'sclaimtobepracticingascientificphilosophy as opposed to Bergson, who is denigrated because he consistently argued against what he took to be Russell's materialism.⁴² Although the defense of Bergson's critique of Einstein's conception of time is exceedingly complex and at times fraught, it is worth pointing out that a significant group of contemporary cosmologists are willing to assert the reality of the arrow of time and uphold the conclusion that laws of nature evolve in time, a thesis that accords with Bergson's view insofar as they argue for a preferred global time.[43]

Russell classifies Bergson's philosophy, along with that of the pragmatists, as a practical philosophy seeking action as the highest good and insists that this manifests Bergson's "revolt" against the authority of Plato, a revolt weirdly aligned with imperialism and the rise of the automobile.[44] Russell takes Bergson to be a crude dualist who inherited the French and Continental Cartesian worldview, thereby dividing the world into incompatible elements: life and matter, instinct and intelligence, intuition and intellect.[45] But his harshest attacks are saved for Bergson's view of continuity and discreteness in relation to mathematics as opposed to human experience.

Russell articulates this in the clearest possible terms: "Mathematics conceives change, even continuous change, as constituted by a series of states; Bergson, on the contrary, contends that no series of states can represent what is continuous, and that in change a thing is never in any state at all."[46] His inevitable conclusion is that insofar as Bergson's concept of continuity and change is not the classical mathematical conception, he is wrong tout court. The argument goes back to Zeno's paradoxes, which leave us with the unfortunate conclusion that if movement and time are infinitely divisible, then neither movement nor time are real. For Bergson, "at bottom, the illusion arises from this, that the movement, once effected, has laid along its course a motionless trajectory on which we can count as many immobilities as we will."[47]

But Russell, true to his mathematical view of the universe, counters that we live in an unchanging world where Zeno's arrow is at rest at every moment of its flight, a view commensurate with mathematically continuous space and time whose only apparently successive states actually and in fact coexist. Russell refuses to relinquish this position even as he recognizes that the world of our experience—actual space and time—is not in the same unchanging state at every single moment.[48] And so, even as Russell reluctantly moderates his views about the unchanging nature of reality, "Russell's logical atomism still makes him inclined to accept the infinite divisibility of space and time and the real existence of points and instants, though he realizes that they are empirically unverifiable."[49]

Russell's logical atomism, although empirically unverifiable, leads him to the conclusion that atoms of time, of minute and invariable duration, are quite adequately represented as cinematographic, the successive projection of static moments onto a screen.[50] He argues that since mathematics conceives of even continuous change as a series of states, the cinema is a perfect representation of its functioning as well as a correct analysis of physical processes.[51] This conclusion has important implications for the nature of time but also, as will become clear, for our understanding of continuity with respect to the experience of duration, a key concept for both Bergson and Deleuze.

MERLEAU-PONTY AND BERGSONISM

In an address to the Congrès Bergson in 1959, Maurice Merleau-Ponty raises the question of "Bergsonism" by acknowledging that there have been not just one but two Bergsonisms.[52] The first is the work of a philosopher of freedom, the enemy of Kant, opposed by the radical party, the university, the religious party, and the far-right Action Français party and thus attacked by his enemies as well as by the enemies of his enemies.[53] The second is an established Bergsonism, "a collection of accepted opinions."[54] Merleau-Ponty disputes this second formulation as a mistaken characterization of Bergson's philosophy in general and especially of his most radical and innovative thinking. He supports this by referring almost immediately to Bergson's greatly maligned criticism of the mathematical conception of time, which was criticized due to Bergson's philosophical position that mathematical time is not real time. Regarding the latter, Merleau-Ponty writes that, according to Bergson, "we do not draw near to time by squeezing it between the reference-points of measurement as if between pincers; but that in order to have an idea of it we must on the contrary let it develop freely, accompanying the continual birth which makes it always anew."[55] The great novelty of this way of thinking, Merleau-Ponty continues, is that, in 1889, it presented a being that is duration in place of an "I think" and, in a reference to Zeno's paradoxes, a duration that is "the world Achilles walks in."[56]

He notes, as well, that in 1959, as in 1924, the physicists "reproach Bergson for introducing the observer into relativity physics, which they say makes time relative only to measuring instruments or the system of reference."[57] Merleau-Ponty goes on to attribute Bergson's position to the role of perception rather than to the Bergsonian concept of duration but nonetheless defends Bergson's conception of intuition against the charge of dualism as a continuum between pure perception and pure memory, as the "'double expansion, toward matter and toward memory."[58]

However, it is in his essay on "Einstein and the Crisis of Reason" that Merleau-Ponty probes the core of the physicist's reproach and the core of Bergson's refusal of that reproach.[59] That refusal lies particularly in the only apparently benign statement that "Einstein himself was a classical thinker."[60] What does this mean? What is it to be a classical thinker if not, as Einstein himself was known to have stated, to be an advocate of the position that truth is in the world and the world is governed by deterministic laws that dictate a preestablished harmony? The classical physicist inhabits a rational world that cannot bring itself into accord with the principles of wave mechanics precisely because they describe the probabilities—a "tissue of probabilities"—arising from wave and particle duality. They do not and cannot address the proper properties of things—things that are or must be physical individuals.[61]

More precisely, Merleau-Ponty identifies classical thought and its ontology with the position advocated by Pierre-Simon Laplace in 1814. The classical conception of science requires, first, causal determinism that, given precise knowledge of nature's elements (their positions and speeds), every future can be inferred; second, the Cartesian idea that complexity can be decomposed into simples; and third, that the world's existence is extensive or spatialized and so excludes becoming.[62]

This is contrasted with what is called "modern science," by which Merleau-Ponty means not relativity but quantum mechanics, and with it a new scientific ontology centered on the impossibility of synthesizing waves and particles and the discontinuous rather than continuous motion of atoms. The former are complementary but mutually exclusive as it is possible to measure either position or velocity but not both at once. Merleau-Ponty draws the significant, relevant conclusion from this situation that "the probability of the presence of a particle . . . does not concern anything but our ignorance. With probabilist indeterminism, we have to deal with pure probability."[63] Determinism is left behind. In contrast to classical determinism, probability is a conception that Merleau-Ponty is willing to admit into what he calls *the fabric of the real*, just as the statistical may be concerned with individual, generic reality.[64] And so we undo the supposition of individual realities and are left with ensembles of movement or theories of species, the indiscernibility of particles.[65]

Merleau-Ponty is perhaps understandably caustic about the nature of the public and scientific acclaim heaped on Einstein. The public, he implies, address the scientist as a miracle worker, as if relativity were "the object of a sixth sense, a beatific vision," as if it did not require much neural energy, as if it makes sense for journalists to consult the "genius" about matters that are the modern equivalent of those asked of the Pythian oracle.[66] Equally peculiar are the pronouncements of the Soviets who condemn relativity as idealistic or bourgeois in opposition to their own questionably named "rational" social doctrine.[67]

Merleau-Ponty notes that when Bergson arrived at the meeting of the Philosophical Society of Paris on April 6, 1922, he came only to listen but was soon pulled into the discussion and so made an effort to clarify his position regarding the distinction between "physical truth and truth." As Bergson had already asserted in *Duration and Simultaneity*, his book contains no "separate theory of relativity, distinct from the one taught by the physicists," but does contain the declaration that it is "studied from the viewpoint of someone responding to a question posed by a philosopher rather than a physicist."[68] That viewpoint is a matter of knowing that there can be a distinction between time perceived and time conceived, real time and measured time, which is to say, *unreal time*, because, as Bergson points out, "it is possible to be an eminent physicist without being adept at handling philosophical ideas" and, more sharply, "philosophy, like anything else, needs to be learnt."[69] And to justify Merleau-Ponty's point of view, Bergson finishes by emphasizing that for physics as well as philosophy, appeals to authority are *worthless*.

But as his critic André Metz points out, even in the second edition of *Duration and Simultaneity*, Bergson is still concerned only with special relativity.[70] Thus, Bergson's objections, as noted previously, are based on what he calls "the simple fact that it is impossible to adopt two frames of reference as the same time in relativity theory."[71] Only one traveler can be the one who lives and measures time and so serves as the frame of reference while the other travels and so is measured. Moreover, for the theory of special relativity, once a traveler is in motion, the theory does not account for his return. Once he has left, he has left for good, and if he were to return, it would have to be at the exact same velocity in the opposite direction, which the theory (specifically the Lorentz equation) does not provide for.[72]

To be clear, Bergson is accepting the constant velocity of light and its mathematical expression, called the Lorentz transformation, as well as Einstein's rejection of an absolute frame of reference (the hypothesis of motionless aether) necessary for the acceptance of complete relativity of motion and the dynamic equivalence of all inertial systems.[73] Physically, this implies the perfect reciprocity of appearances of two systems moving with respect to one another with constant speed. Unfortunately, there is no way to express symbolically the idea that given two clocks, *each one is slower than the other*, so we are forced to say that one of the systems has slowed down with respect to the other.[74] And so, "To speak of such changes as really taking place would mean to slip back into the Lorentz-Newton idea of an absolute frame of reference."[75]

This was Bergson's point. Special relativity demands reciprocity of appearances and not the privileging of the earthbound metric. Dilated time must be understood to mean that a local time is observed from a *privileged frame of reference* such that it is determined from the point of view of that frame of reference. As noted previously, Bergson seems to have cast a stone into this clear pool of thinking, thereby muddying the waters. He states correctly that no observer can experience the dilation of her own local time, but he incorrectly appears to assume that no observer can perceive anything outside her own system, no duration, no length but her own, making of every system a self-contained unit.[76] Direct observations of dilation in other systems refuted this error, but so does Bergson's own philosophy!

Moreover, the reciprocity of appearances in special relativity does not operate within the theory of general relativity, whose calculations allow the traveler to reduce her speed to zero, to turn around, to reaccelerate enormously, and then to return to Earth. Due to time dilation, two years traveling 1/20,000th less than the speed of light turns out to be equivalent to two hundred Earth years. This is because, according to the general theory, effects of acceleration are equivalent to effects of the gravitational field, which "*slows down effectively to the proper or local time,*" undoing the symmetry of appearances.[77] Of course, this possibility, part of the general theory, was just that; it is an "admissible possibility," but Bergson's failure to clearly differentiate between the special and general theories does not give free rein to critics like Metz to denounce Bergson for returning to Newton's conception of absolute motion, particularly since a number of Bergson's critics also failed to make this distinction.[78]

According to the general theory, there are "local time units whose different degree of dilation in different gravitational fields account for different measuring of time in two systems," even though these different measurements do not affect the irreversibility of the underlying structure—for example, that the departure will always precede the return.[79] It has been suggested that this comprehension of time and times in the general theory is not, after all, incompatible with Bergson's own conception of the variability of durations experienced, for example, by someone hallucinating in comparison to someone else who is awake in every normative sense even though they inhabit the same public time.

It appears that we have wandered far from Merleau-Ponty's account of the difficult encounter between the philosopher and the physicist, but this is not without purpose, given that their disagreement over the nature of time is the theater within which Merleau-Ponty situates his defense of Bergson. Here are the twins, Peter and Paul. Peter's time, whether expanding or contracting, does not and cannot express what Paul is living. Each of them experiences the time around himself differently. But the physicist rejects this, ridicules it, and insists that Paul is the absolute, the spectator of the entire universe, invoking mytho-logical time.[80] Merleau-Ponty allows that "relativity could be reconciled with all men's reasoning if only we agreed to treat multiple times as mathematical expressions, and to recognize . . . a philosophical view of the world which is at the same time the view of existing men."[81]

And yet Einstein maintains that lived time has no jurisdiction beyond what each of us sees even as he came to assert that physics is the notation of reality. Merleau-Ponty identifies this, in a manner that recalls Edmund Husserl, as, "the crisis of reason again," where there can be no reason but that of the physicist and no time but that of classical science within which "my present is simultaneous with the future of a different observer sufficiently distant from me, and thereby destroys the very meaning of the future."[82]

Merleau-Ponty's 1956–1957 courses on nature at the Collége de France re-iterate and reinforce his previous remarks. What, he asks, does the science of relativity tell us about time? It tells us, he replies, that time is relative, not abso-lute, and that it is measurable, that it is a variable for thinking but not a separate reality independent of concepts of causality, light, space, and energy—which are an ensemble of concepts, an undivided reality, a rigorous ensemble of con-structed elements—and also that time is not indifferent to nature or events or to the point of view of a subject who is also an observer of time and in time.[83] What is crucial is that we do not confuse the scientific measurement of time with "a trait inherent to the very essence of things."[84] And because the physicist engages in a paradox, stating that the time to come for one twin may be the past for the other, even as one time becomes the measure for the other, the time of relativity physics is thus a semirelativism, the point of view of an observer who sees all points of view at once.[85]

Merleau-Ponty's judgment is that the conception of time of the physicist of relativity is egocentric, a multiplicity of egocentric views in place of a real coexistence of times, thinking the world successively from all points of view but never all at once. But the philosopher must look for the conditions of the possibility of this formulation and wonder how coexistence—that is, how be-longing to the same world—is possible.[86] Moreover, it appears that as physics moves forward, it also moves closer to Bergson with the development of new physics and cosmologies. It is arguable that by 1953, the spacetime continuum was thought by some physicists to indicate a temporalization of space and not a spatialization of time, a temporalization that is not reversible but goes in one direction: the arrow of time.[87] This is the manner in which physics becomes Bergsonian, borrowing from consciousness concepts used by the physicist but not able to be accounted for by physics.

DELEUZE AND BERGSONISM

Gilles Deleuze may well have been the most effective force inaugurating the tremendous renewal of interest in Bergson's philosophy in the twenty-first century, yet his reading of Bergson appears to owe at least something to Russell's criticisms. Deleuze's *Bergsonism* contains no overt references to Russell, but *Difference and Repetition* cites Russell's *The Principles of Mathematics* of 1903 for distinguishing between lengths or extension (extensive quantities divisible into equal parts) and differences or distances (relatively indivisible quantities of intensive origin). The latter are quantities that do not change without also changing their nature, an idea commensurate with Leibniz's account of *spatium*, the innate idea of a necessary relation that does not arise from abstraction.[88] This claim is quite interesting since Russell says that distance generates series whose terms have a simple and irreducible difference from one another and that distance is a case of relations that appear to be derived in some way from perception but are not qualities.

Thus, if we suppose the times series to be one in which there is distance, when an event is said to be more recent than another, it means that its distance from the present was less than that of the other. Thus, recentness is not itself a quality of the time or the event; it quantitatively compares relations or distance, not qualities.[89] This may be at least part of the ground on which Deleuze is retrieving Bergson from Russell's influential criticisms since Deleuze goes on to say that Bergson too defines duration as a multiplicity or divisibility that does not divide without changing its nature, and so duration begins to sound like Russell's concept of distance.[90] This point is discussed in more detail in what follows, as this claim is crucial to understanding exactly how Deleuze is recuperating Bergson's philosophy. Without this recuperation, it is questionable if Bergson would have achieved the status his work now holds in Continental philosophy. Nevertheless, it is not arbitrary, as we proceed, to ask to what extent such recuperation is *Bergsonism*, and therefore central to Deleuze's own ideas, and to what extent it is Bergson.

Let us turn, then, to Bergson's distinction between time and space and from there to that of the tendencies, namely instinct or intuition and intellect.[91] These are among the most fundamental concepts in Bergson scholarship, yet their connection to other aspects of Bergson's thought often remains unclear. What, after all, do time and space have to do with the creative evolutionary forces of instinct, intuition, and intellect? The intent here is to clarify the relations between these different aspects of Bergson's thought and draw out how Deleuze makes use of these structures derived from Bergson's philosophy to clarify in what respect Deleuze differs from Bergson or rereads Bergson in a manner that shields Bergson from Russell's criticisms.

From the beginning, as Bergson states, "Questions relating to subject and object, to their distinction and their union, should be put in terms of time rather than space"—that is, to time as pure duration.[92] Even when philosophers believe they are providing an original or ontological account of time and temporalization, they base their account on a pregiven understanding of static and homogeneous spatiality from which they derive their interpretation of time. This is the mathematical time that for Russell is the true nature of time. But for Bergson, time flows not outside us as identical "any times whatever" but intimately, in relation to our bodily affections, the conscious and unconscious influence of our own sensations. Flowing time, the time of our duration, cannot then be conceptually pregiven and static; it is not an a priori field of identical units. This is due largely to the affectivity of the body.[93]

Every living body with a nervous system is open to a kind of "succession" of qualitative changes. This is not a linear succession whose moments are clearly laid out one after the other but a transformation or translation from one moment *into* another, where each melts into another, each permeating the other without precise outlines and without any tendency to externalize themselves in relation to one another. Bergson refers to this as "multiplicity without divisibility" and "succession without separation."[94] It is impossible for this multiplicity to be cut up into instants and so merely to function as a means to count spaces situated at T1, T2, T3, and so on—spaces that can be set out on a grid exhibiting all past and future times simultaneously following the mathematical model. Thus, he objects to applying the logic of solid bodies to introspective data where there are no sharp boundaries.[95]

Likewise, Bergson does not agree that "multiplicity without divisibility" and "succession without separation" can be understood or reinterpreted as the measure or number of movements, as in Zeno's paradoxes. Such claims lead Bergson to observe that for the paradox of the moving arrow, the arrow is "never moving, but in some miraculous way the change of position has to occur between instants" and movement would then consist of homogeneous immobilities. What happens in the paradox, he explains, is that "the movement, once effected, has laid along its course a motionless trajectory on which we can count as many immobilities as we will."[96] By contrast, Bergson's multiplicity, of which duration is the end or the effect, is pure heterogeneity and becoming, which Deleuze, quite possibly, would like us to understand as difference or, following Russell, distance, is something perhaps not incommensurable with Bergson's account of duration but not necessarily identical to it.

The problem for Bergson's position, in his opposition to the single time of the physicist/mathematician, is how to justify and so make sense of his account of duration. Can it be tested empirically? To this end, Bergson introduces a number of examples such as the prototype of the pendulum clock. He argues that if we count each of the sixty oscillations of a clock's pendulum beating out one minute and *exclude* the sensible and affective recollection, which is the *feeling* of the preceding beats as they reverberate through our body, we will succeed in screening out our experience of duration. We will remain always in the present of each beat—a static, purely cognitive arrangement—in which each beat is without relation to what has come before and what follows.

If we were to imagine the sixty beats set out all at once in a linear order as the mathematicians do, we likewise would forfeit any sense of duration in exchange for an intelligible, spatialized, and homogeneous representation, thereby exchanging our affective memory for cognitive clarity. But if we retain the felt, sensible recollection of the preceding beat along with the current one, if we are attuned to the flow in which each permeates the other like the notes of a tune, they form a "qualitative multiplicity," the image of pure duration that is not quantity but qualities.[97] In space as measured by mathematics and natural science, we count simultaneities; each stroke of the clock on the wall is a homogeneous unit so that nothing of the past position of the hand remains in the new position. But for a being that endures, the past remains in the present.

Deleuze's lecture on the theory of multiplicities in Bergson is instructive here. He asks if Bergson's use of "multiplicity" is a "barely nominalized adjective" or a "substantive" and what difference it makes. For example, in *Time and Free Will*, Bergson argues that numerical multiplicity is the multiplicity of homogeneous units juxtaposed in the homogeneous medium of ideal space. This is why we disregard qualitative differences and common features when we count and instead treat objects as homogeneous units qualitatively identical to one another.[98] It is, on this account, entirely and only their juxtaposition in space that makes these units at all diverse and distinguishable.[99] This can be differentiated from listening to a melody and retaining the sounds in memory without counting them. This *qualitative multiplicity* must be distinguished from treating objects as homogeneous units—that is, as a *numerical multiplicity* that abstracts from the subtle qualitative differences and makes them identical by juxtaposing them in space.[100]

Deleuze rightly insists on the substantive that bypasses the adjective "multiplicity," which is always set in opposition to the "one," as in the claims that being is one or being is a multiplicity.[101] In place of statements of this type, Deleuze notes that, for Bergson, élan vital is neither one nor multiple, but, like duration, it is a type of multiplicity.[102] This allows Deleuze to concur with what was stated previously, that these distinctions rest on the more crucial distinction between numerical or quantitative multiplicity and qualitative multiplicity—in other words, space and duration. Here is where Bergson's and Deleuze's accounts become more complicated. Deleuze argues that for Bergson, number, even unity, is a multiplicity whose elements differ by the position they occupy in space so that as we count one by one, our notion of time has likewise been spatialized as the succession of homogeneous units.[103] Thus, multiplicities may be *discontinuous* and so only *"provisionally* indivisible for the purpose of compounding them with one another," or they may be *continuous*, like "number in its finished state . . . the points have become lines, the divisions have been blotted out, the whole displays all the characteristics of continuity."[104] The former, the provisionally indivisible, is the continuity of spaces, which remain infinitely divisible and homogenous, but the latter, for Deleuze, appears to be commensurate with duration and continuity in Bergson's sense. Crucially, it also expresses Peirce's conception of continuity or generalization, which is, as defined previously, a collection so great that its constituents have no hypothetical existence except in their relations to one another, a field so crowded that units lose identity. With this, the conception of continuity comes to the fore.

PURE SENSATION AND INTENSITY

At this point, the situation has grown more complicated. As noted previously, one of Bergson's significant prototypes is the pendulum clock. If we count each of the sixty oscillations of a clock's pendulum beating out one minute, then exclude the recollection of the preceding beats, we can screen out any experience of duration. The point here is that if we remain in the present of each beat, this yields *discontinuity*, and picturing the sixty beats all at once—a spatialized representation of homogeneous moments—is a type of mathematical *continuity*. As was noted, Bergson opposes both in favor of retaining the recollection of the preceding beat along with the current one, perceiving each permeating the other fluidly and forming a "qualitative multiplicity."[105]

This correlates quite well with Peirce's critique of Cantor's conception of continuity as composed of points and the introduction of Peirce's own version of continuity and discontinuity in chapter 2: "Peirce insists on a synthetical understanding of the *continuum*, as a general whole which cannot be analytically reconstructed by an internal sum of points."[106] Peirce's distinction between Secondness and Thirdness also echoes Bergson's distinction between the discontinuous and duration: "It is a clash between existence and being,

between a discontinuous mark and continuous flow," a general being prior
to the emergence of existing points, a higher generality "on which marks and
number systems are introduced *subsequently*."[107]

Deleuze follows Bergson's assertion of duration as neither mathematically
continuous (consisting of points) nor noncontinuous up to a point. In an odd
comparison with Edmund Husserl's passive, and thus nonintellectual, synthesis—a gestalt phenomenon consisting of a figure on a ground—Deleuze
states that a gestalt-like sensorial aggregate, a passive synthesis, can produce
a nonmathematical multiplicity that is superior in force to the qualities of its
elements although it is dependent on them because it is dependent on their
clarity. This multiplicity arrives as a *surgissement*, an emergence, as when one
looks up to see a lot of stars in the sky, trees in a forest, or columns in a temple.
It may be similar to Peirce's conception, cited in chapter 1, that "we have one
positive direct evidence of continuity and on the first line but one. It is this.
We are immediately aware only of our present feelings—not of the future, nor
of the past."[108] It is the sensation that yields the concept of continuity when it
emerges as a whole.

This appears to also be the case for Bergson, for whom, when we take up any
nonspatialized image such as the sound of tones, we may count the tones and so
reproduce in consciousness the representation that requires space and makes
each of the tones one unit. But if we take up the sound as a purely affective state,
as a sensation, we gather a qualitative impression induced by the whole that is
independent of its elements.[109] Duration, for Bergson, remains independent of its
elements. However, in every example Deleuze provides, the forceful emergence
of a nonnumerical multiplicity can never be separated from its elements. So, for
example, the Idea of color is said to *depend* upon three variables or coordinates
that are defined by *continuous* relations between changes in these variables.[110]
What counts here is that the elements of the multiplicity are determined by
reciprocal relations so that there is *no independence* from its elements: "The
Idea is thus defined as a structure . . . a system of multiple, nonlocalizable connections between differential elements which is incarnated in real relations
and actual terms."[111]

This is not identical to Bergson's conception of qualitative multiplicity but
draws on it and takes it in a different direction via Husserl. In order to count our
states of consciousness, Bergson reminds us, we must represent them symbolically as if they were units in space. But this is discontinuity and not pure affective sensation. Pure affective sensation is duration, and pure affective sensation
is pure quality independent of its elements. But if it is seen through the medium
of extensity—that is, the medium of space, the medium of *discontinuity* or

continuity—it is something else. It becomes the type of quantity called *intensity*.[112] As Bergson states, "Our projection of our psychic states into space in order to form a discrete multiplicity is likely to influence these states themselves and to give them in reflective consciousness a new form, which immediate perception did not attribute to them."[113] They become intensities, and intensities are the projection of our pure affective states into extensive space where they may be measured and quantified. This is the Deleuzian account of difference or distance in every sphere: "Intensity, which envelops distances, is explicated in extensity," and the role of extensity is precisely to exteriorize and make homogeneous those distances.[114]

Bergson provides us with a further opportunity to understand intensity expressed in a manner that is useful to Deleuze. What happens, he asks, "when an obscure desire gradually becomes a deep passion. . . . Little by little it permeates a larger number of psychic elements, tingeing them, so to speak with its own color. . . . How do you become aware of a deep passion once it has taken hold of you, if not by perceiving that the same objects no longer impress you in the same manner?"[115] What has taken place? An image has bypassed perception, which, for Bergson, would lead to action, and penetrated directly into affectivity, into the whole of memory itself, profoundly affecting one's sensibilities and altering perception from within. An intense, deep passion is born. It is a change of quality, but we interpret it spatially, extensively, as a measurable change of "magnitude," as if it were something extended, and we call it an intensity.

We do this, Bergson somewhat severely exclaims, because we like simple thoughts or because our language is a poor companion to the subtleties of psychological analysis.[116] The same state of affairs exists and applies equally to muscular efforts. If you raise your arm and make a tight fist, you feel a complex afferent sensation. You feel contracted muscles, stretched ligaments, compressed joints, possibly an immobilized chest, closed glottis, knit brow, clenched jaws. The greater the effort, the greater the number of muscles contracting in sympathy—that is, more and more of the body is affected. "Intensify" any gesture and what occurs? If your fist is clenched or your hands are thrown up in protest, if your lips are pressed tightly together, you still can only clench your hand so much, your arms only reach so high, and your lips press together only so tightly. You cannot bring your body to the point of exploding into space. What you experience in your hand, arms, and lips remains somewhat constant; what increases is the participation of the rest of your body in the action. Your face and neck grow taut, your arms and legs stiffen, your back may begin to strain. The actual change in the hand, arms, or lips is one of quality; they do not explode, but they begin to feel tired.

The intensified gesture amounts to a simultaneous feeling of increased peripheral sensations and a change in quality. However, as Bergson points out, we tend to resort to an interpretation based on magnitude. We localize the entire gesture with all its resonating sensations to the point where it yields a useful effort, and we focus on the task we are attempting to accomplish.[117] The question is, have we increased the magnitude of effort in any one part of the body? Bergson's unequivocal reply is that we have experienced a combination of a qualitative increase up to a limit point accompanied by an increasing number of muscles and parts of the body. This, too, is the eruption of an intensity.

What about sensations whose cause appears to arise in relation to something outside ourselves? How do we define intensity with regard to heat, weight, or light? Do we resort to the spatialized concept? A more intense heat, such as that of the tropical summer sun, is different in kind—that is, different in quality—from a feeble heat, such as that of a Norwegian winter. As Bergson argues, "A more intense heat is really another kind of heat."[118] Following this, he expresses the hope that there would be no contradiction between the claim that the greatest difference in kind is the difference between intense heat and intense cold and the claim of physiologists that, nevertheless, some points on the body are predisposed to feel heat and others are predisposed to feel cold, for these are also qualitative differences, differences in kind. A pressure of greater and greater intensity against the body, such as experienced when lifting a weight or carrying a child over a long distance, is likewise a matter of qualitative differences, differences in kind: first mere contact, then pressure, then resistance, even pain, extending further and further through the body. The increasing pressure is not, therefore, an increase of sensation but rather, focusing on the immediate affection, a sensation of increase, a different sensation, a difference in kind.[119]

Reducing the difference between heat and cold to measurable magnitude, whether by moving closer to or further from the source of the heat or cold or because different parts of the body perceive heat or cold somewhat exclusively, is, according to Bergson, the effect of our intellectual tendency to externalize the sensation so as to interpret it as a perception, a tendency Deleuze makes use of this to translate Bergson's qualitative multiplicities into Deleuzian multiplicity, "intensity explicated in extensity."[120] Likewise, when we perceive a sensation of increasing resistance and pain because of a heavy object, we interpret this sensation as the perception of magnitude under the influence of the notion of a homogeneous—meaning continuous and uniform—movement in a homogeneous space. This translation extends to all aspects of sensation when it is externalized and translated into perception. It is a mark of our imperceptibility, notes Bergson, that even though we know that changes in light produce remarkable changes in quality with respect to how sharply objects appear, as well as changes in their hues and colors, we still insist that each and every object has its own particular color, hue, and outline.[121] In each and every case, when we experience and speak about the sensation of increase, we tend to explicate it as an increase of sensation and externalize it as a perception.

What we cease to distinguish, according to Bergson, is the difference between what is immediately given as duration and the *physical effect* of passion, gesture, movement, color, sound, light, or weight. A complex feeling or movement as well as an image, sound, or physical force contains many simple affections that, taken as duration, are neither perfectly clear nor perfectly realized. Any psychic state, any duration affected by these many elements, is fluid becoming and not static units. It is not reducible to those elements, even as the psychic state changes as soon as the feelings, movements, images, sounds, and physical forces are felt. As will be addressed in the next chapter, Deleuze continues to resituate Bergson's concepts within the Russellian context that has been traced out here. This effort takes us into the work on cinema, which also and once again links up with Merleau-Ponty and Peirce.

NOTES

1. Andreas Vrahimis, "Russell's Critique of Bergson and the Divide between 'Analytic' and 'Continental' Philosophy," *Balkan Journal of Philosophy* 3, no. 1 (2011): 123–134, https://www.academia.edu/610678/, 9.

2. Vladimir Petrov, "Bertrand Russell's Criticism of Bergson's Views about Continuity and Discreteness," *FILOZOFIA* 68, no. 10 (2013): 890–904, 890. Russell and Alfred North Whitehead are famous for having failed to prove this hypothesis.

3. Vrahimis, "Russell's Critique of Bergson," 12.

4. Petrov, "Bertrand Russell's Criticism of Bergson's Views," 892–893.

5. Petrov, "Bertrand Russell's Criticism of Bergson's Views," 893.

6. Bertrand Russell, "The Philosophy of Bergson. With a Reply by Mr. H. Wildon Carr," published for "The Heretics" by Bowes and Bowes (Cambridge: Macmillan, 1914), 15–16. Cited in Petrov, "Bertrand Russell's Criticism of Bergson's Views," 894.

7. Cited in Petrov, "Bertrand Russell's Criticism of Bergson's Views," 895.

8. Petrov, "Bertrand Russell's Criticism of Bergson's Views," 897–898. See also Milic Capek, *Bergson and Modern Physics: A Reinterpretation and Re-evaluation*, Boston Studies in the Philosophy of Science, vol. 7 (Dordrecht, Netherlands: 1971), 148.

9. Petrov, "Bertrand Russell's Criticism of Bergson's Views," 897.

10. Jimena Canales, *The Physicist and the Philosopher: Einstein, Bergson, and the Debate That Changed our Understanding of Time* (Princeton, NJ: Princeton University Press, 2015), 5.

11. Canales, *The Physicist and the Philosopher*, 56–57.

12. Canales, *The Physicist and the Philosopher*, 58.

13. Lee Smolin, *Time Reborn: From the Crisis in Physics to the Future of the Universe* (Boston: Mariner Books, 2014), 143.

14. Smolin, *Time Reborn*, 144–145.

15. Canales, *The Physicist and the Philosopher*, 20.

16. Smolin, *Time Reborn*, 145, 146.

17. Smolin, *Time Reborn*, 147.

18. Smolin, *Time Reborn*, 148.

19. Smolin, *Time Reborn*, 148.

20. Smolin, *Time Reborn*, 151.

21. Smolin, *Time Reborn*, 174.

22. Smolin, *Time Reborn*, 173.

23. Smolin, *Time Reborn*, 178, 180.

24. Canales, *The Physicist and the Philosopher*, 6.

25. Canales, *The Physicist and the Philosopher*, 11, 19.

26. Capek, *Bergson and Modern Physics*, 91.

27. Canales, *The Physicist and the Philosopher*, 42.

28. Capek, *Bergson and Modern Physics*, 100, 119; Bergson, *Duration and Simultaneity*, trans. Mark Lewis and Robin Durie (London: Clinamen, 1999), 44–45.

29. Canales, *The Physicist and the Philosopher*, 65.

30. Bergson, *Duration and Simultaneity*, 44.

31. Canales, *The Physicist and the Philosopher*, 64.

32. Capek, *Bergson and Modern Physics*, 244; Bergson, *Duration and Simultaneity*, 109–113.

33. Capek, *Bergson and Modern Physics*, 246, 249.

34. Capek, *Bergson and Modern Physics*, 250.

35. Canales, *The Physicist and the Philosopher*, 25.

36. Canales, *The Physicist and the Philosopher*, 44.

37. Canales, *The Physicist and the Philosopher*, 31, 53–54, 132, 140, 152, 153, 162, 169.

38. Canales, *The Physicist and the Philosopher*, 26.

39. Canales, *The Physicist and the Philosopher*, 13, 183, 186.

40. Petrov, "Bertrand Russell's Criticism of Bergson's Views," 890–904.

41. Vrahimis, "Russell's Critique of Bergson," 124.

42. Vrahimis, "Russell's Critique of Bergson," 125–126. It is ironic that philosophers like Élie During, who asserted that Bergson remained an

out-of-touch Newtonian at a conference at the Korean Institute for Advanced Study in August 2015, have now put out a grand "manifesto," titled "We Bergsonians," to determine "who deserves to be regarded as a true Bergsonian." This involves "harnessing" and "directing" Bergson's ideas. One might ask, instead, who, if anyone, has this right? See Élie During and Paul-Antoine Miquel, "We Bergsonians: The Kyoto Manifesto," trans. Barry Dainton, *Parrhesia* 33 (2020): 17–42.

43. Roberto Mangabeira Unger and Lee Smolin, *The Singular Universe and the Reality of Time: A Proposal in Natural Philosophy* (Cambridge, MA: Cambridge University Press, 2015), 415–421.

44. Petrov, "Bertrand Russell's Criticism of Bergson's Views," 892.

45. Petrov, "Bertrand Russell's Criticism of Bergson's Views," 2–3.

46. Petrov, "Bertrand Russell's Criticism of Bergson's Views," 895; Bertrand Russell, "The Philosophy of Bergson, With a Reply by Mr. H. Wildon Carr." Published for "The Heretics" by Bowes and Bowes (Cambridge: Macmillan, 1914), 17.

47. Petrov, "Bertrand Russell's Criticism of Bergson's Views," 895; Henri Bergson, *Creative Evolution*, trans. Arthur Mitchell (New York: University Press of America, 1983), 309. Italics are Bergson's.

48. Petrov, "Bertrand Russell's Criticism of Bergson's Views," 897–898; Capek, *Bergson and Modern Physics*, 330–340.

49. Capek, *Bergson and Modern Physics*, 340; Petrov, "Bertrand Russell's Criticism of Bergson's Views," 899.

50. Capek, *Bergson and Modern Physics*, 343.

51. Capek, *Bergson and Modern Physics*, 343.

52. Maurice Merleau-Ponty, "Bergson in the Making," in *Signs*, trans. Richard C. McCleary (Evanston, IL: Northwestern University Press, 1964), 183.

53. Merleau-Ponty, "Bergson in the Making," 182.

54. Merleau-Ponty, "Bergson in the Making," 183.

55. Merleau-Ponty, "Bergson in the Making," 184.

56. Merleau-Ponty, "Bergson in the Making," 184.

57. Merleau-Ponty, "Bergson in the Making," 185.

58. Merleau-Ponty, "Bergson in the Making," 185.

59. Merleau-Ponty, "Einstein and the Crisis of Reason," in *Signs*, trans. Richard C. McCleary (Evanston, IL: Northwestern University Press, 1964), 192–197.

60. Merleau-Ponty, "Einstein and the Crisis of Reason," 192; Albert Einstein, *The World As I See It*, trans. Alan Harris (San Diego: Book Tree, 2017), 155.

61. Merleau-Ponty, "Einstein and the Crisis of Reason," 193; Albert Einstein and Leopold Infeld, *The Evolution of Physics* (London: Cambridge University Press, 1938), 289.

62. Maurice Merleau-Ponty, *Nature: Course Notes from the Collége de France*, compiled by Dominique Séglard, trans. Robert Vallier (Evanston, IL: Northwestern University Press, 2003), 89. Originally published in French as *La Nature: Notes, Cours Collége de France* (Paris: Éditions du Seuil, 1968), 124. The French original follows the slash.

63. Merleau-Ponty, *Nature*, 91/126–127.

64. Merleau-Ponty, *Nature*, 91/127.

65. Merleau-Ponty, *Nature*, 92/128.

66. Merleau-Ponty, "Einstein and the Crisis of Reason," 194.

67. Merleau-Ponty, "Einstein and the Crisis of Reason," 194.

68. Henri Bergson, *Duration and Simultaneity*, trans. Mark Lewis and Robin Durie (London: Clinamen Press, 1999), 187.

69. Bergson, *Duration and Simultaneity*, 187.

70. P.A.Y. Gunter, "André Metz and Henri Bergson: Exchanges Concerning Bergson's New Edition of *Duration and Simultaneity*," in *Bergson and the Evolution of Modern Physics* (Knoxville: University of Tennessee Press, 1969), 138.

71. Gunter, "André Metz and Henri Bergson," 170.

72. Gunter, "André Metz and Henri Bergson," 172.

73. Capek, *Bergson and Modern Physics*, 239.

74. Capek, *Bergson and Modern Physics*, 240.

75. Capek, *Bergson and Modern Physics*, 241.

76. Capek, *Bergson and Modern Physics*, 244.

77. Capek, *Bergson and Modern Physics*, 246.

78. Capek, *Bergson and Modern Physics*, 246–247.

79. Capek, *Bergson and Modern Physics*, 249.

80. Merleau-Ponty, "Einstein and the Crisis of Reason," 195–196.

81. Merleau-Ponty, "Einstein and the Crisis of Reason," 196.

82. Merleau-Ponty, "Einstein and the Crisis of Reason," 197.

83. Merleau-Ponty, *Nature*, 106–107/145–146.

84. Merleau-Ponty, *Nature*, 107/146.

85. Merleau-Ponty, *Nature*, 107–108/147.

86. Merleau-Ponty, *Nature*, 109/147–148.

87. Merleau-Ponty, *Nature*, 110/149. This is also the thesis put forward by Lee Smolin, Fotini Markopolou, and others who privilege time and argue that space is an emergent property. I have addressed this in Dorothea Olkowski, *The Universal (In the Realm of the Sensible)* (New York: Columbia University Press, 2007), chap. 1.

88. Gilles Deleuze, *Difference and Repetition*, 33n13.

89. Bertrand Russell, *The Principles of Mathematics* (New York: W.W. Norton, 1996), sec. 160, http://fair-use.org/bertrand-russell/the-principles-of-mathematics/s, 160.

90. Gilles Deleuze, *Difference and Repetition*, trans. Paul Patton (New York: Columbia University Press, 1994), 331n14. Originally published in French as *Différence et Répétition* (Paris: Presses Universitaires de France, 1968).

91. In this part of the chapter, I take up and reformulate the reading of Bergson's philosophy that first appeared in my book *Gilles Deleuze and the Ruin of Representation* (Berkeley: University of California Press, 1999), chap. 4, in order to differentiate Bergson's positions more clearly from those attributed to him by Deleuze.

92. Bergson, *Creative Evolution*, 71.

93. Henri Bergson, *Time and Free Will: An Essay on the Immediate Data of Consciousness*, trans. F. L. Pogson (New York: Macmillan, 1959), 104.

94. Bergson, *Duration and Simultaneity*, 44–45.

95. Capek, *Bergson and Modern Physics*, 93; Bergson, *Creative Evolution*, 3–5.

96. Bergson, *Creative Evolution*, 309.

97. Bergson, *Time and Free Will*, 104–105.

98. Bergson, *Time and Free Will*, 76.

99. Capek, *Bergson and Modern Physics*, 178; Bergson, *Time and Free Will*, 127–128.

100. Capek, *Bergson and Modern Physics*, 179.

101. Gilles Deleuze, "Theory of Multiplicities in Bergson," accessed October 2017, http://deleuzelectures.blogspot.com/2007/02/theory-of-multiplicities-in -bergson.html.

102. Deleuze, "Theory of Multiplicities."

103. Deleuze, "Theory of Multiplicities"; Bergson, *Time and Free Will*, 77–79.

104. Deleuze, "Theory of Multiplicities." Some emphasis added; Bergson, *Time and Free Will*, 82–83.

105. Bergson, *Time and Free Will*, 104–105.

106. Fernando Zalamea, *Peirce's Continuum: A Methodological and Mathematical Approach* (Boston: Docent, 2012), http://acervopeirceano.org/wp -content/uploads/2011/09/Zalamea-Peirces-Continuum.pdf, 7.

107. Zalamea, *Peirce's Continuum*, 20.

108. Charles Sanders Peirce, *The Collected Papers of Charles Sanders Peirce*, ed. Charles Hartshorne, Paul Weiss, and Arthur Burks (Cambridge, MA: Harvard University Press, 1931–1935, 1958), 1.167.

109. Bergson, *Time and Free Will*, 87–89.

110. Deleuze, *Difference and Repetition*, 182.

111. Deleuze, *Difference and Repetition*, 183.

112. Bergson, *Time and Free Will*, 90.

113. Bergson, *Time and Free Will*, 90.

114. Deleuze, *Difference and Repetition*, 230.

115. Bergson, *Time and Free Will*, 8.

116. Bergson, *Time and Free Will*, 13.
117. Bergson, *Time and Free Will*, 24–26.
118. Bergson, *Time and Free Will*, 47.
119. Bergson, *Time and Free Will*, 46–48.
120. Deleuze, *Difference and Repetition*, 230.
121. Bergson, *Time and Free Will*, 50–51.

—⁓⁓—

FOUR

Duration, Motion, and Temporalization

Deleuze, Bergson, Merleau-Ponty

DURATION AND MOTION

Deleuze's attempted recuperation of Bergson along Russellian lines is especially evident in the cinema books, which begin with a Bergsonian account of images and then connect it to Peirce's account of signs. The primary encounter with cinema is through the image, but the language of images will be superseded to some extent by the practice of signs. The two fundamental types of cinema image are the movement-image and the time-image, each of which gives rise to other types of image. Although neither type of image is said to be preferred over the other, and neither is more important, beautiful, or profound than the other, there are important structural differences between the two that ultimately influence and are influenced by our understanding of reality. Moreover, while Deleuze expresses no preference for one type of image over the other, it is clear that Bergson does.

Bergson refers to the movement-image as the cinematographic illusion, for which Deleuze reprimands him.[1] For Bergson, the cinema image is a consequence of a mechanistic theory that associates and adds together its elements by constructing a series of immobile images of the same scene with minute variations that follow one another to constitute movement externally.[2] It is an impersonal and abstract movement, the homogeneous movement of externally connected images. For Deleuze, this so-called false movement consists of visual images, which are instantaneous or immobile, and movement, which is uniform thus abstract (twenty-four images per second). However, he objects to the conclusion that the movement-image consists of "immobile sections + abstract movement," insisting instead that it is a section that is mobile—an image beyond the conditions of so-called natural perception (attributed to Merleau-Ponty) but nevertheless a mechanical imitation of natural perception.[3]

This difference in interpretation may be understood as a function of Bergson's resistance to Einstein, but it can also be understood in relation to Bergson's and Deleuze's differing views of the mathematics of differential calculus, which exemplifies the idea of an any-space-whatever. The method of differential calculus involves using a grid defined by Cartesian coordinates, taking minute differences in the x and y directions, and computing the gradients (steepness) of the resultant straight line.[4] As such, "The crucial step . . . was to shift attention from the essentially *static* situation concerning a gradient at a particular point P to the *dynamic* process of successive approximation of the gradient [of the curve] by gradients of straight lines starting at P."[5] This is necessary because, using differential equations, dynamic motion can only be represented mathematically by means of a static function.

Clearly, as Deleuze states, cinema was initially made possible only through the modern scientific method of calculating apparently dynamic motion by means of a static function. Movement along the line from frame to frame is the reproduction of an "any-instant-whatever," an infinitesimal point, a mechanical succession of equidistant instants used by differential calculus to calculate continuous movement on a curve.[6] This modern conception of movement, captured by Edward Muybridge when he filmed the equidistant any-instant-whatevers of a running horse, made cinema possible.

In spite of Bergson's criticism of cinematographic movement as an illusion that does not accurately express our nonmechanical, sensible, and affective experience of change, Deleuze pushes on and derives a second type of image from Bergson's critique. Bergson recognizes that "the mechanism of our ordinary knowledge is of a cinematographic kind" and that perception, intellection, and language, the fundamental *human* relations with the material world, proceed in accordance with the rules of this "cinematograph inside us."[7] Yet, once again, Bergson insists there is a more original sensation, something prior to these any-moment-whatevers, these static points; this more original sensation is duration. Duration is defined as the inner becoming of things and the qualitative heterogeneity of changes that are not equidistant and identical but permeate one another without any tendency toward externalization or extension.[8]

The duration-image does not arise from stringing together identical spaces but from the continuous yet heterogeneous unfolding of qualities, both those of our mental states and those of objects in the world insofar as humans are not isolated from the unfolding world and objects in the world are not isolated from their unfolding environments extending to the stars. Thus, Bergson reveals a cosmological picture of duration. Deleuze sums this up somewhat differently. Our waiting for these qualitative changes to take place, he claims, expresses duration as a mental and spiritual reality as we bear witness to a changing whole, which he calls the time-image.[9] Unlike Bergson, Deleuze first addresses the space and the homogeneous any-space-whatevers of perception, action, and affection. So let us first examine the movement-image, the space within which percepts and affects arise.

THE MOVEMENT-IMAGE

Beginning with the basic structure of the movement-image, Deleuze breaks it into three types of image: the perception-image, the action-image, and the affection-image.[10] Because any space in the movement-image is homogeneous with any other, insofar as they are any-space-whatevers, the film can be played forward as well as backward without a loss of intelligibility in the visual images. Deleuze takes this structure beyond cinema; he takes it to what may be either an ontological or a cosmological level (as Bergson did previously) by echoing Bergson's claim from *Matter and Memory*, thereby exceeding the merely visual image and declaring that truly everything is an image.

An atom is an image. My body is an image, and so an image is understood to be a set of actions and reactions, visual, aural, tactile, or received and responded to in any possible way. My eye and my brain are images, as are the other parts of my body. If the brain is also an image, it cannot *contain* images since it is one image among others.[11] The infinite set of all images is one plane of immanence on which all images exist, but all images are also flowing matter since everything, including all bodies, is an image. Initially, it is not clear if this is the dematerialization of bodies or the materialization of images since the claim is simply that "the material universe, the plane of immanence, is the machine assemblage of movement-images."[12]

Perhaps surprisingly, it is the former because "the identity of image and movement stems from the identity of matter and light."[13] Certainly the theory of relativity led to the identification of light as both particles and waves, and it is perhaps not that difficult to understand images as consisting of light particles or light waves. In order for matter to be light, at least in this iteration, it must also be image. Then, if all flowing matter is light, given the diffusion of light over the entire plane of immanence, the movement-image could then be said to consist wholly of figures of light as in cinema, matter being nothing more than blocs of space-time, a fairly ethereal conception. This also means, according to Deleuze, that consciousness, insofar as it can be said to exist, is also a set of images; it is the light that is immanent to matter, which is, for Deleuze, blocs of space-time, and consciousness cannot be distinguished from the images of light that constitute it as an effect—as decentered—and not as the source of intentional illumination.[14]

Given this structure, there appears to be something inevitable in the development of the cinema of the movement-image, the blocs of space-time, of any-instant-whatevers, which reflect the light immanent to or constitutive of light/matter. It pertains to the laws of the physics of relativity and the privileging of the mathematics of dynamical systems. Moreover, if flowing matter is diffused light on a single plane of immanence, this raises an important question. If everything exists as the reflection of everything else, how is it possible for anything to happen? Why do not all the images on the plane of immanence simply freeze into one infinite static image?

To answer this, Deleuze needs Bergson again, but this time he adheres more closely to Bergson's position. For Bergson, what distinguishes living images from all others is the interval between action and reaction—the zone of indetermination: "The zone of indetermination is that area of affectivity within multidimensional duration in which the organism selects from among the multiplicity of the images that each and every material image is bound up with."[15] For Bergson, any unconscious material point has greater perception than an entity with consciousness. But unlike such entities, in reflecting images, the living being analyzes them with respect to the actions it may exercise upon them, and external objects are thus perceived as objects of virtual action, subject to discernment and choice.[16]

Bergson conceives of the universe as a system of images that exist and influence one another through movement and in which the image of one's own body occupies a central position, but only because everything else changes as the body moves. The entire universe, insofar as it is available to any living creature, is available as images. Every aspect of the body is an image: afferent nerves (transmitting disturbances to nerve centers), efferent nerves (conducting disturbances from the nerve centers to the periphery to set some or all of the body in motion), and the brain. All function without ever producing a single representation of the material universe. Rather, external images influence the "body" image by transmitting *movement* to it. The body image responds by bringing about changes in its surrounding images and giving back movement to them, choosing how it returns what it receives.[17]

Furthermore, such images cannot be construed as knowledge, for they function even in the simplest mass of protoplasm. All life is open to images, no matter how poorly or well-formed they may be, and all life is open to the outside, even though there are as many worlds as there are animals.[18] The openness to the "outside" of living beings makes duration and memory something real; they are not simply psychological phenomenon. In lower organisms, perception can hardly be distinguished from mere touch followed by necessary movement; it is active and passive at once.[19] But even for higher organisms, Bergson affirms "the diffusion or propagation of light on the whole plane of immanence."[20] As such, "A present image . . . act[s] through every one of its points upon all the points of all other images to transmit the whole of what it receives, to oppose to every action an equal and contrary reaction, to be in short, merely a road by which pass, in every direction, the modifications propagated throughout the immensity of the universe."[21]

To make a representation is to detach an image from the process by which it loses itself in other images and in the universe. It is to separate it from the ongoing duration and to thematize it so as to constitute it as static and unchanging.

As centers of indetermination, living beings are what Deleuze, following Bergson, calls the "black screen"—the opacity that stops the movement and light of an image and may reflect that movement and light back into the world—in which case, for Bergson, it indicates the outlines of the object emitting that light, "like the effect of a mirage."[22] This action, a type of discernment, impoverishes the action of all atoms of matter that would otherwise pass through the universe without resistance or loss. In the purely flowing universe, "here is wanting . . . the black screen on which the image could be shown," but with the screen, as the "real action passes through, the virtual action remains."[23] As such, Bergson radically clarifies the sense of action, real action and virtual action. What passes on is real action, and what is left are images that symbolize the indetermination of the will, the zone of indetermination that is an interval. As Bergson laments, when we think about this process, we often incorrectly *detach the image from the nervous system as a whole* and exteriorize it to a point external to it, as a purely external object that conforms to our common sense, when what Bergson wishes to maintain is the integrity of the entire structure as a whole.[24]

All this interests Deleuze greatly, especially the idea that the plane of immanence is the plane of movement and light or the set of movement-images within which an *interval* appears: "And the brain is nothing but this—an interval, a gap between an action and reaction . . . one special image among others."[25] The interval is what receives the action of all the images in the universe on only one facet out of all of them then reacts in the direction of limited parts and so isolates some images from the rest of the universe. Some images are indifferent to the living being and pass through; others are not and are isolated as sensible perceptions by this process, which subtracts them from the whole.

The brain is neither the origin nor the center of the universe of images; it is the center of indetermination in the interval between reception and reaction.[26] In the universe, the brain is an acentered image. In relation to all other images in the universe, an image is a thing, and the thing thereby perceives all other things to the extent that it is subject to their action and as it reacts to them with all of its facets and parts. *Framing* is the term for the filter or facet through which all the other images are received, and framing is the filter or facet that delays reaction—that is, the interval. Deleuze calls a reflection of movement and light an action only if the something unpredictable or new arises out of the process of framing, which is then a true center of indetermination.[27]

In relation to the framing interval of the living being, the image is a perception. In this "first material moment," subjectivity is subtractive, incomplete, and prejudiced, subtracting whatever does not interest it and forming a perception-image for which the world becomes a horizon.[28] One passes imperceptibly from such perceptions to action—the second material moment of subjectivity—but this moment arises only through the intermediary of affection, which takes place between the received perception, the action of images, and a virtual or hesitant action coming from the image that is the living being. It is virtual because the image perceived is separated from the body by an interval and it is only when that interval decreases to the point of urgency or danger that the action becomes real. Affection, for Deleuze, is in the interval; it is the coincidence of subject and object but also the experience a subject has of itself from within and, thus, a third material aspect—a vibration. Bergson states that "the vibration will be passed on to motor elements. . . . The sensitive element retains . . . relative immobility" as it tries to utilize its own motor tendency to set things right even though only the living organism has the capacity to do this, to remove itself from the source of the pain.[29]

For Bergson, unlike Deleuze, the living body is a center of action when it receives the action of some of the objects surrounding it—objects whose movements, when transmitted to the body, might even destroy it. Affection often begins with a perception that increases its action on the body. The experience of pain shows that the body "does not merely reflect action received from without, but it struggles, and absorbs some part of this action. Here is the source of affection."[30] Although originating in a perceptual image, pain itself is pure affectivity; it is the impurity with which perception is alloyed.

For Deleuze, affect must also be characterized as an image. The affection-image, the reaction to the perception of the universe of movement-images, is not action, it is an action-image. Rather than arising from a zone of indetermination, it follows the delay of framing, receiving certain privileged images and eliminating the rest, making possible passage from perception-image to action-image. What is initially reaction becomes action, relating movement to these images by associating them more closely or increasing their distance.[31] But in between the perception-image and the action-image, in the interval, lies the affection-image, a pure quality, and as a quality and not an action, it is the source of expression. Felt from within, *the affection-image may be all that we know of ourselves* outside the interaction of images that is the cinema of life.[32] With these three images, we have a formula for what it is to be a zone of indetermination—that is, "an assemblage of three images, a consolidate of perception-images, action-images, and affection-images."[33]

THE CINEMA OF LIFE

For Deleuze, the system of cinema and the cinema of life occur as the movement-image in its three aspects, which express both the flowing matter of the whole and the interaction of images within that whole by way of the interval where distinct kinds of images are received and acted upon. This material, this plastic mass, is asignifying and asyntactic; it is not formed linguistically, although when language gets hold of it, its utterances tend to replace the images and signs of cinema and life. The system of images and signs that remains independent of language is semiotics—a semiotics of nonlanguage material.[34] This is the point of using Peirce's semiotics—the conception of sign-images.

Deleuze finds in Peirce the signs that relate cognitively to the three types of movement-image. Each sign is itself an image of an image (its object, which is anything that can be thought) by means of a third image: the interpretant (the facet of framing or the brain of subjectivities), which as a sign is subject to the same three-part relation.[35] It becomes apparent that these relations constitute an infinite semiotic system, a cosmos of their own. Although, in the end, Peirce appears to submit semiotics to linguistics, Deleuze does not. He maintains signs as types of images expressed in cinema, in the brain, in the world, and ultimately in the cosmos so that every image acts and reacts on every other. When images relate to the interval of received and executed movement, perception-images are formed, and they may extend into other images so as to constitute a perception of action or an affection of movement (a relation).

Deleuze calls the perception-image the zero degree in that it is prior even to Peirce's Firstness, the sign without reference to subject or object characterized by quality but not yet by relation.[36] As characterized by quality, Deleuze correlates Firstness with the affection-image.[37] Secondness, characterized by action and reaction, is correlated with the action-image, and Thirdness, representation or thought, is correlated with the relation-image, an image external to its terms and external to Firstness and Secondness, which it brings into relation to one another as modes of thought; Thirdness is thought as law or representation.[38] Secondness can overtake both the affection-image and the action-image. Thirdness can encompass all three types of image.[39]

How do these signs function as images? Thirdness, the mental image, is an image of an object of thought but an object whose existence is outside of thought because, after all, it is a sign. These objects are relations, symbolic acts, and intellectual "feelings."[40] Applied, for example, to the films of the Marx brothers, Harpo is Firstness, purely affective; Chico is Secondness, all action; and Groucho is Thirdness, entering into alliance with the other two but as the man of interpretations and symbolic acts, the master of reasoning, arguments, and syllogisms.[41] Or, as in Alfred Hitchcock's *Rear Window*, each image exhibits a mental relation of Thirdness. Characters act, perceive, and experience, yet they are nothing more than effects of camera movements that construct the relation between them. The camera, not the narrative, shows how Jeffries, the news reporter and protagonist of *Rear Window*, has come to have a broken leg, as the camera focuses on the images of a race car and a broken camera.[42] Thirdness, the mental relation, is also the method Hitchcock uses to bring the public into the film; the camera situates the spectator public behind Jeffries and his girlfriend, Lisa, as they gaze out a window at a possible murder scene and makes possible reasoning or reflection on the relation between the camera, the image, and their viewpoint.[43]

THE TIME-IMAGE

Resisting the introduction of linguistic elements, and as if to replicate the infinitesimal any-space-whatever of the mathematical model, Deleuze doubles the types of visible images from three to six by placing an impulse-image between perception and affection and a reflection-image between action and relation, thus adding a relation-image as well. A sign, he argues, is still an image, one that refers to a type of image either from the point of view of its double (and bipolar) composition or from the point of view of its genesis (perception, affection, impulse, reflection, action, relation).[44] Within this structure also arise subsigns, the most important of which, for our purposes, are the opsign and sonsign, purely optical and sound signs, important because they break apart the sensory-motor link of perception, action, and relation-images, *disrupting the movement-image as a whole*, so the sign no longer represents the movement-image. Deleuze cites Andre Bazin, who describes a scene in Vittorio De Sica's

Umberto D. in which a maid enters a kitchen, cleans up, drives away some ants, begins to prepare coffee, then sees the belly of a pregnant woman. At this moment, "it is as though all the misery in the world were going to be born."[45] This is the opsign. This purely optical situation does away with framing; the character does all the viewing, records rather than reacts, and is completely subject to her vision and not engaged in action.[46]

As Deleuze characterizes it, "Some characters, caught in certain pure, optical and sound situations, find themselves condemned to wander about or go off on a trip. These are pure seers, who no longer exist except in the interval of movement."[47] In such situations, *time is out of joint*; time is no longer the sequential tracking of solid bodies in homogenous space. Rather, the image, consisting of pure optical and sound situations, is virtual. Like the movement-image, it is real, but unlike the movement-image (which can only indirectly represent time through changes in the movements of bodies), it is not actualized in a homogeneous spatiality. How is such an image possible at all, especially in film?

The movement-image passes, by association, from one object to another, yielding an indirect image of time—a homogenous, sequential time where everything happens on the same plane.[48] Nothing occurs that is not accessible through the sequential series of camera shots. But what if the camera passes through different planes? This indicates, according to Deleuze, that rather than insisting on the image as the representation of what is habitual; what we expect; what is customary, regular, or routine in such cases; what is habitually inscribed in our sensory-motor associations of one object with another—instead of this—the time-image is a matter of pure optics and pure sound. It is a percept that lacks any intrinsically habitual association; thus, each time it occurs, the time-image is completely new.

Likewise, in the cinema of life, where action is not chosen and perception is *not* gratified, perception cannot seize memory for the sake of action, and the body is pure sensibility. This is the point of claiming that cinema *is* the brain, and the brain is always the boundary where actual and virtual really are inseparable. Thus, the opsign is not merely a manifestation of film. It is the name of that which crystallizes, solidifies, and so acts to break apart the sensory-motor links of perception, action, and thought. Under the opsign, a character in a film or a brain in a living being is forcefully subject to vision but solidifies and does not act, resisting the fact that perception is supposed to exist for the sake of action. This crack up—this breaking apart of perception, action, and thought, this "cracked I"—creates a pattern that proliferates and vibrates, disrupting mere repetition with a bloc of sensation, the reflection of a sensibility that forcefully overtakes that character's actuality.

For Deleuze, this body can be the unthought that forces us to think what has previously been concealed from thought. This body is stubbornly nonthinking. This body is the site of attitudes and postures, of behaviors but never actions.[49] The body is or at least can be a mechanism unable to perform purposive actions, and it may be unable to understand or speak. In cinema, the body suffers the effects of brain damage until it disappears into voices whose sound belongs to no one. It disappears as well into images that move or throb, that take on color or are impossible.[50] This nonthinking body is, for Deleuze, truly a work of art—not just for cinema, but for all the arts—and every human being is merely one of its constructs, not necessarily its greatest either conceptually or aesthetically.

MEMORY-IMAGES

For Deleuze, the time-image arises out of a zone of recollections, dreams, or thoughts that has no access to habitual perception. This follows from Bergson, who argues that there are two forms of memory and so two forms of present experience. The first is the sensory-motor system of the living body, the habitual body that responds to the world to advance its interests in ways that are fairly predictable and socially circumscribed. The second manner in which the past subsists is as virtual in the form of independent memory-images that are the effect of our internal affectivity, our affective as opposed to our active lives. Affection is the action of the body upon itself. It is localized, evidence that the action of external causes threatens to disintegrate the body but evidence also that the body's surface is both perceived and felt.[51]

In any perceptual struggle with an external object, some of the action is absorbed as affection while the rest is reflected back into the world as perception for the sake of action. The absorbed affections are memory-images, but they subsist as virtual, and each subsists as the contraction of the entire past from a certain plane, a certain point of view. Under the conditions of attentive recognition, this second memory, "laden with the whole of the past, responds to the appeal of the present state . . . [by] translation, by which it moves in its entirety to meet experience, thus contracting more or less, though without dividing."[52]

Such "translation" is the process of creating out of Bergson's ontological memory, with its multiple, perhaps infinite virtual levels or regions, each of which is the whole past in a more or less contracted state but from a particular plane or point of view. Emerging into the present, this whole diverges and dissociates. Nevertheless, for Deleuze, when memory-images emerge, they do so only as the powerful optical and sonorous time-images discussed previously, and they arise by means of the ever more complex links. Ever more heterogeneous, qualitative resonances are established in the film between optical-images and sound-images as they arise from memory and the reflection upon that memory as images of time and thought.[53]

Here Deleuze once again follows Bergson in tracing the emergence of subjectivity from the moment of indetermination—the interval between action and reaction—wherein the subject does not react but simply receives the movement as an affection of its own body. As noted previously, Bergson concentrates on the affective and bodily aspect of this moment, but Deleuze emphasizes the interval, the gap, which is filled by a recollection-image, a sort of flashback that operates as a temporal and spiritual image, neither motor nor material.[54] The flashback is a recollection-image; it is the site where subjectivity emerges but only if it is founded in something deeper. That something deeper is Bergson's original affectivity, consisting of feeling-images, dream-images, disturbances of the body, and what Deleuze characterizes as a "failure to act" because the images are cut off from recognition.[55]

But what for Bergson is an indication of choice, a break with determinism and the power of external forces, is, for Deleuze, a break with reality tout court. What the film is left with, then, is "an unstable set of floating memories, images of a past in general which move past at dizzying speed, as if time were achieving a profound freedom"; it is time and not a subjectivity.[56] And due to the speed of these images, the character is powerless to move and powerless to act. Deleuze describes many films that create such an image—films of Fellini and Hitchcock among them—but perhaps it is the case that the dream-image especially characterizes all the films of David Lynch, and to such an extent that there is no subjectivity left because there is no action, only events that happen in a haze of dreams, apparitions, hallucinations, visions, madness, and nightmares. Every character is prey to visual and sound sensations that dissolve any possibility of recognition. Lynch has said that the ear is an opening and a ticket to another world so much so that Jeffrey Beaumont, at the beginning of the film *Blue Velvet*, finds a severed ear in a field, and at the end of the film, the camera zooms out of Jeffrey's own ear as he awakens after having drifted off to sleep in the sun.

Perhaps it's all a dream; possibly the idealized small town, the film's setting, may be the hallucination and the dark nightmarish events that take place at night may be the unrecognizable reality, a past in general that contrasts with the stark white of the picket fence and saturated red of the roses in front of it, which are emblematic of the town, but only on the surface. So when Jeffrey Beaumont hides in Dorothy Vallens's closet, frozen and unable to move as he watches her undress, nothing in his past indicates he would do this. Perhaps it is his dream, but perhaps not. We cannot really tell. Likewise, the film *Mulholland Drive* may be entirely the dream of one of its characters, Betty, a failed actress who lives in the least glamorous part of Hollywood and has succumbed to drug addiction.

Ultimately, one wonders what this means for Deleuze, especially if cinema takes us to philosophy. According to Bergson, the affectivity of our own bodies is what frees us from the determinism of external forces, but, for Deleuze, affective life is full of danger and darkness. It is the beginning of the slide into madness, which Bergson never indicates insofar as the interval is, for him, the site of creativity and choice. Possibly, for Deleuze, creativity and madness are never that distant from one another. One has only to view Marcel Carne's *Daybreak*, whose hero is caught in a multiplicity of circuits that returns him each time to the pure present, where he meets a fatal end.[57] Such a circuit seems to be not determinism but destiny, the pure power of time that overflows all possibility of reaction and defeats, immobilizes, and petrifies figures in their own affectivity, condemning them to a horrendous fate even as it destroys all conventions.

And let us remember that this theory of movement-image and time-image is a theory of the brain and how it functions. Deleuze takes cinema to be the power of putting images in motion in the brain, tracing neuronal circuits, and putting cinema in the place once occupied by psychoanalysis, in place of the human and in place of perception. Gratuitously violent and sexualized images (plentiful in cinema as in life) are localized in the limbic system, which is devoted to generating feeling. These feelings convince us that we are human, that our opinions, our *doxa*, are correct. And, for Deleuze, their effect is like that of numerous other practices—dinner at Mr. Rorty's but also computer science, sociology, marketing, design, advertising—practices that claim to create Ideas but are really only producing *doxa*, opinion.[58]

Deleuze also placed phenomenology among these practices because he claimed it appeals to our feeling because (as seen in chap. 1) it establishes "'natural perception' and its conditions" as its norm, as a sensible form (Gestalt), which organizes the perceptive field as a function of a situated intentional consciousness. We saw, too, that Deleuze replaced the Gestalt with the concept an intelligible form (Idea) *actualized in a content* and that this content is—as seen in this chapter—best characterized as a sign. To repeat, for Deleuze, this is destiny, which is the pure power of time that overflows all possible reaction. It defeats, immobilizes, and petrifies figures in their own affectivity; it sends them to their fate, destroying conventions along the way. For Merleau-Ponty, as for Bergson, acts are still possible in a network of temporal relations so that motion and time are destiny but differently than for Deleuze. Let us look a little further into the nature of these temporal relations to make sense of the distinction between these two philosophers. Once again, Bergson will influence and orient the concepts of Merleau-Ponty, just as he influenced and oriented those of Deleuze.

BERGSON AND MERLEAU-PONTY: THE INNER NECESSITY OF TEMPORALITY

In the *Phenomenology*, Merleau-Ponty notes that Bergson argued that the scientific conception of time "surreptitiously bring[s] in the idea of space" by successively setting states side by side, whereas the time Bergson calls duration is succession *without the mutual externality* of temporal states.[59] Initially, this conception appears to be where Bergson and Merleau-Ponty part ways with respect to the nature of time, yet their differences may be less dramatic than they first appear. Bergson goes on to attribute a *creative evolution* for all phenomena of the world. He argues that evolution first had to overcome the resistance of seemingly inert matter, which changes only under the influence of external forces, where such change is no more than the displacement of parts.[60]

His position is that life does not develop linearly, in accordance with a geometrical, formal model, and that for living things changes are not the displacement of parts that themselves do not change except to split into smaller and smaller parts, molecules, atoms, corpuscles, all of which may return to their original position and are, therefore, time reversible. This would have been the position of classical physics, for which all physical systems are closed to outside influences and are deterministic, in that the position of each particle or entity is specifiable and predictable; reversible, in that the motion of particles can be calculated in either direction; and comprised of atomistic entities.[61] Indeed, as Merleau-Ponty indicates, any state of such a system may be repeated as often as desired; the system has no history, and nothing is created. Thus, what it will be is already there in what it is, and what it is includes all the points of the universe with which it is related.[62]

But this makes the evolution of matter into life seemingly impossible. By contrast, contemporary evolutionary biologists assert that life arose as a phenomenon of energy flow; it is inseparable from energy flow, the process of material exchange in a cosmos bathing in the energy of the stars. Stars provide the energy for life, and the basic operation of life is to trap, store, and convert starlight into energy. For evolutionary biology, the science of nonequilibrium thermodynamics supports the idea that energy flows through structures and organizes them to be more complex than their surroundings and that organized and structured patterns appear out of seemingly random collisions of atoms.[63] From this point of view, there is no purely inert matter.

All the more reason to consider the possibility, as Bergson does, that the simplest forms of matter were initially physical and chemical *and* alive and that life is simply a tendency—a tendency that diverges over and over, sometimes preserved by nature and sometimes disappearing. Bergson clearly contrasted this view of evolution as tendencies to an understanding of evolution as causal mechanism, a theory he rejects.[64] A mechanistic evolutionary theory "means to show us the gradual building up of the machine under the influence of external circumstances [forces] intervening either directly by action on the tissues or indirectly by the selection of better adapted ones."[65] But mechanism and finalism are both constructed in the same manner, which Bergson formulates in terms of cinematographic knowledge.[66]

For his part, Merleau-Ponty initially appears to retain a mechanistic conception, not only to characterize the time of the objective world—the time that belongs to things (even when it appears as a datum of consciousness)—but also to articulate the time that is the subject. Merleau-Ponty states that he wishes to situate the subject at the junction of the *for-itself* and the *in-itself*.[67] This means at the junction of a constituting consciousness—the time of the psychologist—and an unconscious thing-like existence governed by objective time—the time of the physicist and the mathematician. The question this raises is if it will be possible for time to be not time but *temporality* and what that would mean. If temporality is at the *junction* of consciousness and objects, then it is neither—neither a succession of "nows" in consciousness as defined by psychologists nor a product of cerebral traces, bodily mechanisms as defined by physiology.[68] It is something else. What is that something else?

For Merleau-Ponty, the temporal horizons of objects come to our attention not through an idea or concept intuited by a unifying subject but, first, through the preobjective hold our body has upon the world. Is this tantamount to what Deleuze calls "feeling" in the sense of the ground of opinion, or is it something else? It is true that Merleau-Ponty states that parts of space can be said to coexist insofar as they are temporally present to the same perceiving subject but also and prior to this because they are "enveloped in a single *temporal wave*," each one of which gains both unity and individuation because it is "wedged [*pressée*] in between the preceding and following one."[69]

Motion begins in a moving object, but it spreads from there into the visual field, and motion, insofar as it takes place in a *field of relations*, is structural rather than relative. This is why, as we reach the end of the visual field, our sight does not pass into nothingness, as the visual field is a stage in the organization of the world of a particular type—that is, it is lived. We live this organization as the relation between the place in which we dwell, the place that is our abode, and the environment in which our dwelling exists. We also live this relation, insofar as it passes through our body, but it passes through our body only insofar as we are temporality.

This, it seems, is the point of Merleau-Ponty's claim that "we had to acknowledge that spatial perception is a structural phenomenon and is only understood within a perceptual field"—a field in which we are anchored, although not *through* our perceptions.[70] We begin by anchoring ourselves in the prepersonal field of relations and in a space where we cannot affirm our anchorage. To the extent that this is the case, it is impossible to make any commitments, to act in a manner that relieves the ambiguity of perception and allows one to be the temporal wave that moves, particle to particle, through the matter of the world.

We can simulate this by a visit to an unknown place; a city where we have no specific plans produces only highly ambiguous perceptions. If we have no commitments, we must walk through the streets to gather behind ourselves, at each step, even the beginnings of what will be a past and to formulate possible future commitments. Where will we find coffee? Where is a friendly cafe? What is there to see or do? All of this will influence our experience. Are we comfortable with the architecture and plan of this city, or does it leave us feeling isolated and alone? Our choices will, of course, depend on the extent to which we bring along with us the past that we are, a past that is more obscure than if we were at home in familiar territory or busy with a particular task.

Merleau-Ponty points out that schizophrenics and those under the influence of a drug such as mescaline experience a disturbance in the field of relations. For the latter, the person is alone and forlorn in empty space, and the schizophrenic can make no connection between a bird in the garden and the sound of its song. Merleau-Ponty attributes this to the inability of the body to be the passage between the network of relations under these conditions. These situations reflect a profound *collapse of time*, specifically the loss of any sense of time passing and the inability to orient oneself toward a specific future, thus the loss of the ability to act at all.[71] Lacking anchorage in the past and an opening to a future, the individual is alienated from spatial relations and action, and even the daytime becomes an eternal night, contingent and unreal.

In this acknowledgment of the constitutive relation of time and affect to space, it seems that Merleau-Ponty is not so far from the thought of Bergson. Let us recall Bergson's distinction between the duration in which we act, in which our states melt into one another, and the duration in which we *see ourselves acting*, a duration whose elements are dissociated and juxtaposed. Understood as waves, the former is the energy and the latter the matter, and duration unifies our temporality.[72] Our past remains part of the present as desire, will, and action; although only what is useful enters consciousness in any one perception, the entire past that remains is felt, and it is always felt as a tendency.[73]

From this point of view, a body is in space only to the degree that it is an expression of the network of temporal relations of a subject, "the energy with which he tends towards a future through his body and his world."[74] This is why, for Merleau-Ponty, dreams express our temporality—that towards which we tend, sometimes that which we desire. The dreamer knows no objective space; the dreamer possesses only emotions, desires, and bodily attitudes—tendencies—and so the dream is haunted by life and sexuality, and the dreamer feels that toward which her desire goes out, whether past or future.[75] Whether dreaming or awake, for Merleau-Ponty, unlike Deleuze, it is well that we seek a space in which we can feel in touch with our temporality—that is to say, with the great affective entities of our lives. To not do so, to exist as sensitive to any and all spaces, is to be consumed and trapped by mania, with no past or future in relation to space. This is, indeed, the sense in which time and the subject communicate, as Merleau-Ponty claims, from within—that is, in virtue of an inner, interior necessity.

NOTES

1. Gilles Deleuze, *Cinema 1: The Movement-Image*, trans. Hugh Tomlinson and Barbara Habberjam (Minneapolis: University of Minnesota Press, 1986), 1.

2. Henri Bergson, *Creative Evolution*, trans. Arthur Mitchell (New York: University Press of America, 1983), 306.

3. Deleuze, *Cinema 1*, 1–3.

4. Keith Devlin, *Mathematics: The Science of Patterns: The Search for Order in Life, Mind, and the Universe* (New York: Scientific American Library, 1994), 90.

5. Devlin, *Mathematics*, 87, 88. I have covered this extensively in *Postmodern Philosophy and the Scientific Turn* (Bloomington: Indiana University Press, 2012).

6. Deleuze, *Cinema 1*, 4–5.

7. Bergson, *Creative Evolution*, 306.

8. Bergson, *Creative Evolution*, 100, 104.

9. Deleuze, *Cinema 1*, 9.

10. Deleuze, *Cinema 1*, 64–65.

11. Deleuze, *Cinema 1*, 58.

12. Deleuze, *Cinema 1*, 58.

13. Deleuze, *Cinema 1*, 59.

14. Deleuze, *Cinema 1*, 60–61.

15. Dorothea Olkowski, *The Universal (In the Realm of the Sensible)* (New York: Columbia University Press, 2007), 97.

16. Henri Bergson, *Matter and Memory*, trans. N. M. Paul and W. S. Palmer (New York: Zone, 1988), 48–49.

17. Bergson, *Matter and Memory*, 19.

18. Jacob von Uexküll, *Theoretical Biology* (New York: Harcourt & Brace, 1926), 176.

19. Bergson, *Matter and Memory*, 32.

20. Deleuze, *Cinema 1*, 60.

21. Bergson, *Matter and Memory*, 36. This structure is very much like Peirce's Firstness and Secondness in the overall context of Thirdness.

22. Deleuze, *Cinema 1*, 61; Bergson, *Matter and Memory*, 37.

23. Bergson, *Matter and Memory*, 38–39.

24. Bergson, *Matter and Memory*, 43.

25. Deleuze, *Cinema 1*, 62.

26. Deleuze, *Cinema 1*, 63, 64.

27. Deleuze, *Cinema 1*, 62.

28. Deleuze, *Cinema 1*, 62–63.

29. Bergson, *Matter and Memory*, 55–56.

30. Bergson, *Matter and Memory*, 56.

31. Deleuze, *Cinema 1*, 65.

32. Deleuze, *Cinema 1*, 66.

33. Deleuze, *Cinema 1*, 66.

34. Gilles Deleuze, *Cinema 2: The Time-Image*, trans. H. Tomlinson and B. Habberjam (Minneapolis: University of Minnesota Press, 1989), 28–29.

35. Deleuze, *Cinema 2*, 30.

36. Deleuze, *Cinema 2*, 31–32; Charles Sanders Peirce, *Writings*, ed. Houser (Bloomington: Indiana University Press, 1982–2000), 8.328.

37. Deleuze, *Cinema 2*, 32.

38. Peirce, *Writings*, 8.184.

39. Deleuze, *Cinema 2*, 198.

40. Deleuze, *Cinema 2*, 198.

41. Deleuze, *Cinema 2*, 199.

42. Deleuze, *Cinema 2*, 201.

43. Deleuze, *Cinema 2*, 202.

44. Deleuze, *Cinema 2*, 32.

45. Deleuze, *Cinema 2*, 2.

46. Deleuze, *Cinema 2*, 4.

47. Deleuze, *Cinema 2*, 41.

48. Deleuze, *Cinema 2*, 44.

49. Deleuze, *Cinema 2*, 189.

50. Deleuze, *Cinema 2*, 190–191.

51. Bergson, *Matter and Memory*, 56, 57.

52. Dorothea Olkowski, *Gilles Deleuze and the Ruin of Representation* (Berkeley: University of California Press, 1999), 117. In this part of the chapter, I again revisit some ideas in Bergson's philosophy that first appeared in my previous book in order to differentiate Bergson's positions more clearly from those attributed to him by Deleuze.

53. Deleuze, *Cinema 2*, 47.

54. Deleuze, *Cinema 2*, 47–48.

55. Deleuze, *Cinema 2*, 54–55.

56. Deleuze, *Cinema 2*, 55.

57. Deleuze, *Cinema 2*, 48.

58. Gilles Deleuze and Félix Guattari, *What Is Philosophy?*, trans. Hugh Tomlinson and Graham Burchell (New York: Columbia University Press, 1994), 10.

59. Merleau-Ponty credits Bergson with rejecting physiological causal theories of memory but maintains that Bergson posits a theory of psychological preservation of memory. See Maurice Merleau-Ponty, *Phenomenology of Perception*, trans. Donald A. Landes (New York: Routledge, 2012), 412–413. Originally published in French as *Phénoménologie de la perception* (Paris: Gallimard, 1945), 452–453.

60. Bergson, *Creative Evolution*, 8. It seems to me that Bergson is proposing a new image for science, but as he was a philosopher and not a physicist, he was and remains widely misunderstood.

61. David J. Depew and Bruce H. Weber, *Darwinism Evolving: Systems Dynamics and the Genealogy of Natural Selection* (Cambridge, MA: MIT Press, 1995), 92.

62. Bergson, *Creative Evolution*, 6–7. This corresponds to the static view of classical dynamics set forth by Stengers and Prigogine.

63. Lynn Margulis and Dorian Sagan, "The Universe in Heat," in *What Is Sex?* (New York: Simon & Schuster, 1997), 28. Margulis is a well-known evolutionary biologist and Sagan is a science writer. Life is only one example of thermodynamic systems, but, as the authors admit, it is among the most interesting.

64. Bergson, *Creative Evolution*, 102. Margulis and Sagan seem to evade mechanism as well as finalism altogether.

65. Bergson, *Creative Evolution*, 88. This corresponds to what Deleuze calls "force." See Gilles Deleuze, *Difference and Repetition*, trans. Paul Patton (New York: Columbia University Press, 1994), 141. Originally published in French as *Différence et Répétition* (Paris: Presses Universitaires de France, 1968).

66. For this reason, *Creative Evolution* is a thorough critique of empiricism and empirical principles as well as of Kantianism and Kantian principles.

67. Merleau-Ponty, *Phenomenology*, 391/431.

68. Merleau-Ponty, *Phenomenology*, 435/474.

69. Merleau-Ponty, *Phenomenology*, 288/326. Only objective time is made up of successive moments.

70. Merleau-Ponty, *Phenomenology*, 293/332. In part, the idea that we are temporally committed to the spaces we inhabit implies that the network of temporal relations that constitute human spatiality are also the basis of our ethical commitments.

71. Merleau-Ponty, *Phenomenology*, 294–296/333–335.

72. Bergson, *Matter and Memory*, 186.

73. Bergson, *Creative Evolution*, 5.

74. Merleau-Ponty, *Phenomenology*, 296/335. Emphases added.

75. Merleau-Ponty, *Phenomenology*, 296, 297, 298/336, 337.

Phenomenology and the Event

Merleau-Ponty's Radical Concepts:
Reflection, Form, Idea, Multiplicity

REFLECTION

In an address given to the Société française de philosophie shortly after the publication of *Phenomenology of Perception*, Maurice Merleau-Ponty maintains that we can think the world only because we have first experienced it, a position he attributes to Immanuel Kant.[1] This unexpected attribution to Kant, whose a priori faculties of imagination, understanding, and reason might seem to preclude the primacy of perception, provides an opportunity to rethink Merleau-Ponty's account of perception in order to understand in what sense he aligns himself with Kant. Very quickly, Merleau-Ponty elaborates on his position. Our perceptions, taken only as sensations, are private, ours alone, but if we take them as acts of the intellect, they are changed. He states that "if perception is an inspection of the mind, and the perceived object an *idea*, then you and I are talking about the same world."[2] What this means, he clarifies, is that when perception is an *idea*, the world "becomes an ideal existence and is the same for all of us," no different from the mathematical formula known as the Pythagorean theorem.[3]

Merleau-Ponty insists that although neither our sensations nor our ideas are invalid or incorrect, they are not the same as our experience. For experience — as opposed to sensation, which is private, or intellect, which is a shared idea — there is an expectation, if not a demand, that we are somehow seeing or hearing or touching or tasting or smelling the same thing as opposed to sensing or thinking it. Nevertheless, in comparing our perceptions with those of others, it is not all harmony and agreement; in fact, there is often nothing but contradiction. We might conclude from this that the point of thinking and the power of the idea is to erase those contradictions, but what if even thought is full of contradictions? By asking this, Merleau-Ponty undoes our assumptions. Who has not had the experience of "a tissue of concepts which lead to irreducible contradictions due to the irresistible urge to take them in an absolute sense or transfer them into pure being"?[4] For Merleau-Ponty, we have no better evidence for this than the four antinomies Kant places before us both as a warning and in order to untangle their contradictions.

In spite of the contradictions inherent in the absolute or pure use of the intuitions of space and time and the concepts of substance, mechanical causality, and necessary being, these particular contradictions are still *"the very condition of consciousness."*[5] Granted, this contradiction is not the same as that of the law of noncontradiction of formal logic, which is much closer to a system of eternal truths than to perception, but it does make clear the problem of the relation between intellectual and perceptual consciousness, which has been addressed throughout this book. The urgency of this lies in the realization that without *reflection*, not merely perception but life itself "would probably dissipate itself in ignorance of itself or in chaos."[6] Perception needs reflection in order not to just slip away in the chaos of life.

This claim serves as a warning regarding our assumptions about phenomenology, for when we announce our faith in "the primacy of perception," we may not know what we are actually claiming. What does it mean to say that scientific knowledge and physicomathematical relations make sense only insofar as we understand that intellectual knowledge and abstract ideas have the same structures and horizons as our perceptual experience? What this means, Merleau-Ponty clarifies, is that our ideas and our perceptions both have a future and past temporal horizon; both appear to themselves as temporal. We cannot expect to have the same perceptions in the future as in the past any more than we can expect to have the same ideas. Even a mathematical certainty like the Pythagorean theorem, exemplary with respect to mathematical truths, will be resituated as a *partial truth* as our framework for understanding mathematics expands and shifts.[7] As Merleau-Ponty asserts, "And this possibility is always open to us just because we are temporal. . . . What is given is a route, an experience, which gradually clarifies itself, which gradually rectifies itself and proceeds by dialogue with itself and with others."[8]

What does this statement say? It says that our temporality gives us a route. It says that time gives us space and that this order and organization are the basis of the relation between our perception, which is our "nascent *logos*," and our intellectual life—our knowledge and ideas. In this sense, the primacy of perception does not arise prior to our temporality, and it should not be understood only from the point of view of our rational and objective knowledge. The problem this sets out is how to reconcile perception and thought not only with one another but also with time and space, the manner in which we are *être au monde* (being at the world). As Merleau-Ponty states, it is a matter of discovering the structures and horizons that organize both our perceptions and our ideas, as well as our experience of space and time. Let us begin with space in order to see in what sense it is a temporal structure.

FORM

The opening pages of Merleau-Ponty's chapter on space in the *Phenomenology of Perception* focus almost entirely on the *perception* of space, which is identified there as the study of the spatial relations between objects and the geometrical characteristics of objects. In other words, it is an investigation of the nature of human perception for a *disinterested* observer of perception, such as a scientist who is observing or measuring spatial and geometric relations.[9] This analysis of the perception of space initially brought forth questions about the structure of perception that are, for Merleau-Ponty, an aspect of the theory of comportment, which he developed previously in the *Structure of Behavior*.[10]

As Merleau-Ponty argues there, a theory of form can take the place of a theory of real—that is, material physical forces and motor causes, insofar as physical quantity, vital order, and mental signification, the dominant characteristics of matter, life, and mind respectively, all participate, albeit unequally, in the nature of form. Of course, given their different characteristics, there may be no reason to think that physical form and physical reality can have the same properties as physiological and/or mental form.[11] The physical and mental worlds are thought to be unable to participate in a single realm, and the question of whether and how a cause in one universe—that of discourse— can produce an effect in another—that of physical reality—is fraught with difficulties.

It is a profound problem that Merleau-Ponty sets out to resolve by means of a philosophy of form, a philosophy for which there is but one universe. This is the universe of form in which the forms or structures of physical matter, vital life, and the mind are "invested with equal rights" so as to leave aside the ideas of derivation or causality, especially the idea that physical models bring physiological or mental forms into existence.[12] Let us approach the truly difficult question of how successfully and under what restrictions this system functions by first examining the three types of form established by Merleau-Ponty.

PHYSICAL MOLAR FORM

As noted previously, the physical world can be characterized in the manner of the natural sciences and mathematics as consisting of spatial relations between objects and the geometrical characteristics of objects. This is clear from Merleau-Ponty's critique of intellectualism in, for example, the sphere of mental disorders, where it separates itself from the materials in which it is realized, thereby separating us from the "true world."[13] If the scientific characterization of the world is our starting point for understanding reality, this raises an important question: How can the physical world be transformed from a physical and material plenum into a staging ground for behavior through its interactions with one or more of those forms of behavior (*comportement*)?

Merleau-Ponty argues that the variables on which behavior depends are not found in stimuli taken as events in the material and physical order of the world but in a type of relation that does not exist as a material or physical reality. This is due to the distinction between relations constituting behavior—that appear to be temporal as well as spatial—and the spatial mode of existence of physical events. Yet it must be possible to bridge the gap between behavior and physical events. This gap and its bridge rely on our being able to distinguish between physical events as they exist in themselves and the same situation for organisms that feel, perceive, and think. This is particularly the case if we accept the idea that there are structures or forms of behavior according to which each type of organism elaborates physical stimuli.[14] If such structures exist and operate, it may turn out that behavior is not merely a thing, meaning not an effect of physical forces, either according to a crude causality or in the sense of a mathematical function that produces variables.

Merleau-Ponty separates the universe of form into three interacting fields. First, there is matter or quantity, the field of physical forces taken up by physics; second, the physiological field of life engaged in by the so-called sciences of life; and finally, the mental field consisting of mind, value, or signification, the realm of psychology and philosophy. What happens in each field is influenced by what happens in the others so that each local effect is determined by its function, value, and significance in the whole. Nevertheless, if there are no structural differences differentiating the mental, the physiological, and the physical, consciousness would be nothing more than what happens physically in the brain— the index of complex physical structures that alone would be real.[15] The puzzling questions that must be answered are "in what sense *forms* can be said to exist 'in' the physical world and 'in' the living body" and if the concept of form can resolve the antinomy between quantity or matter and mind.[16] Lacking such a resolution, our attempts to transform the physical realm into a staging ground for behavior fail, and we remain mired in an unsolvable dualism.

In tracing this trajectory, we can begin with matter—the physical realm studied by physics—insofar as the ensemble of physical forces is inscribed in a segment of space and can be said to provide the parameters for anything that physically exists. To be clear, "*physical structure* is defined as a set of physical forces in equilibrium . . . physical things in mechanical relations with one another."[17] The model for physical form is a physical construct that physicists and mathematicians call a vector field. Merleau-Ponty characterizes the vector field according to physical principles as an "ensemble of forces in a state of equilibrium or of constant change such that no law is formulable for each part taken separately and such that each *vector* is determined in size and direction by all the others . . . [and such that] each local change in a form will be translated by a redistribution of forces which assures the constancy of their relation."[18] A physical form of this type follows its own *immanent law*. As a whole, he states, it is a *molar individual*, an individual that acts on or by means of large masses or units—large, at least, in comparison with the discernable elements or physical particles that make it up.[19]

This definition and explanation indicates that Merleau-Ponty is interested in the manner in which the particles in a physical field distribute themselves within that field in relation to the external forces acting on them, and it acknowledges that the laws of physics govern the properties of relatively stable wholes or molar individuals rather than particles.[20] For example, the second law of thermodynamics establishes the law of entropy. According to the second law, the aggregate behavior of particles is to become disorganized and lose high-quality energy or organization, a loss they do not regain. Thus, the second law operates, for Merleau-Ponty, as a form determining that, taken as a whole, the motions of particles are not reversible as classical physics determines them to be. Instead, they follow the so-called arrow of time, moving in one direction only, becoming disorganized so that high-quality energy, such as that coming from the sun, is transformed into lower-quality energy, such as that of photosynthesis.

Like gravitation, the second law is a property of relatively stable molar wholes and not an absolute property of individual or molecular particles.[21] An important implication of the second law is the scientific conceptual break with strict determinism, the idea that the future path of bodies can be predicted with certainty in an isolated system, where no new matter or energy enters. This break occurs as an effect of the experiments with gases carried out by the scientist Robert Boyle (1627–1691).[22] Nicolas Leonard Sadi Carnot (1796–1832) formulated the first and second laws of thermodynamics following Boyle's experiments, which were crucial.[23]

Boyle recognized that the motions of *individual or atomistic particles* of gas could not be predicted and that only their behavior in *structures* turned out to be somewhat predictable using methods of statistical sampling when gases were studied as aggregates of particles rather than as individual particles. This was of consequence for philosophy because, following Boyle's experimental refutation of Hobbes's theory of the nature of the air, "no important thinker dared again to promulgate a physics composed of deductions from general principles without careful and exact experimental verification."[24] For our purposes, this early introduction of the concept of structures—the study of the motions of aggregates of particles—rather than atomistic individuals is crucial.

Moreover, as Merleau-Ponty points out, those aggregates, those molar wholes, when compared to the universe and its "history," are really only *partial totalities* because the universe undergoes change—a position also held by Peirce.[25] The laws of physics represent states of equilibrium of forces that constitute partial totalities in the determination of the history of the solar system. This allows us to understand that the scientific conception of space and matter is not simply the idea that the physical world is the effect of intersecting and continuous linear, causal series.[26] *Experiments verify not a single law but a series of conditions, a number of intersecting laws that operate within a cosmological structure.* That nature does not consist of processes that can be known in isolation does not lead to the opposite conclusion that everything literally depends on everything else in a frenzy of fusion. Nevertheless, Merleau-Ponty is cautious. He asks, as we are asking here, what it means to say that physical *forms* exist. In other words, how can the physical and material world participate in the universe of form?

THE IDEA

On the one hand, as noted previously, physical laws are possible only within a particular cosmological structure, and this structure must be posited as "in nature." So, for example, "the *law* of falling bodies is the expression of a property of the terrestrial field which in reality is supported and maintained at each instant by the ensemble of the relations of the universe."[27] The introduction of the term *field* in this context is significant, as the notion of a field is linked through physics and mathematics to structures known as vector fields and vector space. But initially, Merleau-Ponty only ventures to develop the notion of structure, and his claim is that structure can only be maintained by linking it to natural laws. He insists that *there must be structures or forms in natural laws and also natural laws in structures*. However, neither of these phenomena is physical because natural laws are expressed mathematically and structures are expressed as the limit toward which physical knowledge tends. What does this imply?

Although laws are expressed by mathematical equations—the symbols of measurable objects—structures are not. This highlights the distinction between the molar individual (consisting of many molecules) and the molecular. Form serves as the *limit* of the molar, where limit refers to that point toward which tend the separate moments belonging to the *assemblage* of isolable causal actions that are able to be expressed mathematically.[28] Merleau-Ponty's use of the term *limit* correlates very well with its mathematical sense of operating as an attractor. So, form is the attractor, that point toward which the separate moments of a molar individual tend in order to be constituted as the *assemblage* that is a molar individual.[29]

It is easy to understand that the mathematical expression of laws belongs to the universe of thought, insofar as mathematics uses symbols. But this is no less the case for the physical form, which is not expressed symbolically but exists as an idea—a signification—signifying an assemblage or ensemble of molecular facts.[30] So, for example, "Egypt, as an economic, political and social *structure*, remains an object of thought distinct from the multiple facts which have constituted it and brought it into existence. It is *an idea, a signification common to the ensemble of molecular facts*."[31] Likewise, the mathematical expressions of physical objects express physical phenomena only if they are conceived of as laws of certain forms that are concrete wholes.

This is the meaning of saying that laws are laws of forms and that forms are, in turn, determined and oriented by laws.

This chapter earlier posed the question of how to bridge the gap between behavior or comportment and physical events. It was noted that this calls for a distinction between physical events as they exist in themselves and the same situation for organisms that feel, perceive, and think since each type of organism elaborates physical stimuli. This led to the notion of the form that is not a physical reality but *an object of perception*, a perceived whole, that Merleau-Ponty calls knowledge. Knowledge is defined in terms similar to those developed by Immanuel Kant, who claimed that each sensible representation is unified by a transcendental object, a concept for knowledge, which he calls the "object = x." or the "something = x."[32]

Similarly, Merleau-Ponty refers to the unity of the "empty x"—that is, the unity given to nature, existing in space, and distributed in local events. For Kant the "object = x" is an a priori concept. For Merleau-Ponty, the "empty x" is the *idea* under which what happens in several places is brought together. But unlike Kant, for whom this is a priori, for Merleau-Ponty it arises with perception: "This unity is the unity of perceived objects . . . ; it is encountered in physics only to the extent that physics refers us back to perceived things as to that which it is the function of science to express and determine."[33] In other words, it is conceptual but not a priori; it is an idea constructed by a thought confronting the objects of science, and the scientific equations and formulas themselves arise in relation to our perceptions of perceivable things.

The idea, the physical form, is not the foundation or cause of the structure of behavior/comportment. It is the object of knowledge (the empty x) of the fields of force and the dynamic unities of perception. It is dynamic because, just as perceived objects change properties when they change place, so in the physical structure of system wave mechanics, the wave associated with the entire system propagates itself in an abstract configurational space, thereby undergoing change.[34]

The seemingly casual remark, restated from *The Structure of Behavior* is indicative of the ideas Merleau-Ponty is proposing for his conception of structure/form and probably accounts for his use of the concept of a field (*champ*) as well as the reference to waves in the *Phenomenology*. Wave mechanics is not the mechanics of waves; it is a reformulation, in terms of waves, of the branch of physics known as mechanics, which deals with motions of matter. This is needed because "Newtonian mechanics treats matter strictly as localized particles, or of bodies and fluids consisting of such particles. Wave mechanics asserts that when one gets down to the atomic level, *particles sometimes need to be treated as waves*, spread out in space, their location and momentum not known until they interact. Even then, as Heisenberg showed in his uncertainty principle, one can never extract full information."[35]

Adding to the previous discussions of waves, we can say that a wave function is the mathematics that accounts for how the wave varies in space and time.[36] Calculations for the trajectory of the wave are nowhere near as precise as those for the motions of Newtonian atoms and can tell us only the probability that a particle will be found in some particular location when measured at some particular time.[37] In other words, it describes the probable values of the attributes of quantum objects. However, the equation for calculating the quantum wave function "has defied all attempts to give it an interpretation in terms of physically observable entities."[38] Once an actual physical observation/measurement is made, the wave collapses into a single determinate value, and no one seems to know why. It has been suggested that the physicist Erwin Schrödinger, whose equation defines the wave function, takes this to be an epistemological problem and not an ontological one.[39] If so, it would be our knowledge, not physical reality, that is subject to uncertainty; however, this approach would also be antirealist and would deny the efficacy of scientific causal explanations.[40]

Although Merleau-Ponty clearly opposes intellectualist positions insofar as they would make the intellect originary with respect to the world, the position of phenomenology remains murky. For him, physical structures are not to be taken as *in-themselves* but are perceived forms, reaffirming the primacy of perception, which, if it is not idealist, is also explicitly not an empiricist position.[41] The ontological status of phenomenology remains unresolved, but it can probably be characterized as a perceptual epistemology.[42]

In Merleau-Ponty's account, unlike system wave mechanics, classical or Newtonian science first constructed the image of an absolute physical reality and then proposed that perceptual structures are simply manifestations or projections of this fundamental *ontological* foundation. But this is not the case for the concept of form since, although the laws of physical reality conceptualize the perceived world, with respect to form, reference to the perceived world is essential to knowledge of the physical world.[43] In the course "Nature," Merleau-Ponty tries to clarify what he means. The crucial concepts of physics, such as causality, light, space, energy, and even time, have to be understood as an ensemble of concepts subject to experimental verification. Thus, rather than taking them up singly, we encounter them as an "ensemble of parameters," "a massive Being in which whatever time, space, matter, etc. are must appear not so much as juxtaposed realities, but rather as one undivided reality."[44] They are "a rigorous ensemble of constructed terms."[45] So, if our perception of space does, in fact, found our experience of physical reality, what are the philosophical implications of this claim?

SPACE: AN OUTLINE OF MULTIPLICITY

In the *Phenomenology*, the perception of space is said to consist of spatial relationships. The existence of spatial relationships presupposes some notion of a subject in a setting—a someone who inheres in a world where the world is understood to be a spatial field in which the subject is anchored. Yet, following Husserl, Merleau-Ponty argues that *such a subject, one anchored in a spatial field, is still in the "natural attitude" and so does not yet actually have perceptions*—that is, the positing of objects—but rather, this subject undergoes a flow of experiences that imply and explain one another simultaneously and successively.[46]

The analysis of movement is similarly structured. The objective conception of movement defines it in terms of measurable relations within the world, the changing relations between an object and its surroundings.[47] This view takes the experience of the subject for granted and instead corresponds neatly to the calculations of mathematics. Differential calculus, for example, precisely measures the rate of change of one variable quantity in relation to another on which it depends.[48] For calculus, objective movement appears as an accidental attribute of a moving body, a system of relations external to the object in motion. But this is not the only possible view of motion. A different view of motion is that "the identity of the object in motion flows directly from 'experience.'"[49] The identity of the object flows from the experience of "someone" who lives through the object's motions and synthesizes them. It is the experience only of an anonymous someone and not a specific personal someone, which indicates that, on this level, movements take their significance from the natural attitude of the perceiver whose hold on the world orients her movements.[50]

Merleau-Ponty does not dismiss either position—that of objective science or that of the natural attitude—but argues that although each contains an element of truth, it is perception and only perception that allows us to bridge the gap between physical reality and behavior/comportment. This involves both the positing of objects and the experience of a subject. Thinking this through, it seems that the objective view situates an object in terms of its relations with its surroundings so that "movement does not work without an external reference point, and, in short, there is no means of attributing movement exclusively to the 'moving object' rather than to the reference point."[51] Objectively, there must be a moving object and a course through which it moves.

Conversely, the perception of movement is not derived solely from the perception of a moving object, for the successive positions require no transcendental unity to hold them together and identify movement.[52] This is where Husserl's concept of the natural attitude comes into play as a version of the idea of structure or form. Elsewhere, Merleau-Ponty refers to this as an *anonymous flow*, for which there are no states of consciousness but which is not merely a statistical and objective view of consciousness.[53] This version of the natural attitude allows a non-Kantian subject to unify her experience without positing either an objective manifold of space-time oriented purely by physical laws or the unity of consciousness, the "I think" that once was posited to accompany all representations. In place of Kantian synthesis, this is a quasi-synthesis; in place of the unity of what was originally many or diverse, there is a style, "something colored," or "something luminous':[54] It accounts for the idea that this version of the natural attitude underlies the calculations of the logician who thinks the unity of the moving object in terms of a collection of determinate properties[55] It is precisely what Merleau-Ponty earlier characterized as a form.

The natural attitude, understood as an anonymous flow, situates both the moving object and the perceiver in the world. Merleau-Ponty claims explicitly that, "We do not clarify space, movement, and time by discovering an 'inner' layer of experience where their multiplicity is *truly* erased and abolished" insofar as *external* experience, which is sensible perception, is the condition of the possibility of any sort of *internal* experience, and the latter—that is, internal experience—is "ineffable, but only because it is meaningless [*elle ne veut rien dire*]."[56] The problem with pure internal experience is that it has no language insofar as language is an external, cultural product.[57]

THE TEMPORALITY OF SPACE

Kant posited an a priori *intuition* of space and time that is both free of contradiction and able to be constructed mathematically.[58] Borrowing from classical physics, time, for Kant, is transcendentally ideal because it is not only the formal a priori condition of all appearances but also the pure form of all sensible intuition, and what takes place "in time" is simply a sequence of events.[59] By contrast, for Merleau-Ponty, the temporal horizons of objects do not come to our attention by means of the intuition of a unifying subject. From the first, they arise through the preobjective hold of our body upon the world—that is, insofar *as we are perceivers even prior to perceiving anything in particular.* Perceived or not, parts of space can be said to coexist because they are temporally present to the same perceiving subject but also and prior to this because they are "enveloped in one and the same *temporal wave*," each one of which gains both unity and individuation because it is "wedged in [*pressée*] between the preceding and following one."[60]

What is a temporal wave? Merleau-Ponty does not elucidate this concept here, but an obvious analogy might be sound waves. A sound wave is a disturbance that travels through a medium such as a series of interconnected and interacting particles. Sound waves originate with some vibrating object, creating a disturbance that is transported through the air, particle to particle, and for this reason sound waves are said to be mechanical. Mechanical waves require a medium in which to transport their energy, unlike electromagnetic waves, which can travel through a vacuum devoid of particles.[61] Sound waves are a useful image for time because, in wave phenomenon, the wave transports only its energy without transporting matter. Individual particles are displaced only temporarily before returning to their original equilibrium.[62]

In *The Phenomenology of Internal Time Consciousness*, Husserl's analysis of immanent temporal objects is articulated almost entirely in terms of sound and sound waves.[63] The immanent temporal object appears in a continuous flux, which could be called a wave; the sound is continually different but only with respect to *the way it appears*. Of particular importance to the analysis of immanent temporal objects are the "running-off phenomena," which are modes of temporal orientation such as "now" and "past," so that "we know that it [time] is a continuity of constant transformations which form an inseparable unit."[64] No running-off can reoccur as each begins as an upsurge of *now*; every subsequent phase of running-off is also a constantly expanding continuity of pasts; each now changes into a past, each of which sinks deeper into the past; each now passes over into retention, and every now changes continuously from retention to retention such that *every point is a retention for every earlier point* and every retention forms a continuum.[65]

In spite of Merleau-Ponty's eventual concern that Husserl's conception of temporality remains within the framework of Euclidean spatial relations, what is crucial in Husserl's account of running-off is that the phases of running off form a continuum that unifies the experience of temporality without the necessity of positing a transcendental subject to do this.[66] Husserl's concept of retention also distinguishes the real sensation of a sound from the tonal moment in retention, which is *not actually present* but is *primarily remembered in the now*. He states, "The intuition of the past itself . . . is an originary consciousness. . . . It is consciousness of *what has just been* and not mere consciousness of the now-point of the objective thing appearing as having duration."[67]

Of equal importance is the clear distinction Husserl draws between the temporal now that sinks back in retention and the mathematical conception of a *limit*. For modern science, time is an independent variable, a parameter of the spatial manifold useful for calculating the positions of real elements of matter at any-instant-whatever if their current positions are given. From this point of view, each now seeks to found itself moment to moment through the limit or negation of what has come before so as to remain absolutely free of the past. But Husserl insists, "If there were such a boundary point, there would correspond to it a now which nothing preceded, and this is obviously impossible."[68]

A now is an edge-point, but it is an edge-point of an *interval* of time, all of which sinks back. So, for Husserl, the interval is an interval within "the one and unique Objective time," even though, as Merleau-Ponty insists, "we will have to discover beneath the objective thought of movement a pre-objective experience from which it borrows its sense."[69] When bells begin to sound at some objectified temporal point, the sound always corresponds to the temporal point of the sensation. As for any sound wave, Husserl distinguishes between the matter—the primal sensations or primal data through which the wave travels—and the energy, the wave itself—that is, Objectified absolute time—which is identified with a continuity of temporal positions and also with the changing Objectivities that fill it.

Ultimately Husserl differentiates at least three levels of temporality, three components of every temporal wave: (1) the experiential thing of the individual subject in Objective time; (2) the immanent unities of preempirical time; and (3) the absolute, temporally constitutive flux of consciousness. Recalling Merleau-Ponty's concern that internal experience is "incommunicable because meaningless [*elle ne veut rien dire*]," we should not be surprised that he does not concur with the aspect of the temporal wave defined as the intuition of the absolute, temporally constitutive flux of consciousness.[70] Rejecting what he calls a "transcendental I freely positing in front of itself a multiplicity in itself and constituting it from top to bottom," he turns instead to an I that is never conscious of being the creator of time, an I that has the *impression* of mobile entities effecting the passage from one instant to another, an I that is relative and prepersonal and nonetheless provides the basis for space and time.[71]

Merleau-Ponty is also not entirely comfortable with Henri Bergson's account of time as duration. Bergson is critical of Kant for the same reasons as is Merleau-Ponty, which are that Kant posited time as a homogeneous medium whose moments are situated spatially—side by side—and susceptible to the same causality as the outer world. Bergson describes time as pure duration, a lived continuity "wherein our states melt into each other."[72] In some instances, such as when we listen to the "deep notes of a musical scale," we feel the vibration of the notes within our inner continuity; these sensations are pure qualities.[73] Such vibration is nothing other than the movement of atoms. Thus, we grasp at once both the state of our conscious qualitative duration and the reality of movement that contracts into the rhythm of our duration.[74]

Similarly, for Deleuze, the experience of sensations consists of a self that *is* its modifications, which take place in the domain of passive synthesis. The capacity to experience sensations calls for a "contracting machine," a capacity for "contractions, contemplations, pretensions, presumptions, satisfactions," all of which are qualitative differences (Firstness).[75] Former and actual presents are not two successive instants on a timeline. The current or present present reflects itself even as it forms a memory of the former present; thus it is simultaneously reflection and reproduction, recognition and remembrance, and understanding and memory (Secondness). For Deleuze, "The actual present is not treated as the future object of a recollection but rather as that which reflects itself at the same time as it forms the recollection of the old present."[76] The active synthesis is founded in the first synthesis, the passive synthesis, but it is also situated with respect to the past in general, the continuity that is the form of everything that changes and moves (Thirdness or Peirce's continuum); it is the immutable or empty form of change and, as we have seen, of movement.[77]

In his later work, Merleau-Ponty asserts the idea that the past and our consciousness of the past do not coincide except perhaps partially.[78] So he cannot accept the notion of time as intuition (duration) insofar as, for him, this does not leave enough distance or separation (*écart*) between an event in the world and the flux of temporality.[79] Perhaps it is possible to hypothesize that Merleau-Ponty's relative and prepersonal I lies somewhere between Bergson's internal flux of duration and Husserl's transcendental Ego, but always in the context of a structure that is a network of relations. In other words, the supposition is that there must be for space, just as for behavior, a general field within which the perception of spatial entities takes place—a field that orients our perception and gives meaning to spatial phenomena. What Merleau-Ponty takes from Bergson and Husserl is the idea that the general field is time. It is, he maintains, the time within which we act in alignment with the network of relationships that define our acts—acts that are also our abode, the place within which we dwell; and, the place in which we dwell that is also the place from which we form our commitments and assert our freedom.[80]

FREEDOM AND THE GESTALT

In pursuing the problem of how the physical world can be transformed from a physical and material plenum into a staging ground for behavior, the strange solution that emerges is that they are linked by our freedom. Initially, it appears that Merleau-Ponty's account of freedom is a version of his critique of the classical model of the reflex, which appeared in *The Structure of Behavior*. There, he points out that the classical conception of a reflex makes the place of the excitation determine the reaction so that one part of the stimulus should correspond to one part of the response and the same elementary sequences (possibly combined differently) should be found in all reflexes. He objects to this because there is always a complex of stimuli and even the simplest stimulus affects several anatomical elements of the receptors at the same time.[81] He argues that all the stimulations an organism receives are possible only because its preceding movements have culminated in exposing the organism to these external influences so *one could say that the behavior is the first cause of all the stimulations* and that the organism chooses the stimuli in the physical world to which it will be sensitive.[82] This is possible insofar as a living present is open not merely to the past and future but to temporalities outside of lived experience, including those of a social horizon.[83]

He concludes that just as an adequate *stimulus* cannot be defined independently of the *organism as a whole* because it is no mere physical reality but a
physiological or biological whole, so the receptor is also not a mere physio-
chemical agent but also a physiological or biological whole—an occasion, not
merely a response.[84] For this reason, learning is not the process of adding onto
old forms some new connections between stimuli and movements but is a "general" alteration of behavior manifested in a multitude of actions whose content
is variable but whose significance is a constant, by which he means a Gestalt.
This is not the idea of a "form-in-itself" but a revised notion of the Gestalt as
a total process for which everything takes place—for example, as if our eye
movements are what they are in order to take advantage of the situation and in
order to realize certain situations of preferred equilibrium toward which the
forces at work tend.[85]

Regardless of conditioning, useless movements disappear from subsequent
responses. This new behavior should not occur if to learn is merely to repeat, as
the behaviorists claim. To learn is to provide an adapted response to the situation by different means, so it is a matter of an aptitude for resolving a series of
problems of the same form.[86] Perhaps we can refer to this as a *variable* Gestalt;
it will be taken up again in the final chapter.

In the same way, the starting point for setting out the problem of freedom
is the statement that there is no freedom without a field.[87] The English word
field, in the original French text, is *champ*, and its use here is significant insofar
as it refers to the physical and material plenum of physical forms. It was previously stated that Merleau-Ponty designates three interacting fields: matter or
quantity—that is, the field of physical forces; the physiological field of life; and
the mental field consisting of mind, value, or signification. What happens in
each field is influenced by what happens in the others so that each local effect
is determined by its function, value, and significance in the whole. This means
that although we may glimpse ourselves as a molecular, anonymous flow, we are
not simply a material plenum, a field of physical forces, determined by external
factors. We humans are not a molar thing, the object of a statistical and objective view, because there is no material causal relationship between a subject
and the world.[88]

Reflecting on the Sartrean notion of freedom, Merleau-Ponty again emphasizes the role of the field of relations, this time as that site within which
all choices take place. Given his argument that behavior, even the behavior of
physical forces, can be understood as a field—a structure or form—we cannot

objectify ourselves, and other people cannot successfully objectify us. To do so would require precisely what he has ruled out—that is, taking a statistical view of ourselves in order to reach objectivity. Mathematics certainly makes this conceivable, but for that to be possible, we would have to view *ourselves* as a thing to be negated through action.

Freedom is not a matter of degree. One is not a little bit free or unfree either through causal physical forces or through psychological ones such as motivation, which are only possible in the context of the temporal unity of one's projects. After all, Merleau-Ponty points out, the weave of a fabric exists for a subject who observes it from one or another of its sides.[89] For Merleau-Ponty, "I can no longer pretend to be a nihilation [*néant*], and to choose myself continually out of nothing at all," because our choices and acts take place in a field of relations, a universe of structures.[90] In this, he echoes the words of Simone de Beauvoir, who, in *The Ethics of Ambiguity*, also asserts that no existence founds itself only from moment to moment by negating the past and that moral freedom requires a past and a future that belong to the temporal unity of one's current projects that, in turn, may become the starting point for other projects to be carried out by other people, on and on into the infinite future.[91] The emphasis here is dual—that is, freedom is both a temporal phenomenon and a social or historical one.

This resonates with the claims made by Bryan Smyth in his recent book on Merleau-Ponty regarding the interplay between first-person existence and its sublimation into an habitual body whose impersonalization expresses the anonymous, general level of existence.[92] Smyth states, "The lack of an existentially 'healthy' equilibrium between 'actual' and habitual corporeality—and hence freedom—within individual human existence is effectively identical with the lack of 'harmony between the individual [in general] and history,' which Merleau-Ponty regarded as an existential 'postulate of human existence' in the sense of being a necessary condition of the realization of humanity. Inasmuch as the latter can be viewed in terms of freedom construed socially, it follows that for Merleau-Ponty that there is a mutually implicatory relation between the realization of humanity and freedom at the individual level."[93] The body that participates unreservedly in action is the habituated organism, the anonymous and general existence that each one shares with all other beings. And it is because of this that its actions are personally selfless acts of self-sacrifice that are simultaneously a tendency toward universal life—that is to say, toward intersubjective relations.[94]

This is expressed by Merleau-Ponty in a number of ways. It is found, as noted previously, in the Gestalt psychological structure whereby certain shapes, such as cubes and groupings of dots in pairs of six, are favored.[95] It is found, as well, in our relations with history, understood as our way of being in the world within a variety of institutional frameworks.[96] Here, he argues that becoming revolutionary is never the effect of being confronted with a *representation* of revolution. More than likely, no Russian peasants ever expressly represented the transfer of property in 1917, which might have been a terrifying thought. Rather, they found themselves, along with others, engaged in certain projects generalizable as change.[97] There is, Merleau-Ponty notes, a "molecular process," not a molar mechanical causality, at work. This molecular process takes place on the level of the relations that human beings have with one another and with their own lives. It requires coexistence.[98]

Our acts of freedom consist of "the concrete project of a future that is elaborated in social coexistence and in the One [*l'On*]."[99] The anonymity of the One arises when personal existence is *sublimated*—as in chemistry when a substance transitions from a solid to a gas without any intermediate state—and reduced to the molecular field that is the natural, cultural, and historical world. Paradoxically, it is this that sets us free from our first-person existence, from our irrefutable certainties and knowledge, and confirms that we are structures open to the world and to others. It is in this light that we can read the moving conclusion to Merleau-Ponty's *Phenomenology*, which is taken up from the work of Antoine de Saint-Exupery: "Your son is caught in the fire: you are the one who will save him.... You give yourself in exchange.... Your significance shows itself effulgent. It is your duty, your hatred, your love, your steadfastness, your ingenuity.... Man is but a network of relationships."[100]

STRUCTURE OR EVENT?

Phenomenologists familiar with Deleuze's philosophy reading this may be struck by the familiarity of the language usually attributed to Deleuze: reflection, idea, multiplicity, molar, molecular. Are not these radical ideas found in Merleau-Ponty the same ideas utilized by Deleuze? If so, how can Deleuze justify the persistent critique of phenomenology? Let us briefly examine this once again before passing on to Deleuze's reformulation of philosophy in the final chapter.

In his analysis of the paintings of the artist Francis Bacon, Gilles Deleuze makes the bold assertion that the lived body of phenomenology is paltry compared with the almost unlivable power of the body without organs. The phenomenological hypothesis, he notes, is insufficient because it invokes merely the lived body whereas the body without organs, characterized by a *logic of sensation*, arises at the very limit of the lived body.[101] This claim presents us with a distinction and with a comparison, possibly inviting us to choose between two conceptions of the body: that of phenomenology and that of a logic of sensation. It is a choice between a lived body and an almost unlivable one. But on what basis can we possibly choose? Is one obviously true and the other false? Is one saddled to an untenable worldview while the other pushes us forward into brave new worlds of life and thought? Does one inhabit a space of oppression or conformity and the other a space of freedom or endless originality? Perhaps we cannot answer these questions, or perhaps we need to ask different kinds of questions. Let us think about this a bit more.

In Deleuze's account, phenomenology set out to give us perceptions and affections that awaken us to the world. However, as noted, he claims that the lived experience of phenomenological bodies yields nothing but opinion. Phenomenological concepts, Deleuze and Guattari together maintain, are the expression of a three-part set of acts of transcendence that allow the subject to constitute first a sensory world filled with objects; next, an intersubjective world that includes others; and finally, the common ideal world of scientific, mathematical, and logical formations.[102] In this way, they argue, the notion of immanence to nature—what Deleuze calls the vital power—is lost, and what survives is immanence to a subject whose acts are relative to the lived and whose concepts arise out of the lived.[103]

This is why, for Deleuze, these so-called concepts are therefore little more than opinions, *doxa* formulated on the basis of an external perception as the state of the subject and an internal affection as a passage from one state to another. They are thus a function of the perceptive-affective lived experience so that what passes for a phenomenological concept is really only an empirical opinion and phenomenology thereby interprets experience as a sequence of perceptual and affective clichés.[104] And so Deleuze raises the following question: "Should we, along with art, overturn opinion, raising it to the infinite movement that replaces it with, precisely, the concept?"[105] This is apparently what is at stake for Deleuze in the distinction between the lived body and the body without organs, opinion or concept, clichés or unlivable power.

In his book on the paintings of Francis Bacon, Deleuze does not develop his own hypothesis through an immediate critique of phenomenology; rather he plunges boldly ahead with an analysis of the characteristics, or "accidents," he attributes to Bacon's paintings.[106] Deleuze argues that painting does not simply apply laws coming from logic or metaphysics but that it discovers its own "properly aesthetic laws."[107] Relevant to the points being made here is that Deleuze elsewhere maintained that aesthetics designates a theory of sensibility insofar as sensibility is assumed to be the *form of any possible experience*.[108] As the form of any possible experience, aesthetics is clearly situated as an aspect of thought but also as a condition of experience. The type of experience that interests Deleuze is not that of the lived body attributed to phenomenology but that of sensation.

The form of sensation will be a formal structure of well-defined rules that make the system governing experience consistent so that it is not subject to interpretation. A formal system for aesthetics can be thought in relation to sensation as it arises in relation to nature or in relation to sensation produced by a work of art, but it is always without a specific reference to the external events or entities it governs. In addition, Deleuze claims that aesthetics is a theory of art, a reflection of real experience that may include "an aesthetic of the spectator, as in the theory of the judgment of taste; sometimes an aesthetic, or rather a meta-aesthetic, of the creator, as in the theory of genius. Sometimes an aesthetic of the beautiful in nature; sometimes an aesthetic of the beautiful in art."[109]

Although Bacon identified his work with Egyptian painting, Deleuze firmly pushes him in another direction, overturning optical coordinates and tactile connections in a catastrophic break that sweeps away both the optical and the tactile. To understand this, let us return to the first task of aesthetics, aesthetics as a theory of sensibility, where sensibility is assumed to be the form of any possible experience. In a Bacon painting, "like a first catastrophe, the form collapses."[110] The form related to figuration and representation collapses into a form related only to a Figure. Simultaneously, sensation passes from one order, level, or area to another; as "the agent of bodily deformations," sensation acts directly on the nervous system.[111] How are we to understand this catastrophic transformation in which a form related to figuration and narration collapses under the impetus of sensations that act directly on the nervous system? For Deleuze, the form that collapses seems to be situated in relation to the lived body of phenomenology.

In Deleuze's analysis, Bacon's paintings engage the viewer on the level of concepts. They are Events. Before the painter begins, the canvas consists of equally probable any-space-whatevers—a canvas phase space, the ideal space of Events, a field of immanence.[112] The Event consists of real, physical, and effective sensations that bypass imagination and understanding and *directly attack the nervous system*: no intuitions or thought needed.[113] Nevertheless, as a material realization of ideal space, the specific canvas has three dimensions, a center, and boundaries. And then there is the painter with the mysterious "something in his head."[114] This is not to say that the painter thinks about the Figures he paints; rather, everything in his head is already on the canvas, presumably as a representation. What he needs to do is clear it out by sweeping, dilating, contracting, flattening, and elongating. The sensation of manual effort is particularly violent when the deformations concern the face, and the face is cleared out so as to become a head that screams, capturing the invisible and insensible forces, sensations beyond mere pain and feeling.[115]

What response, if any, can phenomenology give to Deleuze's reading of lived experience and the lived body? Is he right that it is mired in clichés and opinions? Although Deleuze's reading of Husserl's phenomenology may certainly be contested, we will confine our inquiry to that of Merleau-Ponty and the claim that only the philosophy of the body without organs creates and maintains concepts and only the logic of sensation describes a superior and powerful, direct and unmediated impact on the nervous system.

Let us examine this first in terms of Deleuze's distinction between the tactile and the visual. In *The Principles of Art History*, Heinrich Wölfflin offers to reduce the difference between the art of Dürer and the art of Rembrandt to its most general formulation: the difference between the tactile and the visual picture, the linear and the painterly. He states, "Linear style sees in lines, painterly in masses. . . . Linear vision, therefore, means . . . that the eye is led along the boundaries and induced to feel along the edges."[116] The difference is between uniformly clear lines that separate and the emancipation of the masses of light and shade.[117] Tracing a figure with an even, clear line is a kind of physical grasping; the movement of the eye resembles the movement of the hand as it feels along a body, and the modeling, with its gradation of light, appeals to the sense of touch. A painterly mass appeals only to the eye and "surrenders" to mere appearance.[118] To say that the linear style represents things as they are and the painterly as they seem to be means the former is fundamentally objective, perceiving and expressing solid, tangible relations, while the latter is subjective, basing the representation on the picture, which retains little resemblance to our conception of the real form of things.[119]

Let us correlate this distinction with the critique leveled against phenomenology previously. If phenomenology is an existential communication that loses touch with the vital power that exceeds every domain of sensation, it is visual and painterly; it is the realm of appearances, and only the philosophy of the concept/Event is objective and tactile. It is the real form of things possessing real vital power.

Deleuze identifies the vital power as an effect of the logic of sensations, describing it as "the world that seizes me by closing in around me, the self that opens to the world and opens the world itself."[120] This occurs in many of Bacon's images when "the flat field closes in around the Figure and when the

Figure contracts or, on the contrary, expands in order to rejoin the field to the point where the Figure merges with the field."[121] But Deleuze attributes this vital power to Paul Cézanne's paintings, as much as to those of Francis Bacon. Similarly, Deleuze argues that Cézanne subordinated all painting techniques to the task of making visible the vital power, the forces of mountains, seeds, or landscapes.[122] Without providing a specific citation, Deleuze attributes the phrase "logic of the senses" to Cézanne. However, in a strikingly similar manner, Merleau-Ponty cites a comment made by Cézanne to Emil Bernard, specifically that "we have to develop an optics, by which I mean a logical vision."[123]

For Merleau-Ponty, when Cézanne says that he is returning to the object, he paints its *arrival* as matter taking on form and manifesting the birth of order, a spontaneous organization. It is with nature as our base, Merleau-Ponty claims, that we construct our sciences rather than the reverse. As Cézanne wrote, this is the manner in which it is possible to confront the sciences with the nature "from which they came."[124]

Still, both Deleuze and Merleau-Ponty claim Cézanne as the source of a logic that defines the senses and sensation. This leaves us with the impression that in a book about Francis Bacon, it is secretly Cézanne's paintings that are the battlefield upon which the contest between the philosophy of the Event and phenomenology takes place. The issue is how we are to frame this contest and if we need to determine which philosophy might be preferable.

In Merleau-Ponty's *The Structure of Behavior*, the primary question has been how to bridge the gap between behavior and physical events. This brought forth the notion of the form that is not a physical reality but rather an object of perception, a perceived whole. This is what Merleau-Ponty calls knowledge. As seen previously, Merleau-Ponty refers to the unity of the "empty x"—that is, the unity given to nature, existing in space, and distributed in local events. It is the unity of perceived objects explicated in physics insofar as physics refers us back to perceived things that science expresses and determines.[125]

For phenomenology, physical form is an object of perception, which can be expressed as an *idea*. The physical form is an object of knowledge (the empty x) of the fields of force and the dynamic unities of perception, thus given that perceived objects change properties when they change place, as in the physical structure of system wave mechanics, still, only the wave associated with the entire system propagates itself in an abstract configurational space.[126]

It has also been noted that, unlike system wave mechanics, classical or Newtonian science, according to Merleau-Ponty, appears to have constructed the image of an absolute physical reality and then proposed that perceptual structures are simply manifestations or projections of this fundamental ontological foundation. This is commensurate with the model Deleuze inherits, but then he proceeds to dismantle its determinations and predictions. This book has examined the effects of this deterritorialization, which is the philosophy of the Event. The question is, can we choose between the philosophy of the Event created out of and celebrating the undoing of the classical model of the universe or a philosophy of structure embracing form but also embodying the uncertainty of quantum wave mechanics? Let us now look further into Deleuze-Guattari's most original formulations to clarify the difference between these two philosophies.

NOTES

1. Maurice Merleau-Ponty, "The Primacy of Perception," trans. James Edie, in *The Primacy of Perception*, ed. James Edie (Evanston, IL: Northwestern University Press, 1964), 12–42, esp. 17.

2. Merleau-Ponty, "The Primacy of Perception," 17.

3. Merleau-Ponty, "The Primacy of Perception," 17.

4. Merleau-Ponty, "The Primacy of Perception," 18.

5. Merleau-Ponty, "The Primacy of Perception," 19.

6. Merleau-Ponty, "The Primacy of Perception," 19.

7. Merleau-Ponty, "The Primacy of Perception," 20, 21.

8. Merleau-Ponty, "The Primacy of Perception," 21.

9. "Normative" perception has been addressed in Dorothea Olkowski, "A Psychoanalysis of Nature?" in *Chiasmi International*, vol. 2, *Merleau-Ponty: From Nature to Ontology* (Paris: Vrin; Milan: Mimesis; Memphis, TN: University of Memphis), 185–205.

10. Maurice Merleau-Ponty, *The Structure of Behavior*, trans. Alden L. Fisher (Boston: Beacon, 1963). Originally published in French as *La structure du comportement* (Paris: Presses Universitaires de France, 1942).

11. Merleau-Ponty, *The Structure of Behavior*, 132–133.

12. Merleau-Ponty, *The Structure of Behavior*, 133–134.

13. Maurice Merleau-Ponty, *Phenomenology of Perception*, trans. Donald A. Landes (New York: Routledge Press, 2012), 127–128/158–159. Originally published in French as *Phénoménologie de la perception* (Paris: Gallimard, 1945). Pages in the French edition appear after the slash.

14. Merleau-Ponty, *The Structure of Behavior*, 129.

15. Merleau-Ponty, *The Structure of Behavior*, 136. Merleau-Ponty stresses that even physical/mental isomorphism is a form of identity or epiphenomenalism.

16. Merleau-Ponty, *The Structure of Behavior*, 137. We cannot simply assume that such a translation is possible. We must prove it.

17. Douglas Low, "Merleau-Ponty on Causality," *Human Studies* 38, no. 3 (July 2015): 2.

18. Merleau-Ponty, *The Structure of Behavior*, 137. This corresponds to the mathematical definition: Given a *complete* set of functions in a given space in differential calculus, each function in that space can be expressed as a combination of that complete set of functions, and functions with the property of completeness can form a vector space under binary operations.

19. The concept of molar individuals has been widely attributed to Gilles Deleuze, who contrasts it with the molecular, but it was clearly utilized by Merleau-Ponty in this context.

20. Merleau-Ponty, *The Structure of Behavior*, 139. This is why, "The law of falling bodies expresses the constitution of a field of relatively stable forces in the neighborhood of the earth" (138).

21. Merleau-Ponty, *The Structure of Behavior*, 138–139.

22. Lynn Margulis and Dorian Sagan, "The Universe in Heat," in *What Is Sex?* (New York: Simon & Schuster, 1997), 28–29. Margulis and Sagan take this as an argument for a universe that is open and complex.

23. Margulis and Sagan, "The Universe in Heat," 29.

24. E. A. Burtt, *The Metaphysical Foundations of Modern Science*, 3rd ed. (New York: Dover Books, 2003), 169, 171. The necessity of experimental proofs affirmed Hume's skepticism with regard to reason but ultimately, once added to mathematics, reinforced its power and authority.

25. Low, "Merleau-Ponty on Causality," 10. Whitehead also held this position. Low states, "Here, in *Nature*, Merleau-Ponty also favorably mentions Whitehead's attempt to evaluate the classical concepts of time, space, causality, and probability. . . . We can make better sense of nature if we regard it as a process, as a continual unfolding" (10).

26. Merleau-Ponty, *The Structure of Behavior*, 138–140. Therefore, experiments verify a system of complementary laws and not a single law.

27. Merleau-Ponty, *The Structure of Behavior*, 141.

28. The mole is the amount of substance of a system that contains as many elementary entities as there are atoms in 0.012 kilogram of carbon 12. "The Mole," accessed August 2021, http://chemistry.bd.psu.edu/jircitano/mole.html.

29. Merleau-Ponty, *The Structure of Behavior*, 142. Unfortunately, there is a lack of precision in Merleau-Ponty's use of the term *limit*, so one can only suggest an adequate reading of it.

30. Merleau-Ponty, *The Structure of Behavior*, 143.

31. Merleau-Ponty, *The Structure of Behavior*, 143. Emphasis added. Readers familiar with the work of Gilles Deleuze will no doubt be surprised that these terms, widely associated with Deleuze, are the ideas of Merleau-Ponty.

32. Immanuel Kant, *Critique of Pure Reason*, trans. Norman Kemp Smith (New York: St. Martin's, 1965), A109. "All our representations are, it is true, referred by the understanding to some object . . . and understanding refers

them to a *something*, as the object of sensible intuition. But this something, thus conceived, is only the transcendental object; and by that is meant a something = x . . . which, as a correlate of the unity of apperception, can serve only for the unity of the manifold in sensible intuition" (A250).

33. Merleau-Ponty, *The Structure of Behavior*, 143–144.

34. Merleau-Ponty, *The Structure of Behavior*, 144. I am assuming that this is a reference to what mathematicians call state space.

35. David P. Stern, "Educational Web Sites on Astronomy, Physics, Spaceflight, and the Earth's Magnetism," Goddard Space Flight Center, accessed August 2017, www.phy6.org/stargaze/Q7.htm. This site is aimed at high school students so may be well useful for the broad spectrum of humanists who have little or no mathematical background.

36. Karen Barad, *Meeting the Universe Halfway: Quantum Physics and the Entanglement of Matter and Meaning* (Durham, NC: Duke University Press, 2007), 453n6. It is highly ironic that Barad interprets the most *antirealist* position in quantum physics as one that is materialist, which is to say physicalist.

37. Barad, *Meeting the Universe Halfway*, 251.

38. John Casti, *Complexification: Explaining a Paradoxical World through the Science of Surprise* (New York: Harper Collins, 1994), 205, 206.

39. Barad, *Meeting the Universe Halfway*, 284.

40. Lee Smolin, *Einstein's Unfinished Revolution: The Search for What Lies Beyond the Quantum* (New York: Penguin, 2019). Smolin proposes the following causal and thus temporal solution to this problem: "I then would propose that each event has a certain quantity of energy and that energy is transmitted from past events to future events along causal relations. An event's energy is the sum of the energies received from the events in its immediate causal past. That energy is divided up and transmitted to the events in its immediate causal future. In this way the law of conservation of energy, according to which energy is never created or destroyed, is respected" (261). If this turns out to be correct, it correlates much more with Bergson's position than with that of Bertrand Russell.

41. Low, "Merleau-Ponty on Causality," 2. Perception is neither the thought of a cube as a solid with six equal sides nor the empirical association of a series of appearances of the cube. Merleau-Ponty, *Phenomenology*, 276/313–314.

42. Seeking to articulate Merleau-Ponty's ontology, Lawrence Hass instead argues that, for Merleau-Ponty, not only language but all life is a form of behavior and expression is the epistemology that knows it, but knows it creatively. Yet, rather than ontology, this appears to be epistemology. See Lawrence Hass, *Singing the World: An Invitation to Merleau-Ponty's Philosophy* (Bloomington: Indiana University Press, 2008), esp. chap. 7.

43. Merleau-Ponty, *The Structure of Behavior*, 145. This reverses the view that Merleau-Ponty holds of the natural sciences, which is that perceptual reality is only a projection of an absolute physical reality.

44. Maurice Merleau-Ponty, *Nature: Course Notes from the Collége de France,* compiled Dominique Séglard, trans. Robert Vallier (Evanston, IL: Northwestern University Press, 2003), 106. Originally published as *La Nature: Notes. Cours de Collège de France* (Paris: Seuil, 1994).

45. Merleau-Ponty, *Nature,* 107.

46. Maurice Merleau-Ponty, *Phenomenology,* 293/332.

47. Merleau-Ponty, *Phenomenology,* 270–271/308–309. He states, "We have to rediscover beneath the objective thought of movement, a pre-objective experience from which it borrows its sense, and where movement, still tied to the person who perceives, is a variation of the subject's hold on his world" (280/317).

48. A simple introduction to calculus can be found at http://wmueller.com/precalculus/.

49. Merleau-Ponty, *Phenomenology,* 285/323. "The perception of movement is not secondary in relation to the perception of the moving object" (285/323).

50. Merleau-Ponty, *Phenomenology,* 267, 268/309–310.

51. Merleau-Ponty, *Phenomenology,* 280/318. The limit of this point of view is that once a *strict* distinction is made between the identical body in motion and movement, the implication is that there are spatial and temporal positions identifiable in themselves (267–268/311).

52. Merleau-Ponty, *Phenomenology,* 285/323. These are not, it seems to me, Merleau-Ponty's most lucid pages.

53. Merleau-Ponty, *Phenomenology,* 293, 458/332, 497. This will be linked to the conception of the anonymous body. Merleau-Ponty defines style for the world as comparable to that of individuals, thus as "a certain way of handling a situation" (342/384).

54. Merleau-Ponty, *Phenomenology,* 287/314–315; 287/324–325. Thus, "Movement is nothing without a moving object that traces it out and that establishes its unity" (285/322). And, "The perception of movement is not secondary to in relation to the perception of the moving object" (285/323). In a footnote Merleau-Ponty refers to the quasi-synthesis as *synopsis,* but this idea does not seem to appear anywhere else in his work (544n60).

55. Merleau-Ponty, *Phenomenology,* 286324. Thus, "Now it is the circle as a thing of the world that possesses, in advance and in itself, all of the properties that analysis [*la pensée thétique*] will discover there" (286/324).

56. Merleau-Ponty, *Phenomenology,* 543–544n60. The positive references to Kant here are striking since Kant is often the recipient of a great deal of Merleau-Ponty's criticism. The bulk of these comments are directed against Henri Bergson, whom Merleau-Ponty reads as a realist with a dualist notion of matter and memory and criticizes as "ambiguous" (*l'équivoque*)!

57. Vladimir Tasić, *Mathematics and the Roots of Postmodern Thought* (Oxford: Oxford University Press, 2001), 55. Phenomenological reduction of experiences of the external world "could potentially be problematic when it comes to

language. It is not immediately clear how the evidence of anything could be collected in a cognizant manner if language were finally bracketed off" (54–55). Even if it turns out that there are universal "deep" language structures, no one speaks without being spoken to.

58. See Gottfried Martin, *Kant's Metaphysics and Theory of Science*, trans. P. G. Lucas (Manchester, UK: Manchester University Press, 1961), 22–23. This clarifies why Kant's explanation of time is modeled on space.

59. Kant, *Critique of Pure Reason*, A26, B42; A34, B50. Cited in Martin, *Kant's Metaphysics*, 39. Merleau-Ponty, *The Structure of Behavior*, 130.

60. Merleau-Ponty, *Phenomenology*, 288/326. Only objective time is made up of successive moments.

61. This useful and clear account of wave behavior can be found at one of the many excellent websites for students: "What Is a Wave," The Physics Classroom, accessed January 2019, http://www.physicsclassroom.com/Class/waves/u10l1b.cfm. I have chosen it deliberately for this reason. Additionally, when two waves meet, the medium changes shape as a result of the net effect of the two individual waves; however, the waves themselves continue unabated on their path.

62. Edmund Husserl, *The Phenomenology of Internal Time Consciousness*, trans. James S. Churchill (Bloomington: Indiana University Press, 1971), 40–46. Husserl is careful to distinguish between the sound that is actually heard and the duration in which the hearing takes place, thus between matter and energy.

63. Husserl, *The Phenomenology of Internal Time Consciousness*, 48.

64. Husserl, *The Phenomenology of Internal Time Consciousness*, 46–52.

65. Husserl, *The Phenomenology of Internal Time Consciousness*, 53–54. Thus, this consciousness is not simply the waning reverberation of the violin note that has just sounded.

66. Maurice Merleau-Ponty, *The Visible and the Invisible*, trans. Alphonso Lingis (Evanston, IL: Northwestern University Press, 1968), 173.

67. Husserl, *The Phenomenology of Internal Time Consciousness*, 95.

68. Husserl, *The Phenomenology of Internal Time Consciousness*, 97.

69. Merleau-Ponty, *Phenomenology*, 280/317.

70. Merleau-Ponty, *Phenomenology*, 543–544n60. The issue in this endnote seems to be that Husserl's consciousness provides too much unity and Bergson's too little.

71. Merleau-Ponty, *Phenomenology*, 543–544n60.

72. Bergson, *Matter and Memory*, 186.

73. Bergson, *Matter and Memory*, 203. Bergson's account corresponds to Peirce's Thirdness (continuity) and Firstness (quality).

74. Bergson, *Matter and Memory*, 203, 204, 205. Bergson states that the smallest interval of time we can detect is 0.002 seconds, although it is highly unlikely that we perceive even this small of an interval (205).

75. Deleuze, *Difference and Repetition*, 78–79.

76. Deleuze, *Difference and Repetition*, 80/109–110. Translation altered.

77. Deleuze, *Difference and Repetition*, 81.

78. Merleau-Ponty, *The Visible and the Invisible*, 122.

79. Merleau-Ponty, *The Visible and the Invisible*, 124.

80. Merleau-Ponty, *Phenomenology*, 279/323. "*C'est une marche au réel.*"

81. Merleau-Ponty, *The Structure of Behavior*, 14.

82. Merleau-Ponty, *The Structure of Behavior*, 10, 11.

83. Merleau-Ponty, *Phenomenology*, 433/472.

84. Merleau-Ponty, *The Structure of Behavior*, 31.

85. Merleau-Ponty, *The Structure of Behavior*, 34–36.

86. Merleau-Ponty, *The Structure of Behavior*, 96.

87. Merleau-Ponty, *Phenomenology*, 438/477. It seems to me that the French term *champ* is incorrectly translated as "room" rather than as *field* in the previous translation of *Phenomenology*, and am pleased to see that the new translation has corrected this.

88. Merleau-Ponty, *Phenomenology*, 434/473.

89. Merleau-Ponty, *Phenomenology*, 454–455/493.

90. Merleau-Ponty, *Phenomenology*, 452/491.

91. Simone de Beauvoir, *The Ethics of Ambiguity*, trans. Bernard Frechtman (New York: Citadel Press, 1976), 27. For this view of Beauvoir's ethics, see my essay "Letting Go the Weight of the Past: Beauvoir and the Joy of Existence," in *Simone de Beauvoir's Philosophy of Age: Gender, Ethics, and Time*, ed. Silvia Stoller (London: Palgrave, 2013).

92. Bryan A. Smyth, *Merleau-Ponty's Existential Phenomenology and the Realization of Philosophy* (London: Bloomsbury, 2013).

93. Smyth, *Merleau-Ponty's Existential Phenomenology*, 172.

94. Smyth, *Merleau-Ponty's Existential Phenomenology*, 168, 170.

95. Merleau-Ponty, *Phenomenology*, 465/504.

96. Merleau-Ponty, *Phenomenology*, 468/506–507.

97. Merleau-Ponty, *Phenomenology*, 470/509.

98. Merleau-Ponty, *Phenomenology*, 471/510.

99. Merleau-Ponty, *Phenomenology*, 476/513.

100. Merleau-Ponty, *Phenomenology*, 483/521. Antoine de Saint-Exupery, *Pilote de Guerre* (Paris: Gallimard, 1972), 171, 174, 176. The role that Saint-Exupery plays in Merleau-Ponty's thought is beautifully and thoroughly explicated by Bryan Smyth in *Merleau-Ponty's Existential Phenomenology*. I am grateful to him for this remarkable book.

101. Gilles Deleuze, *Francis Bacon: The Logic of Sensation*, trans. Daniel W. Smith (London: Continuum, 2004), 44.

102. Deleuze and Guattari attribute this transcendence to Husserl. It is arguably a misrepresentation of Husserlian intuition, intersubjectivity, and cognition.

103. Gilles Deleuze and Félix Guattari, *What Is Philosophy?*, trans. Hugh Tomlinson and Graham Burchell (New York: Columbia University Press, 1994), 142–143.

104. Deleuze and Guattari, *What Is Philosophy?*, 145.

105. Deleuze and Guattari, *What Is Philosophy?*, 150.

106. In *What Is Philosophy?*, Deleuze and Guattari directly critique phenomenology: "Phenomenology wanted to renew our concepts by giving us perceptions and affections that would awaken us to the world. . . . But we do not fight against perceptual and affective clichés if we do not also fight against the machine that produces them" (149–150).

107. Deleuze, *Francis Bacon, Logic of Sensation*, 126. Importantly, these are not material laws but aesthetic ones having to do with aesthesis.

108. Gilles Deleuze, "The Idea of Genesis in Kant's Aesthetics," trans. Daniel W. Smith, *Angelaki: Journal of Theoretical Humanities* 5, no. 3 (December 2000): 59.

109. Gilles Deleuze, "The Idea of Genesis," 59.

110. Deleuze, *Francis Bacon, Logic of Sensation*, 135.

111. Deleuze, *Francis Bacon, Logic of Sensation*, 36.

112. Deleuze, *Francis Bacon, Logic of Sensation*, 93. Phase space is defined as follows: "Because of the complicated motions of the atoms in molecules, [Ludwig] Boltzmann made the distinction between kinds of motion (*Bewegungsart*, such as translational and rotational motion, which contribute to the total energy) and the phase of the motion (*Bewegungsphase*, such as the changing coordinate and momentum values of the motion). That is the defining moment for the word 'phase' in phase space." David D. Nolte, "The Tangled Tale of Phase Space," *Physics Today* 63, no. 4 (2010):33–38, 36, American Institute of Physics, S-0031-9228-1004-010-X.

113. Deleuze, *Francis Bacon, Logic of Sensation*, 15.

114. Deleuze, *Francis Bacon, Logic of Sensation*, 93.

115. Deleuze, *Francis Bacon, Logic of Sensation*, 86, 56–60.

116. Heinrich Wölfflin, *The Principles of Art History: The Problem of the Development of Style in Later Art*, trans. M. D. Hottinger (New York: Henry Holt, 1932), 18.

117. Wölfflin, *The Principles of Art History*, 19.

118. Wölfflin, *The Principles of Art History*, 21.

119. Wölfflin, *The Principles of Art History*, 19.

120. Deleuze, *Francis Bacon, Logic of Sensation*, 43.

121. Deleuze, *Francis Bacon, Logic of Sensation*, 43.

122. Deleuze, *Francis Bacon, Logic of Sensation*, 57.

123. Deleuze provides no attribution for this phrase. Merleau-Ponty cites Paul Bernard, *Souvenirs sur Paul Bernard* (Paris, 1912). Maurice Merleau-Ponty,

"Cezanne's Doubt," in *Sense and Non-Sense,* trans. Patricia Allen Dreyfus (Evanston, IL: Northwestern University Press, 1992), 13.

124. Merleau-Ponty, "Cezanne's Doubt," 13–14.

125. Merleau-Ponty, *The Structure of Behavior,* 143–144. Emphasis added.

126. Merleau-Ponty, *The Structure of Behavior,* 144. This appears to be a reference to state space.

SIX

The Philosophy of the Event

The Dark Precursor, the Chaos, and the Cosmos

I THINK

The idea that a theory of form can take the place of a theory of the real, of material physical forces, seems to bring Merleau-Ponty and Deleuze closer to one another's thinking. However, the structure of Merleau-Ponty's conception of form as something that provides a signification common to an ensemble of molecular facts distinguishes him from Deleuze in a significant way. For Merleau-Ponty, the "empty x" is the *idea* under which what happens in several places is brought together. Merleau-Ponty's version of physical form was said to follow an immanent law—the law of the relatively stable molar individual made up of physical particles. Nature is organized by intersecting laws, expressed mathematically, consisting of and constituting physical forms and, as we recall, not existing symbolically but as an idea—that is, as a signification— signifying an assemblage or ensemble of molecular facts.[1] To signify is defined as "to give meaning." For Merleau-Ponty the idea gives a meaning common to an ensemble. And this meaning is also common to thinkers since, for Merleau-Ponty, if perception is an inspection of the mind and the perceived object an *idea*, "then you and I are talking about the same world."[2] Perceptions differ, but intellect offers a shared idea, which sometimes may lead to contradictions that call for reflection in order not to slip away into chaos.

As noted in chapter 2, what Deleuze refers to as generality belongs to laws. It determines resemblances and equivalences and is defined by the exchange of particulars where this or that particular may participate in the generality insofar as it has some resemblance or equivalence to other particulars. Particulars, however, are opposed by repetition, which is the universality of the singular, but particulars can exist only in relation to generality. Deleuze is not interested in producing or discovering meaning, insisting instead on the existence and relevance of signs. He argues against those philosophers who are in agreement, who reflect principally in order to quell the chaos, stating that they are "minds of goodwill who are in agreement as to the signification of things and words; they communicate under the effect of good will."[3] Philosophy has become for them the expression of a "Universal Mind that is in agreement with itself."[4] This sort of truth is said to be arbitrary and abstract, purely conventional, engaged with possibilities rather than necessities, and so ignorant of the dark regions of the forces acting on thought—that which is not willed but remains involuntary.[5]

Deleuze articulates a version of the empty x when he examines the "I think." As he states in a slightly different context, although "this unity is the unity of perceived objects . . . the *form* of the field must be necessarily and in itself filled with individual differences [as opposed to differences borne by individuals] . . . conditions satisfied in the order of implication of intensities . . . [that] presuppose and express only differential relations; individuals express only Ideas."[6] This form is called the *dark precursor*. What is it, and why does Deleuze posit it?

Deleuze takes up the argument in *Difference and Repetition* that rationalist philosophy appears to have received its orientation from a hidden presupposition, something "everybody knows" and recognizes, which is that "there is a natural capacity for thought endowed with a talent for truth or an affinity with the true. . . . [Thus] everybody is supposed to know implicitly what it means to think."[7] Consequently, "I think, therefore I am" is said to be a universally accessible truth: the truth that everyone knows what it is to think. This prephilosophical and natural Image of thought, this idea of common sense as *Cogitatio natura universalis* along with good sense, which is the affinity for the true, is supposed to give rise to concepts.[8] But, for Deleuze, in whatever form it arises, the natural Image of thought is the ruin of the possibility of thinking concepts, so he calls for "a rigorous struggle against this Image" on the part of repetition without an image.[9]

Such a struggle appears to be both destructive and demoralizing since it is lodged against understanding, reason, and imagination. The struggle takes place against sensibility for its recognition of knowledge, against moral value and aesthetic effect, and (with respect to phenomenology) against sensibility as passive synthesis.[10] Recall that, for Merleau-Ponty, the "empty x" is the *idea* under which what happens in several places is brought together, and its unity is the unity of perceived objects, so that, even in physics, it is encountered only to the extent that physics refers us back to *perceived things* as that which it is the function of science to express and determine.[11] Thus it is a unity—an idea—given over to agreement and goodwill against which Deleuze struggles.

The general term for the natural Image of thought is *representation*, and the "I think" is its most general principle, the source of the unity of the faculties: I conceive, I judge, I imagine, I remember, I perceive.[12] The argument has been stated many times, and it is being restated here primarily in the interest of completeness.[13] Unified by the faculties, "difference becomes an object of representation always in relation to a conceived identity, a judged analogy, an imagined opposition, or a perceived similitude," the latter encompassing the phenomenological approach to the idea.[14] In the end, what is "communicated" by this are only the most conventional thoughts. Even the ideas of a pure intelligence are only logical truths, explicit and conventional, such as "Napoleon was the Emperor of France."[15]

Deleuze maintains that we rarely think because thought requires a shock rather than goodwill and good taste. It requires the jealous partner or the creative interpreter who in the wake of the catastrophe—the disharmony of all the faculties—deciphers the sign in order to develop it into an Idea: "Who would seek the truth if he had not first suffered . . . agonies. . . . Pain forces the intelligence to seek."[16] Thought happens only when there are impressions that *force* us to look, to interpret, and to think—that is, *sensations* that are the signs of laws and Ideas force us to bring what had been felt out of the darkness where it arose.[17] Only the logic of sensation gives us a sign, and only a sign breaks thought away from mere abstract possibilities so that thought must interpret, decipher, and explicate it in an Idea.[18] So, for Deleuze, "To seek truth is to interpret, to decipher, to explicate. But this 'explication' is identified with the development of the sign itself," and what forces us to think is the sign, the violence of an impression, the percepts and affects that bypass the faculties.[19]

Who, then, is the truth seeker? Deleuze attests: "The truth seeker is the jealous man who catches a lying sign on the beloved's face," or "He is the reader, the auditor, in that the work of art emits signs that will perhaps force him to create."[20] In these signs, truth is not an abstraction; it is the impression, the percept and affect that must be *interpreted*. This is how truth betrays itself in the impression, as something to be interpreted or deciphered, putting into free play sensibility, which grasps signs; intelligence, memory, or imagination, which explicates the meaning; and finally pure thought, which conceives the essence, the Idea.

FORM IN ITSELF

At the end of *What Is Philosophy?*, Deleuze and Guattari raise the question of the phenomenological Gestalt in the context of their concept of the brain.

Regarding the nature of the connections in the brain revealed by cerebral mapping, they ask whether such connections—both horizontal connections and vertical integrations—are preestablished and ready-made or self-producing. The former would be localized around hierarchical centers, and the latter would be *Gestalten*, forms that achieve stability and thereby provide a place for a center.[21] The latter theory stands in opposition to the theory of conditioned reflexes and seems to be appropriate for the structure articulated by Merleau-Ponty. Deleuze and Guattari are not convinced that either approach is accurate insofar as both theories rely on a "limited model of recognition"—the ability to recognize objects—so that assumptions about the brain's biology follow from assumptions about the nature of logic.[22]

But something, some association of ideas is needed to "protect us from chaos"—that is, from unimpeded flows of desire, from the body without organs, from infinite speeds at which determinations disappear before any connections can be made, and so from "ideas that fly off" and from "infinite variabilities."[23] But the association of ideas would fail to adhere if there were not also some order in states of affairs, some "objective anti-chaos."[24] And perhaps most importantly, ideas and states of affairs must somehow come together. They do so in sensation, in the repetition of certain sensations: the lightness of feathers, the scent of honey, the weight of a body. Pick up the same object day after day and it feels and looks and often even smells the same, evidence that the past continues into the present. But such sensations are still only opinion, the province of fuzzy logic discussed in chapter 2.

We can ask for more, Deleuze and Guattari insist, and we can get more from art, science, and philosophy, all of which struggle with and turn against opinion as they veer back into the chaos, advancing only through crises, shocks, and catastrophes. Art must always struggle with the power of opinion, in the form of the clichés that inhabit it, to create a composed chaos (chaosmos), the rendering sensory of chaos.[25] Science posits relationships defined by functional variables (in differential calculus) moving from the chaotic state and strange attractors in the direction of fixed points and limit cycles, organizing the chaos with references called Nature.[26] Likewise, philosophical concepts cannot be merely associated ideas or the order of reasons.

If the brain is assumed to function primarily to recognize objects (cubes, pencils, etc.), then mental objects such as philosophy, art, and science—"vital ideas"—have been confined to the realm of opinion—that is, to the kinds of ideas that arise with sensation.[27] Given Merleau-Ponty's conception of the Gestalt, which reflects not merely the lived experience that founds opinion but the experience of a subject as a set of perceptive-affective *variables*—thus as experiencing a *variable Gestalt*, truly Being in the world—this subject remains engaged with perceived forms and so with perception. And although the variability of perceptual forms may distance the subject of phenomenology from the criticism that its determinations are merely hard and fast *doxa*—opinion, the product of habits—this is only to situate it in the realm of the *Urdoxa*, in the role of an original opinion—that of Being in the world and not merely an agent/actor/thinker.[28]

The question this raises is whether the phenomenological Gestalt continues to relegate thought to "man's relations with the world," with which the brain then comes into agreement due to excitations arising from worldly contact, or if, in opposition to phenomenology, it is the brain that thinks and not human beings.[29] This would mean the brain is not a Gestalt, not a *perceived* form, but a *form in itself*, without reference to an external point of view, something Merleau-Ponty explicitly rejected. It would then be a self-survey—that is, the faculty of the creation of concepts and the unmediated recipient of percepts and affects—and so mind, in this limited sense, is the brain, which simultaneously creates concepts and conceptual personae, "thought's aptitude for finding itself and spreading across a plane that passes through me at several places."[30]

We can say this because, for Deleuze and Guattari, there appear to be two brains. There is the neuroscientific brain of connections and secondary integrations, and there is also a brain that says "I is an other."[31] This is the "the long and inexhaustible story" of the "cracked I," the manner in which the mind affects itself or qualifies itself as the affectivity of a passive ego, not the activity of an actor/agent/thinker. The fault, or crack, in the I is also time, the form of interiority that splits the subject.[32] As Deleuze articulates this in *Difference and Repetition*, the receptive ego (*moi*) is in time and so is continuously undergoing change, but the other I (*je*) is an act that synthesizes time along with whatever takes place in time. The I is the force of internal difference in the present. It divides all time into past and future at each instant so that ego and I are split, differentiated in every act of thought by the form of time.[33]

THE CHAOS AND SENSATION

Chapter 2 examined Deleuze and Guattari's critique of logic. Their concern with formal logic, especially Frege, makes sense when we consider Deleuze's critique of Aristotelian representation in *Difference and Representation*. Aristotle's logic can be taken as justification for the manner in which Aristotle establishes his principles—that is, he clearly had to establish the validity of his inferences and did so by means of his logic.[34] Yet, as early as the seventeenth century, philosophers such as Francis Bacon and René Descartes were critical of Aristotelean logic, calling it useless for their needs. Not until Frege did a logic arise that could both analyze mathematical discourse and avoid the inadequacy of language for representing conceptual content, replacing it with the language of pure thought.[35]

It is interesting to note that Frege's symbolic notation did not follow the linear, temporal order of ordinary language but appears two-dimensional, more like "a series of diagrams rather than an arrangement of propositions and formulas."[36] Additionally, Frege intended to show that logic is not a "proper part of mathematics," a particular kind of algebra, but that it is and must be the basis of all reasoning.[37] Frege declared that logic is not about "how and why we judge" but is only concerned with the "conceptual contents of judgments and their interrelations," thereby ensuring the separation of logic and psychology by means of the separation of assertion and predication, the Aristotelean notion of declaring a feature of an object or its nature—that is, the meaning of an object—a property of the object.[38] By contrast and in a significant break with the past, for Frege, assertion is the judgment that grasps a complete thought without affirming or denying, and judging follows as the recognition of the truth of an assertion's content.[39] This takes assertion beyond the semiotics of the Ariekei of chapter 1, which only allows the assertion of true propositions and remains a language built on naturalism.

Deleuze and Guattari's point of view on this is that even though it is detached from predication, Frege's logic remains limited and constrained by recognition and truth telling, specifically the "recognition of truth in the proposition."[40] This position is a consequence of Frege's determination that the psychological aspects of speaking and hearing—both subjective attitudes and expectations—must be sharply differentiated from the proposition's actual objective content—that is, its logical consequences necessary for a correct chain of inferences.[41] As Sluga argues, "Logic for Frege is concerned with the study of the logical relations between the objective contents of judgments" and nothing more.[42]

As Deleuze and Guattari note almost in passing, "Logic seems to be forever struggling with the complex question of how it differs from psychology" so that it sets up an image of thought that evades psychologism but remains normative.[43] They question the value of the recognition of truth in a proposition modeled on calculus, which they liken to a television quiz game, presumably because it is "impoverished and puerile," with respect to the creation of thought.[44]

This brings us to the question of the creation of thought, the creation of concepts, which addresses the chaos and is the rendering consistent of the chaos. What is the dream of capturing a bit of chaos that would make science relinquish all its rational unity in exchange for a little piece of chaos to explore? Sensation does play a role here. The brain that says "I is an other" is the brain that says "I conceive" or "I think," but it is also the brain of sensation, the brain that says "I feel."[45] Are Deleuze and Guattari embracing all they seemed to have rejected? Is this a return to the Kantian schematism, the bringing together of empirical intuition and concepts, or is it a reflection of their Bergsonian beginnings?

Deleuze and Guattari are quite specific. "The artful brain says 'I feel.' It's sensation, both affect and percept, is vibration. Percepts are no longer perceptions; they are independent of a state of those who experience them. Affects are no longer feelings or affections; they go beyond the strength of those who undergo them. Sensations, percepts and affects are *beings* whose validity lies in themselves and exceeds any lived."[46] When the brain feels, its sensation bypasses the senses by going directly to the brain as excitation. It is not the sensation or perception of an actor/agent/subject. As noted in chapter 4, Deleuze and Guattari embrace the idea of the brain as having infinitely greater and more complex perceptions than ordinary human perception. They adopt the Bergsonian view that the brain gathers and transmits, whether directly or indirectly, all the influences, all the movements, of all the points of the material universe, and in so doing, it vibrates. But in the *interval*, sensation persists as vibration and is not returned and dissipated in action. It is the contraction of all that has come before and has not yet disappeared.[47] As Bergson argued, "Even a simple mass of protoplasm is open to the influence of external stimulation."[48]

We can recall how Deleuze initially approached this in *Difference and Repetition*, stating that "we" are all contracted water, earth, light, and air.

> At the level of this vital, primary sensibility, the lived present already constitutes in time a past and future. The future appears, if need be, as an organic form of protentions; the past of retention appears in the cellular heredity. Moreover, these organic syntheses, as they combine with the perceptive syntheses piled upon them, redeploy themselves in the active syntheses of a psycho-organic memory and intelligence. . . . All this forms a rich domain of signs, enveloping the heterogeneous each time and animating behavior. For, each contraction, each passive synthesis, is constitutive of a sign, which is interpreted or deployed in the active syntheses.[49]

It is significant that all this forms a rich domain of *signs* that are then able to be contemplated and reflected upon. With respect to temporality, "this is the Bergsonian idea that each actual present is nothing but the entire past in its most contracted state."[50] For Bergson, who created this concept of time in the face of harsh criticism from the logicians, each contracted past is preserved in itself and in various degrees of expansion and contraction. It is *virtual*—that is, real but not actualized in space—insofar as it can only be actualized by the perception that attracts it and materializes it. But, of course, Deleuze and Guattari are not taking up the perceptual route that operates for the sake of action, and they are bypassing all the organized senses in favor of something else.

For Deleuze and Guattari, the perception-action loop is stymied, leaving contraction as a pure passion. As formulated by David Hume, for whom "ideas are always derived from impressions, and . . . when these impressions disappear, something is left, an idea that 'returns upon the soul,' to produce 'impressions of reflection,' which are again copied or repeated, passions as well as understanding are . . . an effect of reflection, contemplation."[51] As Deleuze articulates this, everything contracts through contemplation: "The lily of the valley . . . sings the glory of heavens. . . . What organism is not made of contemplated and contracted elements and cases of repetition—contemplated and contracted water, nitrogen, carbon, chlorides, sulfates. . . ?"[52] We humans no less than flowers contemplate the elements of matter through sensation. But when sensation is contemplated rather than utilized for action, when it is contracted, then one contemplates the elements that are contracted and creation is possible.[53]

THE CHAOS AND PRAGMATICS

Art, science, and philosophy preeminently cut through the chaos—that is, the potentialities or variables—as forms of thought and creation in the struggle against opinion. Artists wipe away the preexisting clichés to let in the chaos, making way for a vision that is *sensation*. Science limits its variables to two axes for the sake of prediction or allows so many variables that it achieves only probabilities as it veers between equilibrium—fixed points and limit cycles—and chaotic attractors. For Deleuze and Guattari, in order to think at all, philosophy must confront chaos and arrive at mental objects determinable as real beings.[54] Nevertheless, how does this come about?

One way of seeing this (there are others) returns us to Deleuze's interest in and adaptation of Peirce—Peirce the logician and Peirce the pragmaticist. Let us recall how, in chapter 2, Deleuze reformulates the Peircean notion of Thirdness, which refers to an object that is an idea and an idea that remains the same even at different times. In Peirce's thinking, the third "acts as a sign/representamen (a first), to determine another interpretant (another third), through the *Same* object (a second)—and so on . . ." unless an end is reached.[55]

Deleuze, it was noted, utilizes the concept of repetition in place of Thirdness, but for him no end is reached as repetition is an open-ended Thirdness for which "through contemplation we contract as imaginations, generalities, affirmations and self-satisfactions."[56] Underneath the self of action are the selves of contemplation so that "it is always *a third party* who says 'me.'"[57] Yet merely ceasing to say "I" and replacing it with "me" does not guarantee one is not still participating in the "regime of subjectification, . . . [as] a highly stratified semiotic is difficult to get away from."[58]

To address this, Deleuze and Guattari, like Frege before them and like Peirce, began experimenting with the diagram as well as with Peirce's pragmatics, which Peirce defines in a manner that brings it close to Deleuze and Guattari's intensive concept of chapter 2. For Peirce, "Pragmatism is the principle that every theoretical judgment expressible in a sentence in the indicative mood is a confused form of thought whose only meaning, if it has any, lies in its tendency to enforce a corresponding practical maxim expressible as a conditional sentence having its apodosis in the imperative mood."[59] As argued by Kamani Vellodi, Deleuze and Guattari share Peirce's commitment to a pragmatic semiotic, "a theory of signs orientated to their practical bearing on the 'conduct of life.'"[60] Peirce refers to logic as both the science of truth and the science of the general conditions of signs as signs—that is, of the laws of thought and of the evolution of thought—just as Deleuze and Guattari frequently ask what a concept can do.[61]

By this means Peirce sought to resolve one of the central problems raised in this book—that is, the reconciliation of reason with experience, rational ideas with existential facts, generalization with particulars.[62] For this reason, Peirce asserts that thought must be aligned with its "*conceivable* practical effects in the world," and, in addition to this pragmatism, thought must also be understood as a system of signs, a semiotics, wherein each sign/thought is determined only through a process of interpretation—that is, through its effect on another sign/thought.[63]

Peirce wanted a visual means to "illustrate the course of thought . . . any course of thought."[64] For Peirce, reasoners make mental diagrams, which are icons or likenesses, according to which they see that their conclusions are true if their premises are true.[65] The diagram represents the relations of the premise formally—that is, by reducing or suppressing details for the sake of the important features of the reasoning.[66] He states, "We form in the imagination some sort of diagrammatic, that is, iconic, representation of the facts, as skeletonized as possible. . . . [It will be] either . . . geometrical, that is, such that familiar spatial relations stand for the relations asserted in the premisses, or it will be algebraical, where the relations are expressed by objects which are imagined to be subject to certain rules, whether conventional or experiential."[67] The diagram is experimental insofar as it suggests a hypothesis that can be tested, and, if it is found to be necessary, changes can be made to the diagram.[68]

However, although such experimental alterations make the process constructive, they are carried out for the sake of ascertaining that they will always be present in this type of construction. This constitutes a conclusion with universal validity under a specified set of conditions and establishes the diagram as a model for similar hypotheses in a not-yet-determinate universe.[69] Given the hypothetical nature of the diagram, it is important to keep in mind that, for Peirce, "the real world is a part of the ideal world. namely, that part which sufficient experience would tend ultimately (and therefore definitively), to compel Reason to acknowledge as having a being independent of what he may arbitrarily, or willfully, create."[70] This also means that, for Peirce, the diagram is an experimental tool for the attainment of truths. The diagram establishes trajectories of reasoning, which are laws or generalities or universals useful for thought.

Now, when we turn to the matter of Deleuze and Deleuze-Guattari's use of diagrams, we find that it operates somewhat differently. Deleuze's interests in Peirce are usually centered around the two *Cinema* books; however, as this book makes clear, Peirce played a crucial role, even if often unacknowledged, throughout Deleuze's work, and it seems that the turn to pragmatism was intensified and clarified in Deleuze-Guattari's final works together. Vellodi points out that already in the *Cinema* books, Peirce offers Deleuze and Guattari a "dizzyingly comprehensive taxonomy of cinematic signs" even as they reject his "orientation towards meaning."[71] This particular rejection of Peirce's orientation continues in their later work.

In the chapter on several (so presumably not all) regimes of signs in *A Thousand Plateaus*, Deleuze and Guattari point to the difficulty of this trajectory. They isolate "a certain number of semiotics displaying very diverse characteristics," each of which is overcoded, but in different ways, and move along a trajectory indicated by a spiral, a diagram of deterritorialization—shattering the codes—until their line of flight is blocked and negated.[72] But semiotics are mixed, not pure, and "each one necessarily captures fragments of one or more of the other semiotics."[73] The generative component of pragmatics forms mixed semiotics insofar as it reveals how a form of expression on the "language stratum" appeals to several combined regimes.[74] A second component, the transformational component, allows for novelty via the metamorphoses of the forms of expression. In politics and in history, the second element of pragmatics, the transformation of one semiotic into another, occurs constantly.[75] As Deleuze and Guattari state, "A transformational statement marks the way in which a semiotic translates for its own purposes a statement originating elsewhere, and in so doing diverts it, leaving untransformable residues and actively resisting the inverse transformation."[76] Among their examples is the transformation of an African dance into white culture's dance, which exemplifies a mimetic translation accompanied by a power takeover, and they also cite the transformational emergence of Bolshevik statements in the Russian revolution.[77]

The third component of their pragmatics is diagrammatic and "consists in taking regimes of signs or forms of expression and extracting from them particle-signs [molecules] that . . . constitute unformed traits capable of combining with one another."[78] In each case, forms of content and forms of expression—that is, regimes of signs—are abstracted, leaving only unformed traits of content and expression. The final component, the *machinic*, is the assemblage that puts an abstract machine (unformed matter and expression) into play by giving a distinct form to traits of expression and traits of content, each of which operates in relation to the other.[79]

Let us put this to work. Take the proposition "I love you." Begin by asking by what regime of signs it has been taken up and without which its syntactical, semantic, and logical elements would be nothing but empty universal conditions. That is, what in the realm of the nonlinguistic would give the proposition consistency? The presignifying love of the collective (the tribe); the countersignifying love of war and force organized by the war machine against State power (the battle of Achilles and Penthesilea in the Trojan War); the signifying love addressed to a center that must be interpreted and so creates a signifying chain (a relative deterritorialization); or the postsignifying passional love that begins with subjectification (Tristan and Isolde, who incorporate the dominant reality into their cogitos and so are drawn into a black hole of self-consciousness as both are carried toward death).[80] Or one could try to open up the proposition to at least a little bit of chaos, "a patois of sensual delight, physical and semiotic systems in shreds, asubjective affects, signs without significance where syntax, semantics, and logic are in collapse."[81] With this, the point of the critique of formal and fuzzy logic, as well as phenomenology, comes into view.

Let us unpack this a bit more before moving on. Assemblages are molecular or quasimolecular elements. In an assemblage, there are both territories or strata *and* lines of flight, which are movements of deterritorialization and destratification.[82] Each of these, strata and lines of flight, move at measurable speeds: the slowness or viscosity of a strata is stable and makes possible an organism or an organic whole. Semiotically, it is representational and attributable to a subject. Lines of flight are characterized by acceleration and rupture, and they are destabilized and dismantled as an organism and not attributable to a subject. Such an assemblage is *a multiplicity*, a field whose constituents have no existence except in their relations to one another.[83]

Total destratification is what Deleuze calls pure becoming; it is the chaos, and so it exhibits wild destabilization, yet such destabilized matter and expression are not Deleuze's aim. For this reason, *form of expression* and *form of content* are terms of analysis brought into play by Deleuze and Guattari. The first refers to the organization of functions in order to carry out an action, a methodology, or a manner of proceeding, whether it is in writing or in organizing governments. The second refers to so-called raw materials and their qualities, which are always organized in some manner and never just brute material.[84] Substances are formed matters that are coded and organized according to some forms of expression in a regime of signs.

Deleuze and Guattari's account points to their differences with Peirce and also implicates their view of the limits if not failure of formal logic. What makes a proposition or even a word into a statement is not the bare, skeletonized structure (Peirce) or the pure, syntactical ordering of its units (Frege). In every statement there are implicit propositions that cannot be made explicit in this manner, or even at all. Such *incorporeal transformations* indicate what a regime of signs can *do*. This is because the regime of signs is an assemblage with two sides: one, the regime of signs as a semiotic system or form of expression, and two, the semiotic system as the form of content—that is, regimes of bodies or physical systems.

In seeking freedom from the privilege that has been given to language, Deleuze and Guattari revise Peirce through the elimination of the signified-signifier relations of the icon, index, and symbol. As a result, this assemblage, this so-called abstract machine, is neither semiotic nor corporeal, neither form nor substance, but unformed matter and, yes, function, which is not yet semiotically formed: it is purely *diagrammatic*.[85]

Peirce understood diagrams to be icons of relations, a sign that signifies its object by representing the relations of its objects, and diagrams are an icon of the relations by which means some future state could be constructed on the basis of the present state.[86] The diagram signifies its object in the form of a formal presentation of the relations of a given premise.[87] Peirce's additional signs are the *index* and the *symbol*. As noted, the index is a sign whose significance to its object is due to its having a genuine relation to that object, as a knock on the door indicates a visitor.[88] The index forces the attention to the particular object intended without describing it. The symbol is simply the general name or description that signifies its object by means of an association of ideas or habitual connection between the name and the character signified and so requires an interpretant.[89]

The purpose of the diagram is "hypostatic abstraction," the abstracting that skeletonizes to introduce a new object in the transformation—for example, from *good to goodness*—thus making explicit new hidden or new elements of thought.[90] As Peirce insists, "There is no sensuous resemblance between it [the icon or diagram] and its object, but only an analogy between the relations of the parts of each."[91] By observing the diagram, one can interpret—that is, read new information off the diagram, drop unnecessary elements, or creatively insert new ones.[92]

Deleuze and Guattari reject Peirce's view of the diagram as an icon that is the representation of the process of reasoning "through laws, of generals or universals, and oriented towards communication within a community of like-minded thinkers" and of rational relations.[93] They reformulate it even as they reformulate index and symbol by removing them all from the realm of signifiers to that of signs. They state, "First, indexes, icons, and symbols seem to us to be distinguished by territoriality-deterritorialization relations, not signifier-signified relations. Second, the diagram as a result seems to have a distinct role, irreducible to either the icon or the symbol."[94] They hold out for a diagram that does not represent the real but constructs a new reality, the *diagrammatic*, whose transformations "blow apart semiotic systems or regimes of signs on a plane of consistency of a positive, absolute deterritorialization."[95] Deterritorialization is serious and even dangerous because it requires that one "stop the world"—that is, alter the reality of everyday life and interrupt the ordinary flow of interpretation.[96] This means no strata, no stratification, and so no regimes of signs, only particle-signs.[97]

The diagram is distributive; it governs the mutual interactions of expressions and contents. Distribution is usually defined as governing through disjunction, yet the negation of disjunction can be transposed into conjunction with no loss of validity. But here, unlike in mathematics, there are no axioms to subordinate lines of flight and conjunctive traits under unassailable rules.[98] Ultimately, the diagram "plays a piloting role," and "it constructs a real that is yet to come, a new type of reality," by *conjoining*, effecting "conjunctions of deterritorialization (disjunction)" as it produces continuums of intensity (qualitative multiplicity).[99]

And unlike Peirce's diagrams, which produce generalities (Thirdness), Deleuze and Guattari's diagrams create specific names, the name of an artist, a musician, a scientist—they create conceptual personae. Voice and instrument construct a Wagner abstract machine; physics and mathematics construct a Riemann abstract machine; content and expression draw one another along, inseparably.

Yet we must note that like all deterritorializations, these abstract machines—these diagrams—take flight only in the midst of strata and stratification. Abstract machines set things loose on strata in which they are encrusted, ensuring that the "security, tranquility, and homeostatic equilibrium of the strata are thus never completely guaranteed."[100] The nomad and the State, molecular or micropolitical power and fascism, natural history and becomings-animal, linguistics or semiology and pragmatics, Oedipus and the Wolf-Man, the tree and the rhizome, each draws on the other but not equally. As Deleuze and Guattari state:

> Either the abstract machines remain prisoner to stratifications, are enveloped in a certain specific stratum whose program or unity of composition they define (the abstract animal, the abstract chemical Body, Energy in itself) and whose movements of relative deterritorialization they regulate. Or, on the contrary, the abstract machine cuts across all stratifications, develops alone and in its own right on the diagram it constitutes, the same machine at work in astrophysics and in microphysics, in the natural and the artificial, piloting flows of absolute deterritorialization (in no sense of course is unformed matter chaos of any kind).[101]

Nevertheless, it is to this last intimation that we turn.

THE CHAOS AND THE REFRAIN (ON FREEDOM)

Two conceptions guide us to the end of this discussion. The first conception: Onto what does the diagram open? How does it produce new conceptual personae, and are these the beings of freedom? If so, what is the nature of this freedom? The second conception has to do with the Bergsonian thesis that the brain gathers and transmits, whether directly or indirectly, all the influences, all the movements, of all the points of the material universe, and, in so doing, it vibrates; it is a rhythmical vibration, that of differential repetition, that of the Refrain. To follow the Refrain to the open, we begin with the concept of chaos.

How are we to understand chaos if it is not unformed matter? We recall that, for Peirce, continuity is generality understood as conformity to one Idea, yet the continuum is "all that is possible" in a field so crowded that units lose identity and so become continuous.[102] The key here is that the continuum is possibility; it is all that is possible. Of course, Deleuze-Guattari redefine continuity in their own terms. The continuum is that multiplicity that consists of virtual events, or, as they call it, "virtual chaos," and virtuality is the "potential" through which states of affairs take effect.[103] Moreover, we noted that "states of affairs leave the virtual chaos on conditions constituted by the limit (its immanent reference): they are actualities, even though they may not yet be bodies or even things, units, or sets."[104] And further, the continuum consists of real and general possibilities that far exceed anything that exists so that "existence is a rupture," a discontinuity in the continuum.[105] This last is the case, as we have seen, for both Peirce and Deleuze-Guattari.

The plane of consistency does not, then, consist of a chaos of formed matters or unformed matters. There is no "chaotic white knight" or "undifferentiated black knight."[106] There are neither forms nor substances, content nor expression, and not even respective and relative deterritorializations. Forms and substances exist on strata, and, below this, the plane of consistency or abstract machine *"constructs continuums of intensity,"* intensities (qualities) extracted from forms and substances. It *"emits and combines particle-signs"* that set the most asignifying of signs to function in the most deterritorialized of particles, and it conjoins *"flows of deterritorialization."*[107] There are rules not randomness; there is continuity and conjunction.

The rules are the rules of pragmatics as articulated previously, but in what sort of manifold do they function? The universe, the cosmos, Deleuze and Guattari claim, is replete with Refrains (*ritournelles*) linked, as they say, to the problem of territory, entering and exiting territory, territorialization and deterritorialization across nature, animals, elements, deserts, as much as human beings—so let us look there.[108]

Walking in the dark, a child sings softly under his breath to comfort and calm himself. The song takes him from chaos, the virtual full of potential through which states of affairs arise, the virtual that opens the way to something else. Once home, he abandons the forces of chaos as much as possible by leaving them outside and organizes around himself his backpack, his clothing, his homework, each one a small milieu. Possibly he carries with him a little of the chaos in the memory of his fear of the dark or his exaltation at having made his way through it. Conversation with his siblings or parents creates a boundary between them and the outside; the comforting rhythms and sound of their exchanged words are the territory within which they exist. A wrong tone of voice, an empty house, could threaten everything, bring back the chaos and destroy the creator and creation, as even this simple act is a creation.

At some point, the boundary is breached from within by virtue of its own force and someone ventures out onto the future, back into the world, in the direction of the cosmos, improvising as she goes along. All this is the Refrain.

Its three aspects are the chaos, a rhythmic pattern of differential repetition, and the centrifugal force that spirals back out into the cosmos.[109] Clearly, a territory has been established; a territorial assemblage is established as an earthly force (the home) and not as the act of a subject. And we can see that the conversation and the home are also a rhythm and a milieu born out of the chaos.

In each case, *milieus*, blocks of space-time, are created by the rhythm, the vibration, the periodic repetition that holds back the intrusion of chaos, the milieu of all milieus. This means that the milieus are coded, and each serves as the basis for another coding and transcoding as one milieu passes continuously into another through the chaosmos, the rhythm-chaos.[110] Chaos, the virtual, does not always become a rhythm; it does so only if the passage from one milieu to another is heterogeneous, such as the passage from the dark night into the lighted home, carried there by the rhythm of the child's song. Truly it is counterpoint, polyphony, when melodies each play with different codes.

Borrowing from all the transcoding milieus, a territory is formed. Territorialization creates interior zones of shelter, as well as the exterior zones harboring the interior and, beyond that, limits or membranes, intermediary zones, energy reserves, annexes. The Refrain is not directional but dimensional and polyphonic, and, as rhythm, it is expressive. Something is expressed, a mark or signature that makes a territory, and the sign of a rhythm is the expressed. Thus, in the context of nature, we cannot say that there is an instinct to aggressively territorialize but rather a territorialization that creates certain sorts of functions that are reorganized as expressive. The color of birds is functional when connected to actions such as sex or aggression, but as a mark or signature, it is the matter of expression, a quality that expresses a territory and the limits of that territory.[111] The color's functions are secondary and presuppose the territory without which they would not even be possible.

Every such emergence of rhythm—qualities such as color or sound or, in the case of philosophy, sensation—from chaos can be called Art. This characterization connects the Refrain to Deleuze's earliest work on the aesthetics of sensation.[112] It is art to make a mark, to establish a boundary, to express a quality; "it is more profound than being," so it is not the effect of impulses such as subjective impressions or emotions, yet such impulses do play a role.[113] A subject may carry the mark but as a signature or proper name, a domain or abode, which precedes them like a ready-made. This is the effect of expressive qualities—that is, matters of expression in shifting relations with one another expressing the relation of the territory to the interior milieu of impulses, not just a signature but a style or motif, and connected also to the exterior milieu of circumstances, their territorial counterpoints. Of note here is Vinteuil's phrase that reassures Swann of his territory, which is the Bois de Boulogne, and of his possession, Odette, while remaining completely independent of the dramatic circumstances and characters.[114] Such motifs conjoin as the work develops and become their own melodic landscapes and rhythmic characters, beings in their own right, a vast expansion of the notion of conceptual personae.

However, the logical and mathematical structures that have operated throughout Deleuze and Deleuze-Guattari's work have not been abandoned, only reformulated in relation to the chaos and the cosmos by claiming that the virtual chaos, continuity, is pragmatically prior to discontinuity. In this way, by decoding—that is, by situating itself disjunctively [(n)either this (n)or that] between codes and territory; by situating itself on the margins of codes, which are differently determined—territorialization makes differentiation possible and specific differences arise.[115] Milieus pass into one another, then into a territory, the first assemblage, which passes into other assemblages, ceases to be territorial, and becomes social, individual, or species. The bird's colors, for example, may cease to mark territory as it enters a courtship assemblage that is independent of the territory, although within the new assemblage, new reterritorializations may occur.[116] Elements that may have been functional previously—like nest building—may now become merely components of passage (intra-assemblage) into the new interassemblage.

The ease with which something that was stable and territorialized transforms and becomes autonomous is startling. This, above all, characterizes the Refrain. Eventually, all assemblages are abandoned, and the element or elements may enter another plane entirely—that of the deterritorialized Cosmos.[117] The child's song of comfort that territorialized may have transformed into a taunt in the schoolyard and then into an anthem of independence, finally becoming the cosmic, molecular cry of a baby. This is no linear arborescent progression. It is rhizomatic, a molecular consistency that forms on the basis of coordination between centers articulated from within, moving from fuzzy, uncertain aggregates (phenomenology) to creative consolidation beginning "in-between," "intermezzo," and elaborating a rich and consistent material that includes a synthesis of heterogeneities (Bergson).[118] For Deleuze and Guattari, "The varying relations into which a color, sound, gesture, movement, or position enters in the same species and in different species form so many machinic enunciations."[119]

Given the breadth of transformations, such changes cannot be attributed to behavior, to innate tendencies, to drives, or to learning. Innateness decoded and learning territorialized give way to the "natal," not an act or a behavior but the valorization of an object or situation that "stretches" from intra-assemblages to displaced exteriorized centers, to interassemblages, to the Cosmos itself.[120] The concept of behavior remains within a linear construct, while that of the assemblage accounts for the character of the innate and the acquired within the rhizome, both the autonomous aspects coded in centers (innateness) and the acquired links regulated by peripheral sensations (learning).[121] What happens in an assemblage, Deleuze and Guattari like to say, is that a machine is released; in other words, a movement with the real value of a passage deterritorializes the territorial assemblage, drawing out variations and mutations, and opens it to other assemblages, or it may pass through them all, opening to the Cosmos.[122]

Deleuze-Guattari take up this concept, that of the Cosmos, from Paul Klee, whom they cite for saying that one tries to convulsively fly from the Earth and rise above it by centrifugal forces that triumph over gravity.[123] The classical artist also confronted chaos as raw and untamed matter but imposed substance-making forms and milieu-making codes. The romantic artist confronts the Earth, as the mythical hero of the Earth or the people defies God, and acts as a subjectified individual with feelings. But the modern age, the age of the cosmic, no longer confronts chaos or uses the Earth or the people.

The modern artist discerns something behind the forces of chaos, motifs, and earthly things. The modern artist, poet, philosopher, or scientist discerns the immaterial, nonformal, and energetic forces of the Cosmos. The latter are material forces but molecularized and therefore now actually *immaterial*, nonvisible to the artist and scientist and also not thinkable in themselves to the philosopher. The modern artist renders nonvisual forces visible, the composer takes up the synthesizer, which makes the sound process audible; the philosopher abandons a priori synthetic judgment but makes thought into pragmatics, asking what a concept can do, enabling a force of the Cosmos that travels.[124] "We thus leave behind the assemblages to enter the age of the Machine, the immense mechanosphere, the plane of cosmicization of forces to be harnessed."[125] But it must be done soberly, "a sober gesture, an act of consistency, capture, or extraction that works in a material that is not meager but prodigiously simplified, creatively limited, selected."[126] The artist, philosopher, composer, scientist, all must be sober, cosmic artisans whose primary concern is the *technique* necessary to render "a pure and simple line accompanied by the idea of an object" (Klee) or "a simple figure in motion and a plane that is itself mobile" (Edgar Varèse). The fuzzy aggregate, the deterritorialized material, must become consistent so that its disparate elements become discernable without reterritorializing it; that is, Klee's art must not be considered childlike, Artaud's writing is not that of a madman.

It seems we now have passed far beyond the questions with which we began. Is there any thought here of Bergson or Merleau-Ponty? Can we take the fuzzy logic of the phenomenological Gestalt to be a necessary but incomplete trajectory insofar as it limits thought to man's relations with the world—that is, with the Earth alone? Can philosophers now make sense of Bergson's view that duration is immanent to the open universe, which includes the observer?[127] Is fuzzy logic historically coincidental or necessary? What about the zone of indetermination or the hypothesis about freedom? Is Bergson's open universe of duration indicative of the concept of the Cosmos? It is important to reflect on the statement that "all history is really the history of perception," for which there are thresholds of discernibility of given assemblages.[128] There have always been forces of chaos and forces of Earth. Classical content destratified and romantic matters of expression decoded the molecular, freeing it. Becoming is present in every assemblage—but differently.[129] Yet we must be concerned about which thresholds are asserted. We must be concerned because "the processes of destruction and conservation work in bulk, take center stage, occupy the entire cosmos in order to enslave the molecular and to stick it in a conservatory or a bomb."[130]

Why must we take this with utmost seriousness? Because the mass media, the great organizations of various sorts of workers, the governing and educational institutions, including philosophy, have failed to recognize that the Earth is deterritorialized, that it is a point in a galaxy among 200 billion x 10 galaxies, and so they have become machines for the reproduction of ideas, ideologies, positions, and powers. Deleuze-Guattari ask if the people will be trained, controlled, or annihilated by these powers or if there is a possibility that there will be openings to the Cosmos? Can the Earth become cosmic, and can the people of the Earth also become cosmic people? To the extent that this is possible, it is what takes the place of the old concept of freedom.

Within the Refrain, there will always be two milieus, and, for Deleuze-Guattari, their destiny is the destiny of the Earth and its people. One the territorial, related to the Earth, bringing into play folk songs, popular songs, songs of hunters or workers, affective songs of nations. Two, the molecularized, refrains of the sea and the wind, connected to the cosmic. If we hope to make the people of the Earth into cosmic people, we will need the Refrain, especially the musical Refrain. Sound does not communicate or signify or en-lighten. More than painting or science or philosophy, sound has the strongest power of deterritorialization (Bach's "St. Matthew Passion," Piazzola's "Escuelo," Reich's "Music for 18 Musicians," Munir Bashir's "Taqsîm en maqâm: Lâmî") and re-territorialization (national anthems and any signature tune). But as with all pragmatic structures, the Refrain needs first a territorial assemblage Refrain to work with to transform it into the cosmic Refrain. And so, what of philosophy?

Can philosophers envisage a diagram for philosophy such that it is no longer philosophy as we now conceptualize or imagine it? Deleuze and Guattari wait; they wait for philosophy to become pragmatics in order to "produce a deterritorialized refrain as the final end of music, release it in the Cosmos—that is more important than building a new system."[131]

NOTES

1. Maurice Merleau-Ponty, *The Structure of Behavior*, trans. Alden L. Fisher (Boston: Beacon, 1963), 143. Originally published in French as *La structure du comportement* (Paris: Presses Universitaires de France, 1942). He states, "But Egypt, as an economic, political and social structure, remains an object of thought distinct from the multiple facts which have constituted it and brought it into existence."

2. Merleau-Ponty, "The Primacy of Perception," trans. James Edie, in *The Primacy of Perception*, ed. James Edie (Evanston, IL: Northwestern University Press, 1964), 17. Emphasis added.

3. Gilles Deleuze, *Proust and Signs*, trans. Richard Howard (Minneapolis: University of Minnesota Press, 2014), 94–95. Originally published in French as *Proust et les Signes* (Paris: Presses Universitaires de France, 1964).

4. Deleuze, *Proust and Signs*, 95.

5. Deleuze, *Proust and Signs*, 95.

6. Gilles Deleuze, *Difference and Repetition*, trans. Paul Patton (New York: Columbia University Press, 1994), 252. Originally published in French as *Différence et Répétition* (Paris: Presses Universitaires de France, 1968). Emphasis added.

7. Deleuze, *Difference and Repetition*, 131.

8. Deleuze, *Difference and Repetition*, 131.

9. Deleuze, *Difference and Repetition*, 132.

10. Deleuze, *Difference and Repetition*, 137.

11. Merleau-Ponty, *The Structure of Behavior*, 143–144. Emphasis added.

12. Deleuze, *Difference and Repetition*, 138.

13. See Dorothea Olkowski, *Gilles Deleuze and the Ruin of Representation* (Berkeley: University of California Press, 1999), chap. 1.

14. Deleuze, *Difference and Repetition*, 138.

15. Deleuze, *Proust and Signs*, 16. See also chap. 2.

16. Deleuze, *Proust and Signs*, 23.

17. Deleuze, *Proust and Signs*, 95–96.

18. Deleuze, *Proust and Signs*, 98, 100.

19. Deleuze, *Proust and Signs*, 17, 97.

20. Deleuze, *Proust and Signs*, 97.

21. Gilles Deleuze and Félix Guattari, *What Is Philosophy?*, trans. Hugh Tomlinson and Graham Burchell (New York: Columbia University Press, 1994), 208.

22. Deleuze and Guattari, *What Is Philosophy?*, 208.

23. Deleuze and Guattari, *What Is Philosophy?*, 42, 118, 202.

24. Deleuze and Guattari, *What Is Philosophy?*, 202.

25. Deleuze and Guattari, *What Is Philosophy?*, 203, 204.

26. Deleuze and Guattari, *What Is Philosophy?*, 206.

27. Deleuze and Guattari, *What Is Philosophy?*, 209.

28. Deleuze and Guattari, *What Is Philosophy?*, 210. Deleuze suggests that this is the point of Merleau-Ponty's concept of "flesh."

29. Deleuze and Guattari, *What Is Philosophy?*, 210.

30. Deleuze and Guattari, *What Is Philosophy?*, 64.

31. Deleuze and Guattari, *What Is Philosophy?*, 211.

32. See Olkowski, *Gilles Deleuze and the Ruin of Representation*, 137–139, for the relation of the "cracked I" to the pure form of time and temporal syntheses. Deleuze, *Difference and Repetition*, 86–87.

33. See Olkowski, *Gilles Deleuze and the Ruin of Representation*, 137, for the original statement of this claim.

34. Hans Sluga, *Gottlob Frege*, The Arguments of the Philosophers Series (London: Routledge & Kegan Paul, 1980), 65.

35. Sluga, *Frege*, 65.

36. Sluga, *Frege*, 71.

37. Sluga, *Frege*, 72. He states, "In the twentieth century philosophers in general and logicists in particular have tended to uphold the priority of logic over mathematics, while mathematicians in general and in particular those committed to the doctrines of *intuitionism and formalism* have tended to the opposite view" (73). Emphasis added.

38. Ignacio Angelelli, "Predication Theory: Classical vs Modern," in *Relations and Predicates*, ed. Herbert Hochberg and Kevin Mulligan (Frankfurt: Ontos Verlag, 2004), 56.

39. Sluga, *Frege*, 76, 78.

40. Deleuze and Guattari, *What Is Philosophy?*, 139.

41. Deleuze and Guattari, *What Is Philosophy?*, 139.

42. Sluga, *Frege*, 84.

43. Deleuze and Guattari, *What Is Philosophy?*, 139.

44. Deleuze and Guattari, *What Is Philosophy?*, 139.

45. Deleuze and Guattari, *What Is Philosophy?*, 211.

46. Deleuze and Guattari, *What Is Philosophy?*, 164.

47. Deleuze and Guattari, *What Is Philosophy?*, 211.

48. Olkowski, *The Ruin of Representation*, 99n41.

49. Cited in Olkowski, *The Ruin of Representation*, 100n42.

50. Cited in Olkowski, *The Ruin of Representation*, 110. Deleuze, *Difference and Repetition*, 81–82/111.

51. David Hume, *A Treatise of Human Nature* (Oxford: Clarendon Press, 1968), 5, 8. Cited in Olkowski, *The Ruin of Representation*, 106.

52. Cited in Olkowski, *The Ruin of Representation*, 154n20.

53. I have written an extensive version of this process in Olkowski, *The Ruin of Representation*, 147–155.

54. Deleuze and Guattari, *What Is Philosophy?*, 202–208.

55. Kamini Vellodi, "Diagrammatic Thought: Two Forms of Contructivism," in C. S. Peirce and Gilles Deleuze," *Parrhesia*, no. 19 (2014): 89. Vellodi is clear that, for Peirce, an end will be reached, but I prefer to leave the system open, even at the risk of attributing to Peirce a belief he does not hold.

56. Deleuze and Guattari, *What Is Philosophy?*, 74.

57. Deleuze and Guattari, *What Is Philosophy?*, 75. Emphasis added.

58. Gilles Deleuze and Félix Guattari, *A Thousand Plateaus: Capitalism and Schizophrenia*, trans. Brian Massumi (Minneapolis: University of Minnesota Press, 1987), 138.

59. Charles Sanders Peirce, *The Collected Papers of Charles Sanders Peirce*, ed. Charles Hartshorne, Paul Weiss, and Arthur Burks (Cambridge, MA: Harvard University Press, 1931–1935, 1958), 5.18.

60. Vellodi, "Diagrammatic Thought," 81.

61. Peirce, *The Collected Papers*, 1.444.

62. Vellodi, "Diagrammatic Thought," 81.

63. Vellodi, "Diagrammatic Thought," 81. Emphasis added.

64. Peirce, *The Collected Papers*, 4.530.

65. Nathan Houser and Christian Kloesel, eds. *The Essential Peirce*, vol. 1: *Selected Philosophical Writings (1967--1983)* (Bloomington: Indiana University Press, 1992), 9–10.

66. Vellodi, "Diagrammatic Thought," 82.

67. Peirce, *The Collected Papers*, 2.778.

68. Vellodi, "Diagrammatic Thought," 82; Peirce, *The Collected Papers*, 2.778.

69. Vellodi, "Diagrammatic Thought," 83–84.

70. Peirce, *The Collected Papers*, 3.527 marginal note 1908.

71. Vellodi, "Diagrammatic Thought," 85.

72. Deleuze and Guattari, *A Thousand Plateaus*, 135, 137. This is especially apparent in the diagrams that accompany the text.

73. Deleuze and Guattari, *A Thousand Plateaus*, 145.

74. Deleuze and Guattari, *A Thousand Plateaus*, 145, 146.

75. Deleuze and Guattari, *A Thousand Plateaus*, 136.

76. Deleuze and Guattari, *A Thousand Plateaus*, 136.

77. Deleuze and Guattari, *A Thousand Plateaus*, 138. See China Miéville, *October: The Story of the Russian Revolution* (London: Verso, 2017) for an insightful account of this.

78. Deleuze and Guattari, *A Thousand Plateaus*, 145.

79. Deleuze and Guattari, *A Thousand Plateaus*, 146.

80. Deleuze and Guattari, *A Thousand Plateaus*, 133, 129–130.

81. Deleuze and Guattari, *A Thousand Plateaus*, 147.

82. Deleuze and Guattari, *A Thousand Plateaus*, 41.

83. Deleuze and Guattari, *A Thousand Plateaus*, 3–4/9–10. Here we recall the intensive concept of chapter 2.

84. Olkowski, *The Ruin of Representation*, 238n38.

85. Deleuze and Guattari, *A Thousand Plateaus*, 141.

86. Peirce, *The Collected Papers*, 1.53; Vellodi, "Diagrammatic Thought," 83.

87. Peirce, *The Collected Papers*, 3.560; Vellodi, "Diagrammatic Thought," 83.

88. Peirce, *The Collected Papers*, 2.92.

89. Peirce, *The Collected Papers*, 1.370, 2.92.

90. Alexander Gerner, "Diagrammatic Thinking," in *Atlas of Transformation*, ed. Vít Havránek (Zurich: jrp-ringier, 2011), 180.

91. Peirce, *The Collected Papers*, 2.279.

92. Alexander Gerner, "Diagrammatic Thinking," 7.

93. Vellodi, "Diagrammatic Thought," 85.

94. Deleuze and Guattari, *A Thousand Plateaus*, 530n41. Also cited in Vellodi, "Diagrammatic Thought," 85.

95. Deleuze and Guattari, *A Thousand Plateaus*, 136.

96. Deleuze and Guattari, *A Thousand Plateaus*, 142, 139.

97. Deleuze and Guattari, *A Thousand Plateaus*, 142.

98. Deleuze and Guattari, *A Thousand Plateaus*, 143.

99. Deleuze and Guattari, *A Thousand Plateaus*, 142.

100. Deleuze and Guattari, *A Thousand Plateaus*, 144–145.

101. Deleuze and Guattari, *A Thousand Plateaus*, 56.

102. Fernando Zalamea, *Peirce's Continuum: A Methodological and Mathematical Approach* (Boston: Docent, 2012), accessed June 2018, http://acervopeirceano .org/wp-content/uploads/2011/09/Zalamea-Peirces-Continuum.pdf, 15.

103. Deleuze and Guattari, *What Is Philosophy?*, 153.

104. Deleuze and Guattari, *What Is Philosophy?*, 153.

105. Zalamea, *Peirce's Continuum*, 15.

106. Deleuze and Guattari, *A Thousand Plateaus*, 70.

107. Deleuze and Guattari, *A Thousand Plateaus*, 70.

108. Deleuze and Guattari, *A Thousand Plateaus*, 309. See also Gilles Deleuze, *L'Abécédaire de Gilles Deleuze*, produced and directed by Pierre-André Boutang (Paris: Ritournelle, 1988–1989).

109. Deleuze and Guattari, *A Thousand Plateaus*, 311, 312. I have improvised on Deleuze-Guattari's story.

110. Deleuze and Guattari, *A Thousand Plateaus*, 313.

111. Deleuze and Guattari, *A Thousand Plateaus*, 316.

112. See my essay "Deleuze's Aesthetics of Sensation," in *Cambridge Companion to Deleuze*, ed. Daniel Smith (Cambridge: Cambridge University Press, 2012), 265–285.

113. Deleuze and Guattari, *A Thousand Plateaus*, 316, 317.

114. Deleuze and Guattari, *A Thousand Plateaus*, 319.

115. Deleuze and Guattari, *A Thousand Plateaus*, 322.

116. Deleuze and Guattari, *A Thousand Plateaus*, 324.

117. Deleuze and Guattari, *A Thousand Plateaus*, 326.

118. Deleuze and Guattari, *A Thousand Plateaus*, 328, 329, 330.

119. Deleuze and Guattari, *A Thousand Plateaus*, 331.

120. Deleuze and Guattari, *A Thousand Plateaus*, 332, 333. This process appears to exceed if not replace the structure of virtual/real, which Deleuze embraced in earlier work.

121. Deleuze and Guattari, *A Thousand Plateaus*, 332.

122. Deleuze and Guattari, *A Thousand Plateaus*, 333.

123. Deleuze and Guattari, *A Thousand Plateaus*, 337; Paul Klee, *On Modern Art*, trans. Paul Findlay (London: Faber, 1966), 43.

124. Deleuze and Guattari, *A Thousand Plateaus*, 342, 343.

125. Deleuze and Guattari, *A Thousand Plateaus*, 343.

126. Deleuze and Guattari, *A Thousand Plateaus*, 344, 345.

127. Henri Bergson, *Creative Evolution*, trans. Arthur Mitchell (New York: University Press of America, 1983), 10–11.

128. Deleuze and Guattari, *A Thousand Plateaus*, 346–347.

129. Deleuze and Guattari, *A Thousand Plateaus*, 346–347.

130. Deleuze and Guattari, *A Thousand Plateaus*, 346.

131. Deleuze and Guattari, *A Thousand Plateaus*, 350.

BIBLIOGRAPHY

Angelelli, Ignacio. "Predication Theory: Classical vs Modern." In *Relations and Predicates*, edited by Herbert Hochberg and Kevin Mulligan. Frankfurt: Ontos, 2004.

Awody, Steve. "Carnap's Quest for Analyticity." In *Cambridge Companion to Carnap*, edited by Richard Creath and Michael Friedman. Cambridge: Cambridge University Press, 2007.

Barad, Karen. *Meeting the Universe Halfway: Quantum Physics and the Entanglement of Matter and Meaning*. Durham, NC: Duke University Press, 2007.

Barnouw, Jeffrey. *Propositional Perception: Phantasia, Predication and Sign in Plato, Aristotle and the Stoics*. Lanham, MD: University Press of America, 2002.

de Beauvoir, Simone. *The Ethics of Ambiguity*. Translated by Bernard Frechtman. New York: Citadel, 1976.

Bergson, Henri. *Creative Evolution*. Translated by Arthur Mitchell. Lanham, MD: University Press of America, 1983.

———. *Duration and Simultaneity*. Translated by Mark Lewis and Robin Durie. London: Clinamen, 1999.

———. *Matter and Memory*. Translated by Nancy Margaret Paul and W. Scott Palmer. New York: Zone, 1988. Originally published in Henri Bergson, *Oeuvres*. Paris: Presses Universitaires de France, 1963.

———. *Time and Free Will: An Essay on the Immediate Data of Consciousness*. Translated by F. L. Pogson. New York: Macmillan, 1959.

Bernard, Paul. *Souvenirs sur Paul Bernard*. Paris, 1912.

Burtt, E. A. *The Metaphysical Foundations of Modern Science*. 3rd ed. New York: Dover, 2003.

Cajori, Florian. "A History of the Arithmetical Methods of Approximation to the Roots of Numerical Equations of One Unknown Quantity." In Colorado

College Publication, General Series no. 51, Science Series vol. 12 (November 1910): 171–215.

Canales, Jimena. *The Physicist and the Philosopher: Einstein, Bergson, and the Debate That Changed Our Understanding of Time.* Princeton, NJ: Princeton University Press, 2015.

Capek, Milic. *Bergson and Modern Physics: A Reinterpretation and Re-evaluation.* Boston Studies in the Philosophy of Science, vol. 7 (1971): 330–340.

Carnap, Rudolf. *Meaning and Necessity: A Study in the Semantics of Modal Logic.* Chicago: University of Chicago Press, 1956.

Carroll, Lewis. *The Philosopher's Alice in Wonderland and Through the Looking-Glass.* Introduction and notes by Peter Heath. New York: St. Martin's, 1974.

Cartwright, Jon. "Physicists Discover a Whopping 13 New Solutions to Three-Body Problem." *Science,* March 8, 2013. http://www.sciencemag.org/news/2013/03 /physicists-discover-whopping-13-new-solutions-three-body-problem.

Casti, John. *Complexification: Explaining a Paradoxical World through the Science of Surprise.* New York: Harper Collins, 1994.

Deleuze, Gilles. *Cinema 1: The Movement-Image.* Translated by Hugh Tomlinson and Barbara Habberjam. Minneapolis: University of Minnesota Press, 1986. Originally published in French as *Cinéma 1: L'Image-Movement.* Paris: Les Éditions de Minuit, 1983.

———. *Cinema 2: The Time-Image.* Translated by Hugh Tomlinson and Barbara Habberjam. Minneapolis: University of Minnesota Press, 1989. Originally published in French as *Cinéma II: l'Image-temps.* Paris: Les Éditions de Minuit, 1985.

———. *Difference and Repetition.* Translated by Paul Patton. New York: Columbia University Press, 1994. Originally published in French as *Différence et Répétition.* Paris: Presses Universitaires de France, 1968.

———. *Francis Bacon: The Logic of Sensation.* Translated by Daniel W. Smith. London: Continuum, 2004. Originally published in French as *Francis Bacon: Logique de la Sensation.* Paris: Editions de la Difference, 1981.

———. "The Idea of Genesis in Kant's Aesthetics." Translated by Daniel W. Smith. *Angelaki: Journal of Theoretical Humanities* 5, no. 3 (December 2000): 57–70.

———. *L'Abécédaire de Gilles Deleuze.* Produced and directed by Pierre-André Boutan. Paris: Ritournelle, 1988–1989.

———. *The Logic of Sense.* Translated by Mark Lester with Charles Stivale and Constantin V. Boundas. Edited by Constantin V. Boundas. New York: Columbia University Press, 1990. Originally published in French as *Logique du sens.* Paris: Les Éditions de Minuit, 1969.

———. *Proust and Signs.* Translated by Richard Howard. Minneapolis: University of Minnesota Press, 2014. Originally published in French as *Proust et les Signes.* Paris: Presses Universitaires de France, 1964.

———. "Theory of Multiplicities in Bergson." *Lectures by Gilles Deleuze*. Accessed October 2017. http://deleuzelectures.blogspot.com/2007/02/theory-of -multiplicities-in-bergson.html.

Deleuze, Gilles, and Félix Guattari. *A Thousand Plateaus: Capitalism and Schizophrenia*. Translated by Brian Massumi. Minneapolis: University of Minnesota Press, 1987. Originally published in French as *Mille Plateaux: Capitalisme et Schizophrénie*. Paris: Les Éditions de Minuit, 1980.

———. *What Is Philosophy?* Translated by Hugh Tomlinson and Graham Burchell. New York: Columbia University Press, 1994. Originally published in French as *Qu'est-ce que la philosophie?* Paris: Les Editions de Minuit, 1991.

Depew, David J., and Bruce H. Weber. *Darwinism Evolving: Systems Dynamics and the Genealogy of Natural Selection*. Cambridge, MA: MIT Press, 1995.

Devlin, Keith. *Mathematics: The Science of Patterns: The Search for Order in Life, Mind, and the Universe*. New York: Scientific American Library, 1994.

Duffy, Simon B. *Deleuze and the History of Mathematics: In Defense of the New*. London: Bloomsbury, 2014.

During, Élie, and Paul-Antoine Miquel. "We Bergsonians: The Kyoto Manifesto." Translated by Barry Dainton. *Parrhesia* 33 (2020): 17–42.

Einstein, Albert. *The World as I See It*. Translated by Alan Harris. San Diego: Book Tree, 2017.

Einstein, Albert, and Leopold Infeld. *The Evolution of Physics*. London: Cambridge University Press, 1938.

Frege, Gottlob. *Begrijfsscrift*. Edited by I. Angelelli. Hildesheim, Germany: G. Olms, 1964.

———. "Function and Concept." Translated by Peter Geach. Accessed November 2017. http://fitelson.org/proseminar/frege_fac.pdf.

———. *Nachgelassene Schriften*. Edited by H. Hermes and Friedrich Kambartel. Hamburg, Germany: Felix Meiner Verlag, 1969.

———. "On Sense and Reference." In *Meaning and Reference*, edited by A. W. Moore, 23–42. Oxford: Oxford University Press, 1993.

Gerner, Alexander. "Diagrammatic Thinking." In *Atlas of Transformation*, edited by Zbynek Baladrán and Vít Havránek. Zurich: JRP-Ringier, 2011.

Gunter, P. A. Y. "André Metz and Henri Bergson, Exchanges Concerning Bergson's New Edition of *Duration and Simultaneity*." In *Bergson and the Evolution of Modern Physics*. Knoxville: University of Tennessee Press, 1969.

Halliward, Peter. *Concept and Form: The "Cahiers pour l'Analyse" and Contemporary French Thought*. Accessed June 2017. http://cahiers.kingston.ac.uk/names /canguilhem.html.

Hass, Lawrence. *Merleau-Ponty's Philosophy*. Bloomington: Indiana University Press, 2008.

Houser, Nathan, and Christian Kloesel, eds. *The Essential Peirce*. Vol. 1: *Selected Philosophical Writings (1967–1983)*. Bloomington: Indiana University Press, 1992.

Hume, David. *A Treatise of Human Nature*. Oxford: Clarendon Press, 1968.

Husserl, Edmund. *Cartesian Meditations: An Introduction to Phenomenology*. Translated by Dorian Cairnes. The Hague, Netherlands: Martinus Nijhoff, 1973.

———. *Ideas: General Introduction to Pure Phenomenology*. Translated by W. R. Boyce Gibson. New York: Humanities, 1972.

———. *The Phenomenology of Internal Time Consciousness*. Translated by James S. Churchill. Bloomington: Indiana University Press, 1971.

Kant, Immanuel. *Critique of Pure Reason*. Translated by Norman Kemp Smith. New York: St. Martin's, 1965.

Kaufmann, A. *An Introduction to the Theory of Fuzzy Subsets*. Vol. 1. Translated by D. L. Swanson. New York: Academic, 1975.

Kirby, Alan. "The Death of Postmodernism and Beyond." *Philosophy Now*, no. 58 (November/December 2006). https://philosophynow.org/issues/58.

Kisiel, Theodore J., and Joseph J. Kockelmans, eds. *Phenomenology and the Natural Sciences: Essays and Translations*. Evanston, IL: Northwestern University Press, 1970.

Klee, Paul. *On Modern Art*. Translated by Paul Findlay. London: Faber, 1966.

Klein, Morris. *Mathematics in Western Culture*. New York: Galaxy, 1964.

Li, XiaoMing, and ShiJun Liao. "More Than Six Hundred New Families of Newtonian Periodic Planar Collisionless Three-Body Orbits." *Science China Physics, Mechanics & Astronomy* 60 (2017). https://doi.org/10.1007/s11433-017-9078-5.

Livingston, Paul. *The Politics of Logic: Badiou, Wittgenstein, and the Consequences of Formalism*. New York: Routledge, 2011.

Low, Douglas. "Merleau-Ponty on Causality." *Human Studies* 38, no. 3 (July 2015): 1–19.

Ludwig, K. "Carnap, Neurath, and Schlick on Protocol Sentences." *Noûs* 21, no. 4 (1987): 457–470. http://www.jstor.org/stable/2215667.

Margulis, Lynn, and Dorian Sagan. *What Is Sex?* New York: Simon & Schuster, 1999.

Marshall, William. "Frege's Theory of Functions and Objects." *The Philosophical Review* 62 (July 1953): 374–390.

Martin, Gottfried. *Kant's Metaphysics and Theory of Science*. Translated by P. G. Lucas. Manchester, UK: Manchester University Press, 1955.

Merleau-Ponty, Maurice. *Nature: Course Notes from the Collége de France*. Compiled by Dominique Séglard. Translated by Robert Vallier. Evanston, IL: Northwestern University Press, 2003. Originally published as *La Nature: Notes. Cours de Collège de France*. Paris: Seuil, 1994.

———. *Phenomenology of Perception*. Translated by Donald A. Landes. New York: Routledge, 2012. Originally published in French as *Phénoménologie de la perception*. Paris: Gallimard, 1945.

———. "The Primacy of Perception." Translated by James Edie. In *The Primacy of Perception*, edited by James Edie. Evanston, IL: Northwestern University Press, 1964.

———. *Sense and Non-Sense*. Translated by Patricia Allen Dreyfus. Evanston, IL: Northwestern University Press, 1992. Originally published in French as *Sens et Non-Sens*. Paris: Libriarie Gallimard, 1948.

———. *Signs*. Translated by Richard C. McCleary. Evanston, IL: Northwestern University Press, 1964. Originally published in French as *Signes*. Paris: Libriarie Gallimard, 1960.

———. *The Structure of Behavior*. Translated by Alden L. Fisher. Boston: Beacon, 1963. Originally published in French as *La structure du comportement*. Paris: Presses Universitaires de France, 1942.

———. *The Visible and the Invisible*. Translated by Alphonso Lingis. Evanston, IL: Northwestern University Press, 1968. Originally published in French as *Le visible et l'invisible*. Paris: Gallimard, 1964.

Miéville, China. *Embassytown*. London: Del Rey, 2012.

———. *October: The Story of the Russian Revolution*. London: Verso, 2017.

Nirenberg, Ricardo L., and David Nirenberg. "Badiou's Number: A Critique of Mathematics as Ontology." *Critical Inquiry* 37 (Summer 2011): 585–586.

Nolte, David D. "The Tangled Tale of Phase Space." *Physics Today* (2010): 33–38.

Olkowski, Dorothea. "Bergson and Film." In *Film, Theory, and Philosophy: The Key Thinkers*, edited by Felicity Coleman. Durham, NC: Acumen, 2009.

———. "Deleuze's Aesthetics of Sensation." In *Cambridge Companion to Deleuze*, edited by Daniel Smith, 265–285. Cambridge: Cambridge University Press, 2012.

———. *Gilles Deleuze and the Ruin of Representation*. Berkeley: University of California Press, 1999.

———. "Letting Go the Weight of the Past: Beauvoir and the Joy of Existence." In *Simone de Beauvoir's Philosophy of Age: Gender, Ethics, and Time*, edited by Silvia Stoller. London: Palgrave, 2013.

———. *Postmodern Philosophy and the Scientific Turn*. Bloomington: Indiana University Press, 2011.

———. "A Psychoanalysis of Nature?" In *Merleau-Ponty: From Nature to Ontology*. Vol. 2 of *Chiasmi International*, 185–205. Paris: Vrin; Milan: Mimesis; Memphis, TN: University of Memphis.

———. *The Universal (In the Realm of the Sensible)*. New York: Columbia University Press, 2007.

Peirce, Charles Sanders. *The Collected Papers of Charles Sanders Peirce*. Edited by Charles Hartshorne, Paul Weiss, and Arthur Burks. Cambridge, MA: Harvard University Press, 1931–1935, 1958.

———. *New Elements of Mathematics*. The Hague, Netherlands: Mouton, 1976.

———. *Reasoning and the Logic of Things*. Cambridge, MA: Harvard University Press, 1989.

————. *Writings.* Edited by Nathan Houser. Bloomington: Indiana University Press, 1982–2000.

Petrov, Vladimir. "Bertrand Russell's Criticism of Bergson's Views about Continuity and Discreteness." *FILOZOFIA* 68, no. 10 (2013): 890–904.

The Physics Classroom. "What Is a Wave?" http://www.physicsclassroom.com /Class/waves/u10l1b.cfm.

Resnick, Michael. "Review of Hans Sluga's *Gottlob Frege.*" *The Philosophical Review* 92, no. 1 (January 1983).

Rouse, Joseph. "Naturalism and Scientific Practices: A Concluding Scientific Postscript." In *Naturalized Epistemology and Philosophy of Science*, edited by Chienkuo Michael Mi and Ruey-lin Chen, 61–86. Amsterdam: Rodopi, 2007.

Russell, Bertrand. "The Philosophy of Bergson. With a Reply by Mr. H. Wildon Carr." Published for "The Heretics" by Bowes and Bowes. Cambridge: Macmillan, 1914.

————. *The Principles of Mathematics.* Sec. 160. http://fair-use.org/bertrand -russell/the-principles-of-mathematics/s160.

Saint-Exupery, Antoine de. *Pilote de Guerre.* Paris: Gallimard, 1972.

Sluga, Hans. *Gottlob Frege.* London: Routledge, 1980.

Smith, Barry. "Logic and the *Sachverhalt.*" *The Monist* 72, no. 1 (January 1989): 52–69.

Smith, David Woodruff, and Ronald McIntyre. *Husserl and Intentionality: A Study of Mind, Meaning, and Language.* Dordrecht, Netherlands: D. Reidel, 1982.

Smolin, Lee. *Einstein's Unfinished Revolution: The Search for What Lies Beyond the Quantum.* New York: Penguin, 2019.

————. *Time Reborn: From the Crisis in Physics to the Future of the Universe.* Boston: Mariner, 2014.

Smyth, Bryan A. *Merleau-Ponty's Existential Phenomenology and the Realization of Philosophy.* London: Bloomsbury, 2013.

Stern, David P. "Educational Web Sites on Astronomy, Physics, Spaceflight, and the Earth's Magnetism." Goddard Space Flight Center. Accessed August 2017. http://www.phy6.org/stargaze/Q7.htm.

Tasić, Vladimir. *Mathematics and the Roots of Postmodern Thought.* Oxford: Oxford University Press, 2001.

Tiles, Mary. *Mathematics and the Image of Reason.* London: Routledge, 1991.

————. *The Philosophy of Set Theory: An Introduction to Cantor's Paradise.* London: Blackwell, 1989.

Uexküll, Jacob von. *Theoretical Biology.* New York: Harcourt & Brace, 1926.

Vellodi, Kamini. "Diagrammatic Thought: Two Forms of Contructivism in C. S. Peirce and Gilles Deleuze." *Parrhesia*, no. 19 (2014): 79–95.

Vrahimis, Andreas. "Russell's Critique of Bergson and the Divide between 'Analytic' and 'Continental' Philosophy." *Balkan Journal of Philosophy* 3, no. 1 (2011): 123–134, 9. www.academia.edu/610678/.

Weiner, Joan. *Frege Explained: From Arithmetic to Analytic Philosophy.* Chicago: Open Court Press, 2004.

Weisstein, Eric W. "Russell's Antinomy." From *MathWorld*—A Wolfram Web Resource. Accessed June 2017. http://mathworld.wolfram.com /RussellsAntinomy.html.

Wetzel, Linda. "Frege and the Philosophy of Mathematics by Michael D. Resnik." *The Philosophical Review* 92, no. 1 (January 1983): 114–116.

Wölfflin, Heinrich. *The Principles of Art History: The Problem of the Development of Style in Later Art.* Translated by M. D. Hottinger. New York: Henry Holt, 1932.

Zadeh, L. A. Foreword to *An Introduction to the Theory of Fuzzy Subsets,* by A. Kaufmann. Vol. 1. Translated by D. L. Swanson. New York: Academic, 1975.

Zalamea, Fernando. *Peirce's Continuum: A Methodological and Mathematical Approach.* Boston: Docent, 2012. https://uberty.org/wp-content/uploads /2015/07/Zalamea-Peirces-Continuum.pdf.

INDEX

DOROTHEA OLKOWSKI is Professor and former Chair of Philosophy at the University of Colorado, Colorado Springs; Director of Humanities; Director of the Cognitive Studies Program; and former Director of Women's Studies. She is author of more than one hundred articles and twelve books, including *Postmodern Philosophy and the Scientific Turn*, *The Universal (In the Realm of the Sensible)*, *Feminist Phenomenology Futures* (with Helen Fielding), *Deleuze and Guattari's Philosophy of Freedom: Freedom's Refrains* (with Eftechios Pirovolakis), and *Deleuze at the End of the World: A South-American Perspective on the Sources of His Thought* (with Juilán Ferreyra).

CPSIA information can be obtained
at www.ICGtesting.com
Printed in the USA
LVHW110409261021
701556LV00004B/471